Mometrix TEST PREPARATION

NYSTCE®

Family and Consumer Sciences (072) Test Secrets Study Guide

I0880291

DEAR FUTURE EXAM SUCCESS STORY

First of all, **THANK YOU** for purchasing Mometrix study materials!

Second, congratulations! You are one of the few determined test-takers who are committed to doing whatever it takes to excel on your exam. **You have come to the right place.** We developed these study materials with one goal in mind: to deliver you the information you need in a format that's concise and easy to use.

In addition to optimizing your guide for the content of the test, we've outlined our recommended steps for breaking down the preparation process into small, attainable goals so you can make sure you stay on track.

We've also analyzed the entire test-taking process, identifying the most common pitfalls and showing how you can overcome them and be ready for any curveball the test throws you.

Standardized testing is one of the biggest obstacles on your road to success, which only increases the importance of doing well in the high-pressure, high-stakes environment of test day. Your results on this test could have a significant impact on your future, and this guide provides the information and practical advice to help you achieve your full potential on test day.

Your success is our success

We would love to hear from you! If you would like to share the story of your exam success or if you have any questions or comments in regard to our products, please contact us at **800-673-8175** or **support@mometrix.com**.

Thanks again for your business and we wish you continued success!

Sincerely,
The Mometrix Test Preparation Team

Need more help? Check out our flashcards at:
http://MometrixFlashcards.com/NYSTCE

Written and edited by the Mometrix Exam Secrets Test Prep Team
Printed in the United States of America

TABLE OF CONTENTS

Introduction

Thank you for purchasing this resource! You have made the choice to prepare yourself for a test that could have a huge impact on your future, and this guide is designed to help you be fully ready for test day. Obviously, it's important to have a solid understanding of the test material, but you also need to be prepared for the unique environment and stressors of the test, so that you can perform to the best of your abilities.

For this purpose, the first section that appears in this guide is the **Secret Keys**. We've devoted countless hours to meticulously researching what works and what doesn't, and we've boiled down our findings to the five most impactful steps you can take to improve your performance on the test. We start at the beginning with study planning and move through the preparation process, all the way to the testing strategies that will help you get the most out of what you know when you're finally sitting in front of the test.

We recommend that you start preparing for your test as far in advance as possible. However, if you've bought this guide as a last-minute study resource and only have a few days before your test, we recommend that you skip over the first two Secret Keys since they address a long-term study plan.

If you struggle with **test anxiety**, we strongly encourage you to check out our recommendations for how you can overcome it. Test anxiety is a formidable foe, but it can be beaten, and we want to make sure you have the tools you need to defeat it.

Secret Key #1 – Plan Big, Study Small

There's a lot riding on your performance. If you want to ace this test, you're going to need to keep your skills sharp and the material fresh in your mind. You need a plan that lets you review everything you need to know while still fitting in your schedule. We'll break this strategy down into three categories.

Information Organization

Start with the information you already have: the official test outline. From this, you can make a complete list of all the concepts you need to cover before the test. Organize these concepts into groups that can be studied together, and create a list of any related vocabulary you need to learn so you can brush up on any difficult terms. You'll want to keep this vocabulary list handy once you actually start studying since you may need to add to it along the way.

Time Management

Once you have your set of study concepts, decide how to spread them out over the time you have left before the test. Break your study plan into small, clear goals so you have a manageable task for each day and know exactly what you're doing. Then just focus on one small step at a time. When you manage your time this way, you don't need to spend hours at a time studying. Studying a small block of content for a short period each day helps you retain information better and avoid stressing over how much you have left to do. You can relax knowing that you have a plan to cover everything in time. In order for this strategy to be effective though, you have to start studying early and stick to your schedule. Avoid the exhaustion and futility that comes from last-minute cramming!

Study Environment

The environment you study in has a big impact on your learning. Studying in a coffee shop, while probably more enjoyable, is not likely to be as fruitful as studying in a quiet room. It's important to keep distractions to a minimum. You're only planning to study for a short block of time, so make the most of it. Don't pause to check your phone or get up to find a snack. It's also important to **avoid multitasking**. Research has consistently shown that multitasking will make your studying dramatically less effective. Your study area should also be comfortable and well-lit so you don't have the distraction of straining your eyes or sitting on an uncomfortable chair.

The time of day you study is also important. You want to be rested and alert. Don't wait until just before bedtime. Study when you'll be most likely to comprehend and remember. Even better, if you know what time of day your test will be, set that time aside for study. That way your brain will be used to working on that subject at that specific time and you'll have a better chance of recalling information.

Finally, it can be helpful to team up with others who are studying for the same test. Your actual studying should be done in as isolated an environment as possible, but the work of organizing the information and setting up the study plan can be divided up. In between study sessions, you can discuss with your teammates the concepts that you're all studying and quiz each other on the details. Just be sure that your teammates are as serious about the test as you are. If you find that your study time is being replaced with social time, you might need to find a new team.

Secret Key #2 – Make Your Studying Count

You're devoting a lot of time and effort to preparing for this test, so you want to be absolutely certain it will pay off. This means doing more than just reading the content and hoping you can remember it on test day. It's important to make every minute of study count. There are two main areas you can focus on to make your studying count.

Retention

It doesn't matter how much time you study if you can't remember the material. You need to make sure you are retaining the concepts. To check your retention of the information you're learning, try recalling it at later times with minimal prompting. Try carrying around flashcards and glance at one or two from time to time or ask a friend who's also studying for the test to quiz you.

To enhance your retention, look for ways to put the information into practice so that you can apply it rather than simply recalling it. If you're using the information in practical ways, it will be much easier to remember. Similarly, it helps to solidify a concept in your mind if you're not only reading it to yourself but also explaining it to someone else. Ask a friend to let you teach them about a concept you're a little shaky on (or speak aloud to an imaginary audience if necessary). As you try to summarize, define, give examples, and answer your friend's questions, you'll understand the concepts better and they will stay with you longer. Finally, step back for a big picture view and ask yourself how each piece of information fits with the whole subject. When you link the different concepts together and see them working together as a whole, it's easier to remember the individual components.

Finally, practice showing your work on any multi-step problems, even if you're just studying. Writing out each step you take to solve a problem will help solidify the process in your mind, and you'll be more likely to remember it during the test.

Modality

Modality simply refers to the means or method by which you study. Choosing a study modality that fits your own individual learning style is crucial. No two people learn best in exactly the same way, so it's important to know your strengths and use them to your advantage.

For example, if you learn best by visualization, focus on visualizing a concept in your mind and draw an image or a diagram. Try color-coding your notes, illustrating them, or creating symbols that will trigger your mind to recall a learned concept. If you learn best by hearing or discussing information, find a study partner who learns the same way or read aloud to yourself. Think about how to put the information in your own words. Imagine that you are giving a lecture on the topic and record yourself so you can listen to it later.

For any learning style, flashcards can be helpful. Organize the information so you can take advantage of spare moments to review. Underline key words or phrases. Use different colors for different categories. Mnemonic devices (such as creating a short list in which every item starts with the same letter) can also help with retention. Find what works best for you and use it to store the information in your mind most effectively and easily.

Secret Key #3 – Practice the Right Way

Your success on test day depends not only on how many hours you put into preparing, but also on whether you prepared the right way. It's good to check along the way to see if your studying is paying off. One of the most effective ways to do this is by taking practice tests to evaluate your progress. Practice tests are useful because they show exactly where you need to improve. Every time you take a practice test, pay special attention to these three groups of questions:

- The questions you got wrong
- The questions you had to guess on, even if you guessed right
- The questions you found difficult or slow to work through

This will show you exactly what your weak areas are, and where you need to devote more study time. Ask yourself why each of these questions gave you trouble. Was it because you didn't understand the material? Was it because you didn't remember the vocabulary? Do you need more repetitions on this type of question to build speed and confidence? Dig into those questions and figure out how you can strengthen your weak areas as you go back to review the material.

Additionally, many practice tests have a section explaining the answer choices. It can be tempting to read the explanation and think that you now have a good understanding of the concept. However, an explanation likely only covers part of the question's broader context. Even if the explanation makes perfect sense, **go back and investigate** every concept related to the question until you're positive you have a thorough understanding.

As you go along, keep in mind that the practice test is just that: practice. Memorizing these questions and answers will not be very helpful on the actual test because it is unlikely to have any of the same exact questions. If you only know the right answers to the sample questions, you won't be prepared for the real thing. **Study the concepts** until you understand them fully, and then you'll be able to answer any question that shows up on the test.

It's important to wait on the practice tests until you're ready. If you take a test on your first day of study, you may be overwhelmed by the amount of material covered and how much you need to learn. Work up to it gradually.

On test day, you'll need to be prepared for answering questions, managing your time, and using the test-taking strategies you've learned. It's a lot to balance, like a mental marathon that will have a big impact on your future. Like training for a marathon, you'll need to start slowly and work your way up. When test day arrives, you'll be ready.

Start with the strategies you've read in the first two Secret Keys—plan your course and study in the way that works best for you. If you have time, consider using multiple study resources to get different approaches to the same concepts. It can be helpful to see difficult concepts from more than one angle. Then find a good source for practice tests. Many times, the test website will suggest potential study resources or provide sample tests.

Practice Test Strategy

If you're able to find at least three practice tests, we recommend this strategy:

UNTIMED AND OPEN-BOOK PRACTICE

Take the first test with no time constraints and with your notes and study guide handy. Take your time and focus on applying the strategies you've learned.

TIMED AND OPEN-BOOK PRACTICE

Take the second practice test open-book as well, but set a timer and practice pacing yourself to finish in time.

TIMED AND CLOSED-BOOK PRACTICE

Take any other practice tests as if it were test day. Set a timer and put away your study materials. Sit at a table or desk in a quiet room, imagine yourself at the testing center, and answer questions as quickly and accurately as possible.

Keep repeating timed and closed-book tests on a regular basis until you run out of practice tests or it's time for the actual test. Your mind will be ready for the schedule and stress of test day, and you'll be able to focus on recalling the material you've learned.

Secret Key #4 – Pace Yourself

Once you're fully prepared for the material on the test, your biggest challenge on test day will be managing your time. Just knowing that the clock is ticking can make you panic even if you have plenty of time left. Work on pacing yourself so you can build confidence against the time constraints of the exam. Pacing is a difficult skill to master, especially in a high-pressure environment, so **practice is vital**.

Set time expectations for your pace based on how much time is available. For example, if a section has 60 questions and the time limit is 30 minutes, you know you have to average 30 seconds or less per question in order to answer them all. Although 30 seconds is the hard limit, set 25 seconds per question as your goal, so you reserve extra time to spend on harder questions. When you budget extra time for the harder questions, you no longer have any reason to stress when those questions take longer to answer.

Don't let this time expectation distract you from working through the test at a calm, steady pace, but keep it in mind so you don't spend too much time on any one question. Recognize that taking extra time on one question you don't understand may keep you from answering two that you do understand later in the test. If your time limit for a question is up and you're still not sure of the answer, mark it and move on, and come back to it later if the time and the test format allow. If the testing format doesn't allow you to return to earlier questions, just make an educated guess; then put it out of your mind and move on.

On the easier questions, be careful not to rush. It may seem wise to hurry through them so you have more time for the challenging ones, but it's not worth missing one if you know the concept and just didn't take the time to read the question fully. Work efficiently but make sure you understand the question and have looked at all of the answer choices, since more than one may seem right at first.

Even if you're paying attention to the time, you may find yourself a little behind at some point. You should speed up to get back on track, but do so wisely. Don't panic; just take a few seconds less on each question until you're caught up. Don't guess without thinking, but do look through the answer choices and eliminate any you know are wrong. If you can get down to two choices, it is often worthwhile to guess from those. Once you've chosen an answer, move on and don't dwell on any that you skipped or had to hurry through. If a question was taking too long, chances are it was one of the harder ones, so you weren't as likely to get it right anyway.

On the other hand, if you find yourself getting ahead of schedule, it may be beneficial to slow down a little. The more quickly you work, the more likely you are to make a careless mistake that will affect your score. You've budgeted time for each question, so don't be afraid to spend that time. Practice an efficient but careful pace to get the most out of the time you have.

Secret Key #5 – Have a Plan for Guessing

When you're taking the test, you may find yourself stuck on a question. Some of the answer choices seem better than others, but you don't see the one answer choice that is obviously correct. What do you do?

The scenario described above is very common, yet most test takers have not effectively prepared for it. Developing and practicing a plan for guessing may be one of the single most effective uses of your time as you get ready for the exam.

In developing your plan for guessing, there are three questions to address:

- When should you start the guessing process?
- How should you narrow down the choices?
- Which answer should you choose?

When to Start the Guessing Process

Unless your plan for guessing is to select C every time (which, despite its merits, is not what we recommend), you need to leave yourself enough time to apply your answer elimination strategies. Since you have a limited amount of time for each question, that means that if you're going to give yourself the best shot at guessing correctly, you have to decide quickly whether or not you will guess.

Of course, the best-case scenario is that you don't have to guess at all, so first, see if you can answer the question based on your knowledge of the subject and basic reasoning skills. Focus on the key words in the question and try to jog your memory of related topics. Give yourself a chance to bring the knowledge to mind, but once you realize that you don't have (or you can't access) the knowledge you need to answer the question, it's time to start the guessing process.

It's almost always better to start the guessing process too early than too late. It only takes a few seconds to remember something and answer the question from knowledge. Carefully eliminating wrong answer choices takes longer. Plus, going through the process of eliminating answer choices can actually help jog your memory.

Summary: Start the guessing process as soon as you decide that you can't answer the question based on your knowledge.

How to Narrow Down the Choices

The next chapter in this book (**Test-Taking Strategies**) includes a wide range of strategies for how to approach questions and how to look for answer choices to eliminate. You will definitely want to read those carefully, practice them, and figure out which ones work best for you. Here though, we're going to address a mindset rather than a particular strategy.

Your odds of guessing an answer correctly depend on how many options you are choosing from.

Number of options left	5	4	3	2	1
Odds of guessing correctly	20%	25%	33%	50%	100%

You can see from this chart just how valuable it is to be able to eliminate incorrect answers and make an educated guess, but there are two things that many test takers do that cause them to miss out on the benefits of guessing:

- Accidentally eliminating the correct answer
- Selecting an answer based on an impression

We'll look at the first one here, and the second one in the next section.

To avoid accidentally eliminating the correct answer, we recommend a thought exercise called **the $5 challenge**. In this challenge, you only eliminate an answer choice from contention if you are willing to bet $5 on it being wrong. Why $5? Five dollars is a small but not insignificant amount of money. It's an amount you could afford to lose but wouldn't want to throw away. And while losing $5 once might not hurt too much, doing it twenty times will set you back $100. In the same way, each small decision you make—eliminating a choice here, guessing on a question there—won't by itself impact your score very much, but when you put them all together, they can make a big difference. By holding each answer choice elimination decision to a higher standard, you can reduce the risk of accidentally eliminating the correct answer.

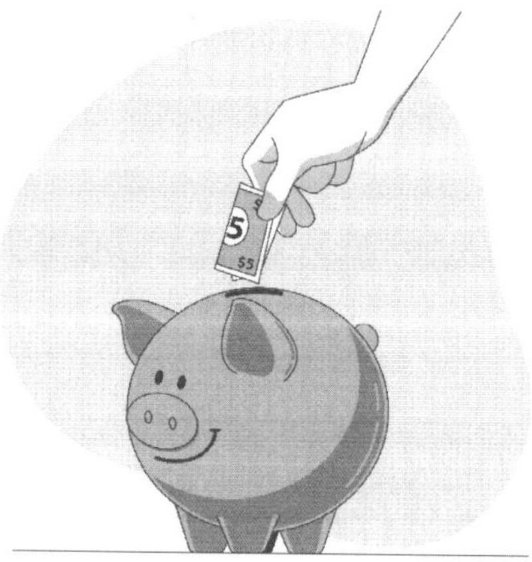

The $5 challenge can also be applied in a positive sense: If you are willing to bet $5 that an answer choice *is* correct, go ahead and mark it as correct.

Summary: Only eliminate an answer choice if you are willing to bet $5 that it is wrong.

Which Answer to Choose

You're taking the test. You've run into a hard question and decided you'll have to guess. You've eliminated all the answer choices you're willing to bet $5 on. Now you have to pick an answer. Why do we even need to talk about this? Why can't you just pick whichever one you feel like when the time comes?

The answer to these questions is that if you don't come into the test with a plan, you'll rely on your impression to select an answer choice, and if you do that, you risk falling into a trap. The test writers know that everyone who takes their test will be guessing on some of the questions, so they intentionally write wrong answer choices to seem plausible. You still have to pick an answer though, and if the wrong answer choices are designed to look right, how can you ever be sure that you're not falling for their trap? The best solution we've found to this dilemma is to take the decision out of your hands entirely. Here is the process we recommend:

Once you've eliminated any choices that you are confident (willing to bet $5) are wrong, select the first remaining choice as your answer.

Whether you choose to select the first remaining choice, the second, or the last, the important thing is that you use some preselected standard. Using this approach guarantees that you will not be enticed into selecting an answer choice that looks right, because you are not basing your decision on how the answer choices look.

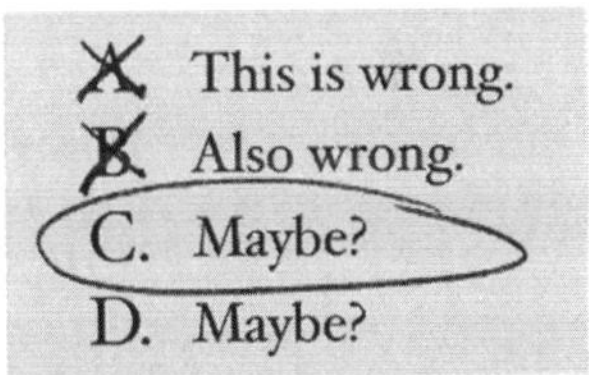

This is not meant to make you question your knowledge. Instead, it is to help you recognize the difference between your knowledge and your impressions. There's a huge difference between thinking an answer is right because of what you know, and thinking an answer is right because it looks or sounds like it should be right.

Summary: To ensure that your selection is appropriately random, make a predetermined selection from among all answer choices you have not eliminated.

Test-Taking Strategies

This section contains a list of test-taking strategies that you may find helpful as you work through the test. By taking what you know and applying logical thought, you can maximize your chances of answering any question correctly!

It is very important to realize that every question is different and every person is different: no single strategy will work on every question, and no single strategy will work for every person. That's why we've included all of them here, so you can try them out and determine which ones work best for different types of questions and which ones work best for you.

Question Strategies

✓ Read Carefully

Read the question and the answer choices carefully. Don't miss the question because you misread the terms. You have plenty of time to read each question thoroughly and make sure you understand what is being asked. Yet a happy medium must be attained, so don't waste too much time. You must read carefully and efficiently.

✓ Contextual Clues

Look for contextual clues. If the question includes a word you are not familiar with, look at the immediate context for some indication of what the word might mean. Contextual clues can often give you all the information you need to decipher the meaning of an unfamiliar word. Even if you can't determine the meaning, you may be able to narrow down the possibilities enough to make a solid guess at the answer to the question.

✓ Prefixes

If you're having trouble with a word in the question or answer choices, try dissecting it. Take advantage of every clue that the word might include. Prefixes can be a huge help. Usually, they allow you to determine a basic meaning. *Pre-* means before, *post-* means after, *pro-* is positive, *de-* is negative. From prefixes, you can get an idea of the general meaning of the word and try to put it into context.

✓ Hedge Words

Watch out for critical hedge words, such as *likely, may, can, often, almost, mostly, usually, generally, rarely,* and *sometimes.* Question writers insert these hedge phrases to cover every possibility. Often an answer choice will be wrong simply because it leaves no room for exception. Be on guard for answer choices that have definitive words such as *exactly* and *always.*

✓ Switchback Words

Stay alert for *switchbacks.* These are the words and phrases frequently used to alert you to shifts in thought. The most common switchback words are *but, although,* and *however.* Others include *nevertheless, on the other hand, even though, while, in spite of, despite,* and *regardless of.* Switchback words are important to catch because they can change the direction of the question or an answer choice.

✓ Face Value

When in doubt, use common sense. Accept the situation in the problem at face value. Don't read too much into it. These problems will not require you to make wild assumptions. If you have to go beyond creativity and warp time or space in order to have an answer choice fit the question, then you should move on and consider the other answer choices. These are normal problems rooted in reality. The applicable relationship or explanation may not be readily apparent, but it is there for you to figure out. Use your common sense to interpret anything that isn't clear.

Answer Choice Strategies

✓ Answer Selection

The most thorough way to pick an answer choice is to identify and eliminate wrong answers until only one is left, then confirm it is the correct answer. Sometimes an answer choice may immediately seem right, but be careful. The test writers will usually put more than one reasonable answer choice on each question, so take a second to read all of them and make sure that the other choices are not equally obvious. As long as you have time left, it is better to read every answer choice than to pick the first one that looks right without checking the others.

✓ Answer Choice Families

An answer choice family consists of two (in rare cases, three) answer choices that are very similar in construction and cannot all be true at the same time. If you see two answer choices that are direct opposites or parallels, one of them is usually the correct answer. For instance, if one answer choice says that quantity *x* increases and another either says that quantity *x* decreases (opposite) or says that quantity *y* increases (parallel), then those answer choices would fall into the same family. An answer choice that doesn't match the construction of the answer choice family is more likely to be incorrect. Most questions will not have answer choice families, but when they do appear, you should be prepared to recognize them.

✓ Eliminate Answers

Eliminate answer choices as soon as you realize they are wrong, but make sure you consider all possibilities. If you are eliminating answer choices and realize that the last one you are left with is also wrong, don't panic. Start over and consider each choice again. There may be something you missed the first time that you will realize on the second pass.

✓ Avoid Fact Traps

Don't be distracted by an answer choice that is factually true but doesn't answer the question. You are looking for the choice that answers the question. Stay focused on what the question is asking for so you don't accidentally pick an answer that is true but incorrect. Always go back to the question and make sure the answer choice you've selected actually answers the question and is not merely a true statement.

✓ Extreme Statements

In general, you should avoid answers that put forth extreme actions as standard practice or proclaim controversial ideas as established fact. An answer choice that states the "process should be used in certain situations, if..." is much more likely to be correct than one that states the "process should be discontinued completely." The first is a calm rational statement and doesn't even make a definitive, uncompromising stance, using a hedge word *if* to provide wiggle room, whereas the second choice is far more extreme.

⊘ Benchmark

As you read through the answer choices and you come across one that seems to answer the question well, mentally select that answer choice. This is not your final answer, but it's the one that will help you evaluate the other answer choices. The one that you selected is your benchmark or standard for judging each of the other answer choices. Every other answer choice must be compared to your benchmark. That choice is correct until proven otherwise by another answer choice beating it. If you find a better answer, then that one becomes your new benchmark. Once you've decided that no other choice answers the question as well as your benchmark, you have your final answer.

⊘ Predict the Answer

Before you even start looking at the answer choices, it is often best to try to predict the answer. When you come up with the answer on your own, it is easier to avoid distractions and traps because you will know exactly what to look for. The right answer choice is unlikely to be word-for-word what you came up with, but it should be a close match. Even if you are confident that you have the right answer, you should still take the time to read each option before moving on.

General Strategies

⊘ Tough Questions

If you are stumped on a problem or it appears too hard or too difficult, don't waste time. Move on! Remember though, if you can quickly check for obviously incorrect answer choices, your chances of guessing correctly are greatly improved. Before you completely give up, at least try to knock out a couple of possible answers. Eliminate what you can and then guess at the remaining answer choices before moving on.

⊘ Check Your Work

Since you will probably not know every term listed and the answer to every question, it is important that you get credit for the ones that you do know. Don't miss any questions through careless mistakes. If at all possible, try to take a second to look back over your answer selection and make sure you've selected the correct answer choice and haven't made a costly careless mistake (such as marking an answer choice that you didn't mean to mark). This quick double check should more than pay for itself in caught mistakes for the time it costs.

⊘ Pace Yourself

It's easy to be overwhelmed when you're looking at a page full of questions; your mind is confused and full of random thoughts, and the clock is ticking down faster than you would like. Calm down and maintain the pace that you have set for yourself. Especially as you get down to the last few minutes of the test, don't let the small numbers on the clock make you panic. As long as you are on track by monitoring your pace, you are guaranteed to have time for each question.

⊘ Don't Rush

It is very easy to make errors when you are in a hurry. Maintaining a fast pace in answering questions is pointless if it makes you miss questions that you would have gotten right otherwise. Test writers like to include distracting information and wrong answers that seem right. Taking a little extra time to avoid careless mistakes can make all the difference in your test score. Find a pace that allows you to be confident in the answers that you select.

✅ Keep Moving

Panicking will not help you pass the test, so do your best to stay calm and keep moving. Taking deep breaths and going through the answer elimination steps you practiced can help to break through a stress barrier and keep your pace.

Final Notes

The combination of a solid foundation of content knowledge and the confidence that comes from practicing your plan for applying that knowledge is the key to maximizing your performance on test day. As your foundation of content knowledge is built up and strengthened, you'll find that the strategies included in this chapter become more and more effective in helping you quickly sift through the distractions and traps of the test to isolate the correct answer.

Now that you're preparing to move forward into the test content chapters of this book, be sure to keep your goal in mind. As you read, think about how you will be able to apply this information on the test. If you've already seen sample questions for the test and you have an idea of the question format and style, try to come up with questions of your own that you can answer based on what you're reading. This will give you valuable practice applying your knowledge in the same ways you can expect to on test day.

Good luck and good studying!

Nutrition, Food, and Wellness

Nutrition and Wellness

Preventing Anorexia, Bulimia, and Obesity

Unfortunately, there is no known way of completely eliminating the risk of an individual developing an eating-related condition such as **anorexia**, **bulimia**, and **obesity**, but it has been shown that some methods may significantly lower the risk of developing these conditions. The best way to reduce the risk of developing eating disorders or becoming obese is for parents to interact more with their children and make sure that they are teaching them good eating habits early on. It is also important that parents attempt to build-up the self-esteem of their children through interactions that show high esteem in both the parents and child. Children who have been taught good eating habits by their parents and who have been taught to have high self-esteem have been shown to eat more carefully, and therefore are at a significantly lower risk of becoming obese or developing eating disorders such as anorexia and bulimia.

Anorexia is an eating disorder in which an individual views their own body as being overweight, even though they are not, which causes the person to have an extreme, unfounded fear of gaining additional weight. This fear can lead individuals to use desperate and unhealthy methods to reduce their weight below what would normally be healthy. These methods include deliberate vomiting, limiting their food intake, exercising excessively without eating enough food, and using medications to flush their system. Anorexia is commonly found to affect young women, specifically during adolescence. It can pose a serious risk to an individual's health as the obsessive attempts to reduce body weight can affect the health of the heart, brain, immune system, muscles, and other organs. Anorexia can be extremely difficult to treat as it is a complicated psychological condition, but it has been shown that psychotherapy may be able to help the individual overcome the inaccurate perceptions she or he has regarding their own body.

Bulimia is an eating disorder, similar to anorexia, in which an individual views their own body as being unattractive or overweight, but lacks the ability to control their own eating. Bulimic individuals regularly eat an unhealthily large amount of food and then attempt to flush their systems to prevent themselves from gaining additional weight. Some of the methods individuals suffering from bulimia might use to flush food from their systems include deliberate vomiting, excessive exercise, and using diet pills, laxatives, ipecac, and other medications. Bulimia is most commonly found in women, especially younger women from ages 12 to 19, and can have a significant impact on the health of the individual. It can cause problems such as anemia, weakness, muscle and heart problems, dehydration, malnutrition, damage to the stomach, and a wide range of other problems. Bulimia is difficult to treat, but a combination of group psychotherapy and low doses of anti-psychotic medications have been shown to help.

Anorexia and bulimia are very similar disorders, but the one major difference between the two conditions is control. An individual suffering from anorexia is usually already below a healthy weight, still perceives that their own weight is unacceptable, and therefore attempts to lower that weight further by limiting food intake. Bulimic individuals, on the other hand, have no sense of control over their eating habits. They instead eat excessively and then attempt to overcompensate for their excessive food intake. In short, individuals suffering from anorexia are usually below what would normally be considered a healthy weight for their age and size and attempt to control their eating to reduce their weight further. Bulimic individuals, however, are usually above a healthy weight as they have no control over their own eating.

Obesity is a condition of the body where the individual has increased their own body weight significantly beyond what is normally considered healthy, usually by excessive eating. Obesity occurs because the individual takes in more food than their body can actually use, and the excess food is stored as fat. Overeating is the primary cause of obesity, but obesity can also be tied to family history, genetic factors, stress and lack of sleep, various illnesses and conditions, and many other causes. An individual who is obese is at a significantly higher risk for certain health problems, including problems with the heart, stomach, muscles, lungs, skin, nervous system, and many other areas of the body. The best way to treat obesity is through a well-balanced diet that eliminates excessive food intake and a rigorous exercise program. In extreme cases, individuals may also use medication or even surgery to help lower their weight.

Diabetes

Diabetes is a disease that prevents the body from producing or using a hormone called insulin, which the body needs to process sugar and use it as energy for the cells of the body. Since an individual with diabetes cannot produce insulin or cannot use what is produced, the body is unable to appropriately use the sugar that the cells need to survive. Instead the sugar builds up in the body, leading to a high sugar concentration in the blood, which is a condition known as hyperglycemia. Diabetes can lead to a series of dangerous health problems including the potential failure of the heart, kidneys, nerves, and eyes as well as conditions such as high blood pressure, blindness, poor healing of wounds, and many other dangerous conditions. There is currently no cure for diabetes, but the negative effects of diabetes can be controlled through careful monitoring of blood sugar levels, the use of a specific diet to maintain the individual's blood sugar, and through the use of certain drugs and/or insulin shots.

The three types of diabetes are **type 1**, **type 2**, and **gestational diabetes**. Type 1 diabetes is a form of diabetes in which the individual's own immune system mistakes the beta cells of the pancreas, which are the cells responsible for producing insulin, as being harmful and therefore attacks and destroys them. Type 1 diabetes prevents the individual from actually producing insulin. It is treated primarily through the use of a carefully constructed diet and insulin injections or the use of an insulin pump. Both type 2 diabetes and gestational diabetes are conditions in which the individual is either unable to produce enough insulin for the body or the cells of the body are unable to use the insulin correctly. Type 2 and gestational diabetes can both be treated through the use of a carefully monitored diet along with medication to help the body use the insulin appropriately. The only major difference between type 2 diabetes and gestational diabetes is that gestational diabetes occurs specifically due to hormones present during pregnancy.

There is currently no way to completely prevent an individual from developing diabetes, but the risk of developing certain forms of diabetes can be reduced. The risk of type 2 diabetes and gestational diabetes can be reduced by eating a more healthy diet high in fiber and whole grains, exercising regularly, and lowering the amount of high-fat foods that the individual eats. It has also been suggested that the risk of a mother developing gestational diabetes may be reduced through breast-feeding as it allows the mother to release some of the excess hormones present in her body as a result of the pregnancy. The risk of type 2 and gestational diabetes can be reduced, but there is, unfortunately, no known way of preventing type 1 diabetes, as researchers know very little about the exact causes of the disease.

Review Video: Diabetes Mellitus
Visit mometrix.com/academy and enter code: 501396

Hypertension

Hypertension is a condition in which an individual's blood pressure is regularly higher than the range that is normally acceptable. The blood pressure of a healthy individual should be somewhere between 90/50 and 120/80, and anything over 140/90 is considered to be a high blood pressure. Anything between 120/80 and 140/90 is considered to be prehypertension, in which the individual does not yet have dangerously high blood pressure, but is at significant risk of developing hypertension if steps are not taken to lower the blood pressure. Hypertension can significantly impact virtually every part of the body as the increased force of the blood against the artery walls can severely damage the body's organs, including the heart, brain, eyes, and kidneys, if it goes untreated. Usually there are no apparent symptoms associated with hypertension, but individuals with extremely high blood pressure might experience headaches, vomiting, and difficulty seeing clearly.

Hypertension can usually be treated through the use of a low-salt and low-fat diet along with exercise to bring the individual's blood pressure back down to a reasonable level. People who are being treated for hypertension are usually also advised to stop smoking and drinking to excess, unless it is believed that ceasing these activities will actually put too much additional stress on the individual's body. Persons with significantly higher blood pressures are also often prescribed medication that will help reduce their blood pressure further. There is no way to completely eliminate the risk of hypertension and some factors, including age, race, and family history, can make the individual more predisposed to developing hypertension. However, there are certain factors that individuals can eliminate from their daily activities to significantly lower their risk of developing hypertension. These activities include excessive drinking, smoking, regularly consuming high-salt foods, regular involvement in high-stress activities, and other similar factors that put additional stress on the body.

Dietary Guidelines for Americans

The **Dietary Guidelines for Americans** is a combined publication of the United States Department of Health and Human Services and the United States Department of Agriculture that offers advice to consumers about dietary choices that promote good health and reduce the risk of certain diseases, including hypertension, anemia, and osteoporosis. The Dietary Guidelines for Americans offers advice to consumers on a variety of topics such as weight management, appropriate exercise, food safety, and examples of good sources of certain nutrients. This publication is important because it offers a detailed outline of the kinds of foods that an individual should have in their diets, so they do not need to use additional supplements and vitamins. It also informs consumers of the types of exercise that are necessary for an individual to stay healthy as well as the appropriate manner in which to handle and prepare certain foods to minimize the risk of foodborne illness.

Importance of Vitamins

Vitamin C, also known as ascorbic acid, is important because it helps protect the health of the skin, bones, teeth, cartilage, and blood vessels. Vitamin C protects these areas of the body primarily by acting as an antioxidant that helps reduce the negative effects that oxygen reactions within the body can have on the cells. Vitamin C is also necessary in the production of collagen, which is a protein necessary for skin and cartilage health. Significant vitamin C deficiencies can result in a number of serious health problems including a disorder known as scurvy, in which the body lacks the collagen it requires to maintain the health of the skin. Scurvy ultimately leads to the formation of liver spots on the skin and gums, and can also cause bleeding from all the body's mucous membranes including the nose, lips, ears, and other areas. Common sources of vitamin C include strawberries, oranges, lemons, limes, mangos, grapes, broccoli, potatoes, spinach, liver, and milk.

Vitamin E, and its form tocopherol, is important primarily because it aids in maintaining proper brain function and eye health. It has also been suggested that vitamin E may help reduce the risk of cancer, cataracts, heart disease, and other health conditions as well as helping treat patients that have Parkinson's or Alzheimer's Disease. A significant vitamin E deficiency can result in muscle weakness, blindness, and neurological problems as a result of the body transmitting nerve impulses incorrectly. Common sources of vitamin E include peanuts, hazelnuts, coconuts, corn, asparagus, carrots, tomatoes, fish, peanut butter, and vegetable oils. There are also many multivitamins and supplements that supply vitamin E, but some studies have shown that some synthetic vitamins and supplements may actually be significantly less beneficial or even have a negative impact on the individual when taken in large doses. However, both men and women do require vitamin E, in similar amounts, to continue functioning normally.

B12, and its synthetic form cyanocobalamin, is important because it is necessary for the production of blood cells and aids in maintaining the health of the nervous system. A severe lack of B12 within the body can lead to a variety of conditions including megaloblastic anemia, a condition in which the red blood cells have less hemoglobin and therefore have more difficulty functioning properly. A significant lack of B12 can also lead to severe problems with the nervous system because the lack of B12 causes the disintegration and death of nerve cells. Individuals who lack significant quantities of B12 may develop symptoms such as numbness, tingling, and difficulty with muscle control. Some common sources of B12 include chicken, beef, pork, liver, fish, shellfish, certain breakfast cereals, milk, cheese, eggs, and yogurt. Vegetarians may have difficulty getting enough B12 since the primary sources of B12 are meat products, but B12 supplements and multivitamins can be a good option as well.

Vitamin A, and its derivative retinol, is important because it aids in bone growth, skin health, and the ability to reproduce. Vitamin A also promotes eye health and aids in the production of tears, which prevents the eyes from drying out and washes away bacteria that might cause infections. A vitamin A deficiency can cause the eyes to deteriorate and may lead to conditions such as night blindness, also known as nyctalopia, in which an individual has difficulty seeing in low light environments. Common sources of vitamin A include carrots, sweet potatoes, pumpkins, spinach, beef, pork, chicken, eggs, and broccoli. Both men and women require similar amounts of vitamin A for their bodies to function normally, but men usually require slightly more than women do.

Importance of Fiber

Fiber is an important part of an individual's diet because it helps with bowel movements, digestion, and immune responses. Fiber has also been shown to lower blood cholesterol, help prevent obesity, lower the risk of certain types of cancer including colon cancer, and lower the risk of type 2 diabetes. A significant lack of fiber in an individual's diet can lead to symptoms such as constipation and slower digestion and can cause an individual to have a higher risk of developing certain diseases. Some common sources of fiber include certain breakfast cereals, oatmeal, whole-wheat bread, beans, apples, pears, strawberries, bananas, potatoes, onions, and green beans. Both men and women require similar amounts of fiber to continue functioning properly.

Importance of Protein

Protein is important to the functioning of a healthy individual because it is necessary for the body to produce the amino acids it needs to continue functioning. Most of the amino acids that the body needs are already present in the body, but certain amino acids, known as essential amino acids, can only be produced when the body digests protein. A severe lack of protein is usually caused by malnutrition and can lead to reduced brain function, intellectual disabilities, and an overall weakening of the immune system due to a decrease in the number of white blood cells. It has also been suggested that a significant lack of protein may lead to conditions such as kwashiorkor, which causes significant weight loss, thinning and discolored hair, swelling of the organs, and weakens the responses of the immune system. Some common sources of protein include chicken, beef, wheat, rice, milk, cheese, eggs, peas, beans, peanuts, and peanut butter.

Importance of Iron

Iron is important because it aids in the proper functioning of virtually all the muscles and organs. Iron also allows the body to form hemoglobin, which is a protein in red blood cells that carries oxygen throughout the body. If an individual does not have enough iron in their diet, anemia can result, a condition in which the body is unable to produce hemoglobin. The body may also be unable to produce additional red blood cells if there is a lack of iron, and the individual will be more likely to become fatigued and develop other symptoms and conditions. Common sources of iron include oatmeal, spaghetti, whole wheat bread, sunflower seeds, broccoli, green beans, beets, peas, potatoes, green leafy vegetables, beef, pork, and chicken. Women usually require more iron than men do partially because of the regular blood loss associated with menstruation.

Importance of Calcium

Calcium is important to the development and maintenance of bones and teeth, since a lack of calcium can result in osteoporosis and other bone problems. Calcium is also important to the production of lymph, which is a fluid similar to interstitial fluid that aids in the overall operation of the body, specifically the immune system. Common sources of calcium are milk, cheese, eggs, orange juice, oranges, broccoli, rutabagas, almonds, and other nuts. Calcium can also be obtained through supplements and multivitamins, which can be a good source for people who are allergic to dairy products or have a significant calcium deficiency. Both men and women require similar amounts of calcium, but the amount of calcium required increases as an individual ages.

RDA and RDI

RDA stands for recommended dietary allowance, which is the amount of each vitamin, mineral, or other nutrient that health professionals believe an individual needs to receive daily in order to stay healthy. The RDA has been replaced by the now more commonly used **RDI** or reference daily intake. The RDI is similar to the RDA, but does not recommend different nutrient intakes based on gender and age as the RDA does. The RDI is used to determine the RDV, or recommended daily value, which is printed on virtually every food product in the United States and Canada to inform consumers of the nutritional value, or the lack thereof, that each product offers. These recommended daily values are usually based on a 2000-calorie diet, and since the RDI recommends the same nutrient intake for everyone, there is no difference shown between the intakes necessary for individuals of different age groups or genders. Both the RDA and RDI are important because they allow consumers to determine which foods are best for their diet.

Low Activity and High Activity Individuals

A **low activity** individual is usually considered to be anyone who does not exercise regularly and gets less than 30 minutes of exercise on any given day. A **high activity** individual is usually considered to be anyone who exercises regularly and gets at least 30 to 60 minutes of exercise 4 to 5 times a week. An individual can also be considered high activity if they are in a profession that is physically intense such as warehouse workers, moving company workers, gym teachers, etc. Individuals who exercise more than 30 minutes at a time, but do so only once or twice a week are usually considered mid-level activity persons rather than high or low activity individuals.

Nutritional needs change in a variety of ways as an individual ages, but the major changes involve which vitamins and the number of calories the body requires to keep functioning. Young children usually require around 1000 to 1500 calories a day, but the amount of calories a child requires increases as the child grows. Young teens usually require somewhere between 1600 and 2200 calories a day, depending on their gender and other factors. Individuals entering young adulthood usually require between 2000 and 2400 calories a day. However, after a person reaches age 30, the calorie requirement begins to decrease and continues to do so as they get older. People also require progressively more Vitamins A, C, and E as well as iron and fiber as they age. Individuals over age 50 also require significantly more calcium.

An individual that is more active requires more calories than a person who is less active. A young active child usually requires about the same number of calories as a less active child, but the difference between the calorie needs increases substantially as the children grow. Active young teens require 1600 to 2600 calories, depending on gender and other factors, and active individuals entering young adulthood usually require between 2000 and 3200 calories. As these age ranges show, the calorie needs of an active individual is usually between 400–800 calories higher than a less active person. Active people also require more protein than less active individuals, but usually require similar amounts of Vitamins A, C, and E as well as iron and fiber.

Factors Affecting Nutritional Needs

Some of the major factors that can affect an individual's nutritional needs include:

- **Age of the individual**: The age of an individual plays a major role in the nutritional needs that person has in several ways. As a child grows, for instance, the number of calories the child needs also increases, but after the individual passes a certain age, the number of calories they need decreases. A person's need for specific vitamins and minerals also increases as they get older.
- **Individual's gender**: Gender can affect an individual's nutritional needs; men typically require more protein and more calories than women do, while women usually require significantly more iron than men.
- **Individual's level of activity**: Level of activity also plays a large role in their nutritional needs because an individual who is more active will require a larger number of calories than an individual who less active.

Cholesterol

Cholesterol is a lipid, a type of fat that the body uses to produce both new cells and bile, a substance secreted by the liver that helps the body digest fat. Although the body requires a certain amount of cholesterol to continue functioning normally, excessive amounts of cholesterol can lead to heart and circulatory problems, including a condition known as atherosclerosis, a dangerous condition in which arteries are clogged by deposits of cholesterol. Clogged arteries can cause a variety of other serious problems, such as heart attacks and strokes, because the heart, brain, and many other vital organs cannot receive enough blood to function properly. One of the best ways to avoid too much cholesterol is to stay away from foods that contain high concentrations of saturated fats. Some examples of foods that are high in cholesterol and saturated fats are beef, pork, eggs, milk, butter, cheese, and most snack foods. Some examples of foods that are low in cholesterol and saturated fats include oatmeal, fish, rice, and most fruits and vegetables.

Carbohydrates

Carbohydrates, also known as saccharides, are a group of simple and complex sugars and starches that form an important class of foods in an individual's nutritional needs by supplying energy for the body. Such carbohydrates as the sugar glucose are transported throughout the body via the bloodstream and broken down into energy that keeps the body functioning. Carbohydrates are also important in the function and regulation of the body's immune system and reproductive system. In addition, because carbohydrates aid a person's blood in clotting effectively, they play an essential role in the body's ability to heal. Although many of the body's functions that carbohydrates play a role in can be carried out by proteins and fats as well, carbohydrates are easier for the body to digest and contain less cholesterol than proteins and saturated fats. Examples of foods that are high in carbohydrates include bread, beans, cereals, pasta, potatoes, and rice.

Review Video: Carbohydrates
Visit mometrix.com/academy and enter code: 601714

Fats

Fats are important to the healthy functioning of the body because they allow certain vitamins, including vitamins A, D, E, and K, to be digested and absorbed by the body. These fat-soluble vitamins can be broken down and used by the body only when enough fat is present. In addition, a lack of certain fats in an individual can lead to other vitamin deficiencies. Fats also help maintain the body's temperature; help promote hair, skin, and overall cell health; protect the body's organs; help protect against some diseases; and act as a means of storing energy for the body to use later. However, an excessive amount of fat in the body can adversely affect an individual's health, as an abundance of saturated fats and trans fats can greatly increase the cholesterol level in the blood, which in turn increases an individual's risk of certain heart conditions and other health problems. Some foods that individuals may want to avoid eating in excess because they are high in fat include butter, cream, cheese, lard, milk, and snack foods.

Iodine

Relatively small amounts of **iodine** are important to an individual's health because the element iodine is necessary for the production of thyroid hormones, which the body needs to function normally. A lack of iodine in an individual's diet or an excessive amount of iodine in the body can lead to a variety of symptoms and conditions including depression, fatigue, mental slowness or intellectual disability, excessive weight gain, and goiter, which is an enlargement of the thyroid gland characterized by an extremely swollen neck. Iodine deficiencies are fairly uncommon in the United States and other developed countries because most of the salt used in cooking has been treated with iodine to make sure that individuals ingest enough iodine on a daily basis. Other foods that have high concentrations of iodine include fish, kelp, and most dairy products.

Food

Food is essential for the health of an individual, because it satisfies an individual's nutritional needs. Additionally, food provides many people some degree of psychological satisfaction as well. Food is a basic necessity for the successful functioning of an individual; therefore, the body makes a person aware of its need for food by creating a feeling of hunger. When the individual satisfies this hunger by consuming various foods, the body releases hormones that result in the person's feeling a sensation of being full, an indication that the body's need for sustenance has been assuaged. Certain types of foods satisfy an individual's hunger more effectively than other foods. Foods that are high in fiber, protein, and water usually will make an individual feel more satiated, or full. If an individual's body lacks a specific type of nutrient, the body will cause that person to experience a craving for foods that will satisfy that particular nutritional need.

The New Pyramid

The New Pyramid is the current federal healthy eating guide, formerly MyPlate and the Food Pyramid. It was introduced for the 2025-2030 Dietary Guidelines for Americans. While MyPlate mainly focused on showing how a meal could be divided into different food groups, The New

Pyramid looks more closely at the kinds of foods people choose. It encourages everyone to eat real, whole, nutrient-dense foods as often as possible. This includes such foods as protein, dairy, vegetables, fruits, healthy fats, and whole grains, especially when they are in their natural or minimally processed forms. The guidelines also remind people to limit foods and drinks that are heavily processed or high in added sugars, refined carbohydrates, excess sodium, unhealthy fats, and artificial ingredients. Overall, The New Pyramid is not just about how much of each food group is on the plate. It mainly focuses on the quality of the food chosen and encourages people to build meals around choices that provide important nutrients and support better health throughout their lives.

History of American Dietary Guidelines

Early in 1977, the US Senate Select Committee on Nutrition and Human Needs, then chaired by Senator George McGovern, following extensive reviews of science and discussions, recommended dietary goals consisting of recommendations concerning food and nutrients. The first goal recommended Americans only eat as much energy from food (i.e., calories) as they expended. This goal addressed obesity through balanced consumption. Regarding nutrients, the committee recommended eating more complex carbohydrates and fewer simple (i.e., processed or refined) carbohydrates and decreasing total fat, saturated fat, cholesterol, and sodium. Food goals also included eating more vegetables, fruits, and whole grains and replacing more saturated fats with unsaturated fats. Due to controversy and skepticism from industrial and scientific groups, the US Departments of Agriculture and Health and Human Services (formerly Health, Education, and Welfare) jointly issued a nutrition and health brochure in 1980, partly based on the Surgeon General's 1979 report on health promotion and disease prevention and reflecting research findings about relationships between diet and health. However, this too met with debate.

Despite their straightforward, scientific basis, US Dietary Guidelines issued in 1980 encountered arguments from various industrial and scientific quarters. In response, Congress directed the Departments of Agriculture (USDA) and Health and Human Services (HHS, formerly HEW) to form an advisory committee to solicit formal and informal outside and private-sector advice for subsequent editions. Though the 1985 edition of the Guidelines did not incorporate extensive changes, adding non-federal scientists' input resulted in far less controversy and wider adoption. HHS and USDA formed a second scientific advisory committee in 1989 to review and revise the Guidelines. The 1990 edition reinforced earlier editions' principles, but additionally suggested numerical targets for saturated and total fat amounts, emphasizing these did not apply to a single food or meal, but to eating choices over multiple days. While these first three editions were voluntarily issued, the 1990 National Nutrition Monitoring and related Research Act first legally mandated the Dietary Guidelines report, required a new report every five years, and established a Dietary Guidelines Advisory Committee for that purpose. The 2005 committee adopted systematic methods to review scientific evidence and literature. The 2010 committee extended these, also establishing the Nutrition Evidence Library to support its work with a comprehensive, evidence-based review process.

Nutrients, Carbohydrates, Fats, Protein, Vitamins, and Minerals Found in Foods

Carbohydrates are starches, fibers, and sugars in foods from which the body manufactures glucose, the blood sugar used to fuel all activities of the body, including the brain. Glucose is accessed immediately, or stored in the muscles and liver for future use. Fats are necessary to normal bodily functions, but only 20-35 percent of the human diet need be from fats (preferably oils, not solid fats; and unsaturated, not saturated or trans fats). USDA recommends eating below 10 percent of calories in saturated fats, and avoiding trans fats. (Trans fats are found in partially hydrogenated oils.) Humans need to eat foods with protein, which our bodies digest into amino acids to rebuild all organs, tissues, and cells, which contain protein that is continually broken down and replaced. Animal proteins are complete protein sources with all essential amino acids. Vegetable proteins are incomplete sources, but combining complementary vegetable proteins can yield complete protein. Ten to 35 percent of daily calories should be protein; Americans typically eat enough. Vitamins and minerals are important to health; for instance, vitamin D aids calcium absorption, and calcium promotes strong bone formation. Supplements are available, but eating a nutritious and varied diet usually provides enough vitamins and minerals.

Fat

Fats are divided into two main categories: saturated and unsaturated. Saturated fats are mostly found in meat, lard, butter, coconut, and palm oil. Doctors consider these fats to be the most hazardous to health because they increase the risk of heart disease and certain kinds of cancer. Unsaturated fats include sunflower oil, corn oil, olive oil, and canola oil. The last two oils are called monounsaturated fats and are particularly good for the body because they lower cholesterol. Recent research has concluded that the most harmful kinds of fats are trans fats, which are formed when liquid vegetable oil is processed to make table spreads and cooking fats. Trans fats have been consistently shown to create buildup in arteries, a process which can impair heart health.

Many fats can increase cholesterol, a substance in the body which has consistently been linked with heart disease. Cholesterol has many positive uses in the body, like helping the liver operate and helping to form many hormones, but if cholesterol becomes too abundant, it can build up in the arteries and impede the flow of blood. Research has shown that saturated fats cause a more significant buildup of cholesterol than unsaturated fats or other foods that contain cholesterol. In order to minimize cholesterol in the diet, individuals should cut back on fats altogether, but especially limit their intake of saturated fats. Monounsaturated fats, like canola and olive oil, are a good, low-cholesterol source of fat.

Fiber

Whole grains, fruits, and vegetables are all excellent sources of fiber. Fiber can be either insoluble or soluble. Insoluble fibers (cellulose and lignin, for example) speed digestion and can reduce the risk of colon cancer and heart disease. Wheat and corn bran, leafy vegetables, and fruit and vegetable skins are all great sources of insoluble fiber. Soluble fibers (pectins and gums, for example) lower cholesterol levels and help manage the level of blood sugar. They can be found in the pulp of fruits and in vegetables, oats, beans, and barley. Doctors warn that most Americans do not eat nearly enough fiber. However, increasing fiber in your diet should be done gradually, as a sudden increase in fiber can result in bloating, cramps, and diarrhea.

Water

A person should drink 7 to 10 average sized glasses of water daily. Water is probably the most important substance a person can consume. Water carries nutrients throughout the body and regulates body temperature. Water lubricates joints, aids digestion, and helps speed waste matter out of the body. Losing even 5% of the body's water causes immediate physical symptoms, like dizziness, fatigue, and headache; losing 15% of the body's water can be fatal. The normal daily loss is between 64 and 80 ounces of water a day, which is equal to about 9 large glasses of water. Many fruits and vegetables contain helpful water, but people should still consume the recommended amount of water each day. People who are active, live at a high altitude, or travel a great deal should be sure to drink even more water.

Water Supply

Even though Americans have generally been able to rely on the water supply, in recent years some concerns have been raised about the prevalence of potentially dangerous chemicals in water. Fluoride, which has greatly improved dental health by strengthening teeth since it was added to the water supply, may be damaging to bone strength if it is consumed in great volume. Chlorine, which is often added to water to kill bacteria, may increase the risk of bladder cancer. One of the most dangerous chemicals that can affect water is lead, which is known to leach from pipes and enter the drinking supply. High amounts of lead in the body can cause serious damage to the brain and heart.

Review Video: Dehydration
Visit mometrix.com/academy and enter code: 283651

Alcoholism

The National Council on Alcoholism and Drug Dependence considers alcoholism as a disease that is influenced by social, environmental, and genetic factors. The common features of alcoholism are the inability to control consumption, continued drinking despite negative consequences, and distorted thinking patterns (like irrational denial). It is important to note that alcoholism is not simply the result of a weak will but is a physiological state that requires medical treatment so that it can be controlled. Many individuals may have a problem with alcoholism but not realize it if they are still functioning well overall and only drink in social situations. Alcoholics tend to be those who, even when they aren't drinking, place an undue amount of psychological emphasis on alcohol.

Drug Abuse

A drug is any chemical substance that changes the way a person acts or feels. Drugs may affect a person's mental, physical, or emotional state. Though many drugs are taken to improve the condition of the body or to remedy personal problems, drugs can also undermine health by distorting a person's mind and weakening a person's body. According to the World Health Organization, drug abuse is any excessive drug use that is not approved by the medical profession. The use of some drugs in any quantity is considered abuse; other drugs must be taken in large quantities before they are considered to have been abused. There are health risks involved with the use of any drug, legal or illegal, insofar as they introduce a foreign substance into the balanced system of physical health.

Appetite

The feeling of hunger can be caused by up to 12 different hormones and areas of the brain. There is even some speculation that the size of an individual's fat cells may cause them to feel hungry. The appetite is the physiological desire to eat, and though it is thought to be the body's means of avoiding failure, it can also be stimulated when the body does not really need food. Humans tend to stop eating when they reach the point of satiety, in which they are no longer hungry and feel full. Scientists have advanced the set-point theory of appetite, which contends that each individual has an internal system that is geared to regulate hunger and satiety so as to keep body fat at a certain rate.

Health and Wellness

Health

Quite simply, **health** is the state of being sound in mind, body, and spirit. According to the World Health Organization, health is not only the absence of disease, but the presence of physical, mental, and social well-being. When assessing an individual's health, a professional is likely to examine them from a physical, psychological, spiritual, social, intellectual, or environmental standpoint. Although every individual has their own standard of health, it is common for people to recognize the following characteristics as healthy: an optimistic outlook in life, the ability to relax, a supportive home life, a clean environment, a satisfying job, freedom from pain and illness, and the energy necessary to enjoy life.

Wellness

Health professionals refer to the highest state of health as **wellness**. Wellness has a number of definitions: it may mean enjoying life, or having a defined purpose in life and being able to work towards it, or it may mean deliberately taking the steps necessary to avoid disease and maximize health. Wellness is different from health in that it means actively enhancing health, not just maintaining good health. Total wellness depends on psychological, physical, and social factors. In the general model for wellness, all of these factors combine to produce the individual's complete level of wellness. Indeed, part of the reason why health professionals promote the idea of wellness is to show people that all the areas of their lives depend on one another.

Psychological Health

In order to achieve **psychological health**, you must have an accurate and favorable impression of yourself. Having healthy self-esteem does not mean overestimating your talents and value; it means feeling good about your role in life and expecting that you will have the personal resources to deal with any adversity. A person who has a reasonable concept of themselves will be able to tolerate the faults of others, based upon the knowledge gained from self-reflection. Part of establishing a realistic but positive view of the world is accepting that there are many things that you will be unable to change in life, and that rather than making yourself miserable about them, you can direct your attention to those things that are under your control.

Physical Education

The meaning of the phrase "**physical education**" may seem obvious at first glance, but it is quite possible for individuals to have very distinct ideas of what physical education entails. Physical education, by most accounts, is composed of exercise (the use of the body), play (the action generated by the exertion of the body), games (competitions of any kind), leisure (freedom from the responsibilities of work), recreation (any activity that refreshes the mind and body after work), sport (physical activities performed for pleasure or achievement), and athletics (organized, competitive activities). So, a general definition of physical education might be that it is the process whereby an individual improves their physical, mental, and social skill through physical activity.

Personal Fitness

Personal fitness is particular to the individual. Some people may be considered fit when they can run for a mile without stopping, while others may be athletic enough to accomplish that feat without really being in shape. Most people will acquire a sense of their own fitness only after spending a great deal of time exercising, setting fitness goals, and working to achieve them. However, those who want more objective data on their physical condition may submit to testing at a sports medicine laboratory. There, they will have their muscular and cardiovascular endurance measured on a treadmill, their body fat measured in a submersion tank, and their flexibility tested through a variety of trials.

Cardiovascular Fitness

An individual's **cardiovascular fitness** is the ability of their heart to pump blood through the body at the necessary rate. Proper cardiovascular fitness can be achieved through aerobic exercise: that is, any activity during which the amount of oxygen taken into the body is equal to or more than the amount the body is using. Jogging, walking, or riding a bike are all examples of aerobic activity. The heart also gets an excellent workout during anaerobic exercise, in which the body takes in less oxygen than it needs to maintain the activity. Sprinting or swimming fast can be anaerobic exercises, if they leave the person breathless. Nonaerobic exercise, like bowling or golf, does not challenge the heart and lungs and therefore will not improve cardiovascular fitness.

Muscle Strength and Endurance

Developing healthy muscles is not simply a matter of lifting the heaviest possible object. The ability to use your muscles over and over without getting tired is also an important part of physical fitness. Developing **muscular strength** and **endurance** will help make body tissue firmer and more resilient. Well-maintained muscles tend to work more efficiently, and they can withstand more strain. Furthermore, muscular development aids in circulation, with the result that the whole body absorbs and makes use of nutrients in the blood more quickly. Strength and endurance training has also been shown to be one of the most effective ways to lose weight, as developed muscles burn more calories than fat does.

Exercising Muscles

Muscles are in a constant state of change. If muscles are not used, they will atrophy and weaken; on the other hand, if they are regularly exercised, they will grow stronger and possibly larger. Muscles are best exercised when they are overloaded or asked to do more than they usually do. When you are training your muscles, you will need to gradually increase the amount of the weight or the number of repetitions to ensure that your muscles are always receiving a challenge. Many fitness professionals contend that a good muscular workout will be somewhat painful because muscles can only be developed by exceeding their normal requirements. However, not every kind of pain is profitable for a muscular workout, and individuals should be careful to distinguish muscular fatigue from injury, particularly when they are lifting heavy loads.

Recreation Safety Laws

A number of laws exist to ensure the safety of individuals when they engage in recreational activities. For instance, an individual may not be intoxicated while driving a boat. There are also laws governing the use of jet-skis, wave runners, snowmobiles, and all-terrain vehicles. The federal government cites these last vehicles as particularly dangerous for young, untrained, or intoxicated drivers. A set of regulations governs the use of the national and state parks (e.g., restrictions on the building of fires). The federal government recently reported a sharp increase in the number of in-line skating and skateboarding injuries; skaters are now denied access to many recreational areas because of the increased safety risk.

Vital Signs

Every individual should be able to identify the **vital signs** and know how to measure them. The four common measures considered to be vital signs are body temperature, blood pressure, pulse rate, and respiration rate. Body temperature can be taken with a thermometer and should register between 96º and 99.9º Fahrenheit, depending on the time of day and sex (women tend to have slightly higher temperatures). Measuring blood pressure requires some equipment; a normal blood pressure is between 120/70 and 140/90, depending on age and sex. A normal pulse rate is ranges between 60 and 80 beats per minute. For athletes, resting pulse rates can be even lower. A normal respiration rate is between 15 to 20 breaths a minute.

Warming Up and Cooling Down

There are important reasons for warming up before and cooling down after exercise. For one thing, performance is always enhanced by warming up. Muscles tend to work more effectively when their temperature has been slightly raised; they are also more resistant to strains and tears at a higher temperature. Warming up directs the blood to working muscles and gives the heart time to adjust to the increased demands of the muscles. Warming up also stimulates the secretion of synovial fluid into the joints, which makes them less likely to suffer wear and tear. Warming up should include slow stretching and low-impact cardiovascular exercise. Cooling down is important for easing the body's transition to a normal resting condition. By stretching and slowly decreasing cardiovascular workload, the heart is aided in its readjustment.

Recreation Versus Competition

One of the perennial issues facing physical educators is whether activities should be promoted as forms of recreation or as competition. If competition is to be the dominant feature, then activities must have explicit rules, a formal way of keeping score, and identifiable winners and losers. When students are taught activities for competition, the emphasis will be on practicing specific skills and avoiding mistakes as much as possible. When sports are taught as recreation, participation is the most important factor for students. Each student should get an equal amount of experience and performance time, regardless of their skill level. Although score is typically not kept in strictly recreational activities, students may receive certificates for good sportsmanship or diligent participation.

Health Education as a Community Service

In a general sense, all of health education can be seen as community service. By teaching positive health behaviors and promoting good health to students, health teachers are improving the quality of life for everyone in the community. More specifically, though, the Center for Disease Control has recommended that health educators use their special training to improve health through work outside of school. Many health educators participate in fundraising for health charities, give speeches on health-related topics, or work in the community to generate enthusiasm for exercise and nutrition. According to the Code of Ethics for health educators, it is imperative for those with knowledge and skills to advance positive health behaviors whenever possible and, thus, help their community.

Aerobic Fitness

A minimum of **aerobic fitness** has been achieved when you are able to exercise three times a week at 65% of your maximum heart rate. The easiest means of achieving this level of fitness is by running for 30 minutes three or four times a week. Moderate aerobic fitness is achieved by exercising four or more times a week for at least 30 minutes at a heart rate that is 75% or more of maximum. This level of aerobic fitness is appropriate for athletes who are seeking to play vigorous sports like football or tennis. Maximum aerobic fitness can only be achieved by working close to maximum heart rate several times a week and by exercising vigorously almost every day. In order to achieve this level of fitness, you must consistently work beyond your anaerobic threshold. A good way to do this is having interval training or brief, high-intensity workouts.

Skeletal System

The **skeletal system** is composed of about 200 bones which, along with the attached ligaments and tendons, create a protective and supportive network for the body's muscles and soft tissues. There are two main components of the skeletal system: the axial skeleton and the appendicular skeleton. The axial skeleton includes the skull, spine, ribs, and sternum; the appendicular skeleton includes the pelvis, shoulders, and the various arm and leg bones attached to these. The skeleton does not move, but it is pulled in various directions by the muscles. There are few differences between the male and female skeleton: the bones of a male tend to be a bit larger and heavier than those of the female, who will have a wider pelvic cavity.

Review Video: Skeletal System
Visit mometrix.com/academy and enter code: 256447

Lymphatic System

The **lymphatic system** is connected to the cardiovascular system through a network of capillaries. The lymphatic system filters out organisms that cause disease, controls the production of disease-fighting antibodies, and produces white blood cells. The lymphatic system also prevents body tissues from swelling by draining fluids from them. Two of the most important areas in this system are the right lymphatic duct and the thoracic duct. The right lymphatic duct moves the immunity-bolstering lymph fluid through the top half of the body, while the thoracic duct moves lymph throughout the lower half. The spleen, thymus, and lymph nodes all generate and store the chemicals which form lymph and which are essential to protecting the body from disease.

Nervous System

The **nervous system** collects information for the body and indicates what the body should do to survive in the present conditions. For instance, it is the nervous system that administers a bad feeling when the body is cold, and then sends a more positive message when a person warms up. These important messages are sent by the nerves, which vary in size and cover the entire body. The central nervous system is composed of the brain and spinal cord, and the peripheral nervous system is composed of the rest of the body, including those organs which a person does not voluntarily control. The peripheral nervous system is divided into sympathetic and parasympathetic systems, which counterbalance one another to allow for smooth function.

Review Video: Function of the Nervous System
Visit mometrix.com/academy and enter code: 708428

Digestive System

The **digestive system** is composed of organs that convert food into energy. This process begins with the teeth, which grind food into small particles that are easy to digest. Food is then carried through the pharynx (throat) and esophagus to the stomach. In the stomach, it is partially digested by strong acids and enzymes. From there, food passes through the small and large intestines, the rectum, and out through the anus. On this journey, it will be mixed with numerous chemicals so that it can be absorbed into the blood and lymph system. Some food will be converted into immediate energy, and some will be stored for future use; whatever cannot be used by the body will be expelled as waste.

Review Video: Gastrointestinal System
Visit mometrix.com/academy and enter code: 378740

Muscular System

The muscles of the body are attached to the skeleton by tendons and other connective tissues. Muscles exert force and move the bones of the body by converting chemical energy into contractions. Every muscular act is the result of some muscle growing shorter. The muscles themselves are composed of millions of tiny proteins. Muscles are stimulated by nerves that link them to the brain and spinal cord. There are three types of muscles: cardiac muscles are found only in the heart and pump the blood through the body; smooth muscles surround or are part of internal organs; skeletal muscles are those a person controls voluntarily. Skeletal muscles are the most common tissue in the body, accounting for between 25 and 40% of body weight.

Review Video: Muscular System
Visit mometrix.com/academy and enter code: 967216

Endocrine System

The **endocrine system** creates and secretes the hormones that accomplish a wide variety of tasks in the body. The endocrine system is made up of glands. These glands produce chemicals that regulate metabolism, growth, and sexual development. Glands release hormones directly into the bloodstream, where they are then directed to the various organs and tissues of the body. The endocrine system is generally considered to include the pituitary, thyroid, parathyroid, and adrenal glands, as well as the pancreas, ovaries, and testes. The endocrine system regulates its level of hormone production by monitoring the activity of hormones; when it senses that a certain hormone is active, it reduces or stops production of that hormone.

Review Video: Endocrine System
Visit mometrix.com/academy and enter code: 678939

Circulatory System

The **circulatory system** is composed of the heart, the blood vessels, and the blood. This system circulates the blood throughout the body, giving nutrients and other essential materials to the body cells and removing waste products. Arteries carry blood away from the heart, and veins carry blood back to the heart. Within body tissues, tiny capillaries distribute blood to the various body cells. The heart takes oxygenated blood from the lungs and distributes it to the body; when blood comes back bearing carbon dioxide, the heart sends it to the lungs to be expelled. Other organs not always considered to be a part of this system (for instance, the kidneys and spleen) help to remove some impurities from the blood.

Review Video: Cardiovascular System
Visit mometrix.com/academy and enter code: 376581

Hormone System

Hormones are the chemicals that motivate the body to do certain things. They are produced in the organs that make up the endocrine system. With the exception of the sex organs, males and females have identical endocrine systems. The actions of the hormones are determined by the hypothalamus, an area of the brain about the size of a pea. The hypothalamus sends messages to the pituitary gland, which is directly beneath it. The pituitary gland turns on and off the various glands that produce hormones. Hormones, once released, are carried to their targets by the bloodstream, at which point they motivate cells and organs to action. Hormones can influence the way a person looks, feels, behaves, or matures.

Cartilage

The areas of bones that are close to joints are covered in a shiny connective tissue known as **cartilage**. Cartilage supports the joint structure and protects the fragile bone tissue underneath. Cartilage is susceptible to injury because it is subject to gravitational pressure as well as pressure born of joint movement itself. Long-term stress to cartilage can result in rheumatoid arthritis and osteoarthritis. There are no blood vessels in cartilage; nutrients are delivered by the synovial fluid, and from nearby blood vessels. Cartilage contains a huge number of spongy fibers because it needs to absorb a great deal of shock. Especially resilient cartilage, known as fibrocartilage, is found between the vertebrae and in the knees, among other places.

LIGAMENTS

Ligaments are dense bundles of fibers running parallel to one another from one bone in a joint to another. Ligaments are a part of the joint capsule, although they may also connect to other nearby bones that are not part of the joint. Ligaments are not like muscles; they cannot contract. Instead, ligaments passively strengthen and support the joints by absorbing some of the tension of movement. Ligaments do contain nerve cells which are sensitive to position and speed of movement, and so ligaments can hurt. One function of this pain is to alert the person to an unnatural or dangerous movement of the joint. Ligaments may also be strained or rupture if they are placed under unnecessary or violent stress.

MUSCLE TISSUE

Muscle tissue is made up of bundles of fibers which are held in position and separated by various partitions. These partitions range from large (deep fascia, epimysium) to small (perimysium, endomysium), and often extend beyond the length of the muscle and form tendons connecting to a bone. Each muscle cell is extremely long and has a large amount of nuclei. Every muscle cell contains a number of smaller units called sarcomeres; these contain thick filaments of the protein myosin and thin filaments of the protein actin. Muscle tissue contracts when a nerve stimulates the muscle and the thin filaments compress within the sarcomere, causing a general muscle contraction.

SETTING GOALS

Individuals who are most likely to make positive permanent changes in their health set realistic goals along the way. When setting goals, individuals should identify what resources (time, money, and effort) are available to achieve them. Individuals should also identify the potential barriers to success and consider ways to minimize or remove these problems. It is always better to set a number of small, attainable goals rather than goals that may be difficult to achieve.

PHYSICAL FITNESS

Physical fitness is the body's ability to perform all of its tasks and still have some reserve energy in case of an emergency. People who are physically fit can meet all of their daily physical needs, have a realistic and positive image of themselves, and are working to protect themselves against future health problems. Physical fitness has three main components: flexibility, cardiovascular fitness, and muscular strength or endurance. Some other factors, like agility and balance, are also often considered when assessing physical fitness. The benefits of pursuing physical fitness throughout life are not only physical but mental and emotional; regular exercise is proven to reduce the risk of disease and increase life expectancy.

FLEXIBILITY

A person's **flexibility** is their range of motion around particular joints. An individual's flexibility will vary according to age, gender, and posture. Some individuals may be less flexible because of bone spurs, and some individuals may be less flexible because they are overweight. Typically, an individual's flexibility will increase through childhood until adolescence, at which point joint mobility slows and diminishes for the rest of the individual's life. Muscles and the connective tissue around them (tendons and ligaments) will contract and become tighter if they are not used to their potential. Lack of flexibility can lead to a buildup of tension in the muscles and can increase the risk of injury during exercise.

Heart, Lungs, and Bones

Maintaining physical fitness has a number of advantages besides improving personal appearance. It has been shown time and again that habitual exercise is the best way to prevent coronary death. In fact, individuals who don't exercise are twice as likely as active individuals to die of a heart attack. Exercise makes the lungs more efficient, as they are able to take in more oxygen and make better use of it. This provides the body with more available energy. Exercise also benefits the bones. Individuals who do not exercise are more likely to have weak or brittle bones, and they are more prone to osteoporosis, in which bones lose their mineral density and become dangerously soft.

Mood, Disease Prevention, and Body Weight

The benefits of regular exercise are both physical and mental. It is well documented that frequent exercise improves a person's mood, increases energy, focus, and alertness, and reduces anxiety. In fact, long workouts cause the release of mood-elevating chemicals called endorphins into the brain. Exercise also reduces the risk of disease. By aiding in the proper digestion, exercise reduces the risk of colon and rectal cancers. Studies have also indicated that women who exercise are less likely to develop breast cancer. Finally, exercise is beneficial because it helps people lose weight and keep it off. The body's metabolism remains elevated for a prolonged period after exercise, which means food is processed more quickly and efficiently. In addition, regular exercise helps suppress the appetite.

Nutrition and Exercise

For most people, the balanced diet depicted in realfood.gov's New Pyramid will supply all the healthy nutrients the body needs to maintain a program of physical fitness. However, individuals who are seriously testing their endurance by exercising for periods of more than an hour at a time will need to increase their intake of complex carbohydrates, which keep the level of blood sugar stable and increase the amount of available glycogen. Contrary to popular thought, heavy workouts do not require a diet high in protein, and in fact, consuming too much protein can put a severe strain on the kidneys and liver. Similarly, most health experts discourage the use of dietary supplements and body-building foods unless under supervision because these products can easily result in nutritional imbalances.

Water and Exercise

Water is the most important thing for a person to consume before, during, and after exercise. On hot days, active people can sweat up to a quart of water. If you become dehydrated, your heart will have a difficult time providing oxygen and nutrients to muscles. Even sports drinks cannot provide the hydrating effect of cool water because the sodium, sugar, and potassium in them delay their absorption into the body. Salt tablets should be avoided as well; they are potentially dangerous and unnecessary. Although people do lose a bit of sodium when they sweat, this is more than offset by the huge amount of salt in the average American diet.

Review Video: Dehydration
Visit mometrix.com/academy and enter code: 283651

First-Aid Tips and Supplies

Since it is necessary to act fast when an emergency happens, it is a good idea to think ahead and have a plan in place. If you are in a public place, you may want to begin by shouting for help to see if a doctor is available. Someone should immediately dial 911. Do not attempt any resuscitation techniques unless you are trained. If you have a car and it is appropriate, you should immediately take the victim to the nearest hospital. Furthermore, every home should have some basic first-aid supplies. A good first-aid kit will include bandages, sterile gauze pads, scissors, adhesive tape, calamine lotion, cotton balls, thermometer, ipecac syrup (to induce vomiting), a sharp needle, and safety pins.

Smog

Smog is the informal name given to the combination of smoke, gases, and fog that accumulates in major industrial or metropolitan areas. Most smog is created by motor vehicles, wood-burning stoves, industrial factories, and electric utilities plants. Gray smog, which is mainly sulfur dioxide, is common in the eastern United States because of the high concentration of industry. This kind of smog acts like cigarette smoke on the lungs, impairing the ability of the cilia to expel particulates. Brown smog comes from automobiles and is mainly composed of nitrogen dioxide. Ozone, one of the other components of brown smog, can impair the immune system. Automobiles are also known to produce carbon monoxide, which diminishes the ability of the red blood cells to carry oxygen.

Pollution

Many people do not consider **pollution** a personal health issue, but polluted air and water can affect every aspect of a person's life. Scientists define pollution as any change in the air, soil, or water that impairs its ability to host life. Most pollution is the byproduct of human acts. Some of the common health problems associated with pollution are nasal discharge, eye irritation, constricted air passages, birth defects, nausea, coughing, and cancer. Environmental agents that change the DNA of living cells are called mutagens, and they can lead to the development of cancer. Pollutants that can pass through the placenta of a woman and cause damage to an unborn child are called teratogens.

Exercise and Weight Loss

Despite the appeal of quick solutions to obesity, exercise remains the best way to reduce weight and maintain weight loss. Many people think that increasing exercise will make them want to eat more; in actuality, frequent exercise tends to reduce the appetite, and since it raises the rate of metabolism, it also helps keep weight off. There are numerous other advantages to exercise in regard to weight; exercise burns off fat reserves and increases muscle mass. Since muscle tends to use calories more quickly than fat, this means it will be more difficult for the individual to put on pounds of fat. In study after study, individuals who exercise regularly are shown to be more likely to lose weight and keep it off.

Communicable and Non-Communicable Diseases

Communicable diseases are those that are caused by microorganisms and can be transferred from one infected person or animal to a previously uninfected person or animal. Although some diseases are passed on by direct contact with an infected individual, many can be spread through close proximity: airborne bacteria or viruses account for most communication of disease. Some examples of communicable disease are measles, smallpox, influenza, and scarlet fever. Some communicable diseases require specific circumstances for transmission; for instance, tetanus requires the presence of infected soil or dirt. Any disease that cannot be transferred from one person or animal to another is considered non-communicable.

Infectious and Non-Infectious Diseases

Infectious diseases are those that are caused by a virus, bacterium, or parasite. Infectious diseases are distinguished from **non-infectious diseases** in that they stem from biological causes, rather than from physical or chemical causes (as in the case of burns or poisoning). An infectious disease will always have an agent (something that has the disease and spreads it to others) and a vector (a way of transmitting the disease). In the case of malaria, for instance, a parasite contains the disease, and it is introduced to the body when a mosquito carrying it places it in the bloodstream. The vector of an infectious disease does not need to be biological; many diseases are transmitted through water, for example.

Viruses

Viruses are the smallest of the pathogens, but they are also the most difficult to destroy. Viruses consist of a small bit of nucleic acid (either DNA or RNA) inside a coating of protein. Viruses are unable to reproduce by themselves, so they infest the reproductive systems of cells already in the body and command them to make new viral cells. These new cells are then sent to other parts of the body. Some of the most common viruses are influenza, herpes, hepatitis, and papilloma. It is difficult to treat viruses without also damaging the cells that they are using. Antibiotics, for instance, have no effect on viruses. Special antiviral drugs must be taken, and even these do not entirely eliminate the presence of the virus.

Bacteria

Bacteria are simple, one-celled organisms and are the most common microorganism and pathogen. Most bacteria do not cause disease; in fact, many bacteria are important to body processes. Bacteria can harm the body when they release enzymes that digest other body cells or when they produce toxins. Since bacteria are quite different from normal body cells, they can usually be effectively treated with antibiotics. However, not just any antibiotic can be used to treat every bacterial infection; a doctor must determine the particular strain of bacteria that is causing the problem before they write a prescription. Over time, bacteria may become resistant to antibiotics, so it is best not to take too much of this effective treatment.

Immune System

The body uses a number of different weapons to try to defeat infections. Most obviously, the skin repels most invaders. Many substances produced by the body (like mucus, saliva, and tears) also fight against infection. When these methods are ineffective, however, the **immune system** goes to work. The immune system consists of parts of the lymphatic system like the spleen, thymus gland, and lymph nodes, and vessels called lymphatics that work to filter impurities out of the body. The spleen is where antibodies are made, as well as the place where old red blood cells are disposed. The thymus gland fortifies white blood cells with the ability to find and destroy invaders. The lymph nodes filter our bacteria and other pathogens.

Whenever an antigen, or infecting substance, enters the body, the immune system immediately goes to work to defeat it. Initially, the T cells fight the antigen while assisted by macrophages (cells that scavenge for foreign or weakened cells). While this battle is raging, the B cells create antibodies to join in. Many pathogens will be transported to the lymph nodes, where a reserve store of antibodies will eliminate them. It is for this reason that the lymph nodes often become swollen during cold and flu season. If the antigens find some success, the body will rush a greater blood supply to the infected area, enriching the supply of oxygen and nutrients. In the event that the pathogens are able to contaminate the blood stream, the infection becomes systemic and much more dangerous.

Review Video: Immune System
Visit mometrix.com/academy and enter code: 622899

Allergies

An **allergy** is a hypersensitivity or overreaction to some substance in a person's environment or diet; it is the most common kind of immune disorder. There are many different symptoms of an allergic reaction, but the most common are sneezing, hives, eye irritation, vomiting, and nasal congestion. In some extreme cases, the person may collapse and even die. Allergic triggers, or allergens, can be anything from peanuts to pollen, or from insect bites to mold. Although there is no way to reverse or eliminate a personal allergy, science has made progress in treating the allergic reaction. These days, it is possible to be treated for an allergic reaction without becoming drowsy or sluggish.

Immunizations

Despite the overwhelming evidence supporting the use of **immunization** in preventing potentially life-threatening diseases, many Americans still neglect to get the basic immunizations. At present, the American Academy of Pediatrics recommends that every child be immunized against measles, mumps, smallpox, rubella, diphtheria, tetanus, and hepatitis B. Some vaccinations will need to be repeated on a certain schedule. Basically, a vaccination is the intentional introduction of a small amount of an antigen into the body. This stimulates the immune system to learn how to fight that particular antigen. There are certain vaccinations that a pregnant woman should not get, and a person should never be vaccinated if they are currently sick.

Common Cold

The **common cold** is one of the most pesky and irritating of viruses, though it is rarely a great risk to long-term health. One reason the cold is so difficult to fight is that there are over 200 varieties of the virus, so the body is never able to develop a comprehensive immunity. The cold virus is typically spread through the air or through contact. There is no completely effective medical treatment, either. Indeed, doctors warn that taking aspirin and acetaminophen may actually suppress the antibodies that the body needs to fight the infection and may therefore contribute to some symptoms. There is also no conclusive evidence to support taking vitamin C in large doses. Antihistamines, which many people credit with relieving the symptoms of the common cold, may make the user drowsy.

Cancer

Cancer is the uncontrolled growth and spread of abnormal cells throughout the body. Cancer cells, unlike the regular cells of the body, do not follow the instructions encoded in the body's DNA. Instead, these cells reproduce themselves quickly, creating neoplasms, or tumors. A tumor may be either benign, when it is not considered dangerous, or malignant (cancerous). Unless they are stopped, cancer cells continue to grow, crowding out normal cells in a process called infiltration. Cancer cells can also metastasize, or spread to the other parts of the body by entering the bloodstream or lymphatic system. The gradual overtaking of the body by these cancer cells will eventually make it impossible to sustain human life.

Every cancer has some characteristics in common with other cancers, but it may be more or less treatable depending on its particular nature. The most common forms of cancer are carcinoma, sarcoma, leukemia, and lymphoma. **Carcinoma** is the most common kind of cancer; it originates in the cells that line the internal organs and the outside of the body. **Sarcomas** are those cancers that develop in the connective and supportive tissues of the body, namely bones, muscles, and blood vessels. **Leukemias** are cancers that originate in the blood-creating parts of the body: the spleen, bone marrow, and the lymph nodes. **Lymphomas** are cancers that originate in the cells of the lymph system where impurities are filtered out.

By now, most Americans are aware that the risk of developing cancer is increased more by cigarette smoking than by any other single behavior. Not only do cigarettes lead to lung cancer, but they also lead to cancer of the mouth, pharynx, larynx, esophagus, pancreas, and bladder. The risk of developing cancer is not limited to cigarettes: pipes, smokeless tobacco, and cigars all put a person at risk. Second-hand smoke has a similar effect; scientists have shown that individuals who are exposed to environmental smoke for more than three hours a day are three times more likely to develop cancer than those not exposed. In addition to tobacco, other acknowledged carcinogens are asbestos, dark hair dye, nickel, and vinyl chloride. Individuals should always try to make certain their living and working spaces are well ventilated to reduce the harmful substances in the air.

Hygiene

Besides helping you maintain an attractive appearance, **hygiene** is essential for keeping you healthy and free of disease. The body is usually covered with a certain amount of bacteria, but if this number is allowed to grow too high, you may place yourself at risk for disease. Individuals who fail to regularly wash their hair are more likely to have head lice, and those who fail to properly clean their genitals are more susceptible to urinary tract infections. Good hygiene also reduces an individual's contagiousness when sick. Hygiene is especially important when dealing with food: failing to wash everything involved in the preparation of a meal can result in the spread of bacterial infections like *E. coli* and hepatitis A.

To stay clean and reduce the risk of disease, students should practice daily basic hygiene. Everyone should wash hair and body daily and should wash the hands more frequently than that. Teeth should be brushed between one and three times daily. Always wash hands before eating, avoid spitting or nose-picking, and cover your mouth when sneezing. Try to avoid coming into contact with any bodily fluids, and keep clothes and living space clean. Finally, avoid putting your fingers in your mouth, and try not to touch any animals before eating.

Similarities Between Basic Food Preparation and Medical Hygiene

There are a few basic hygiene habits that every individual should practice when preparing food or performing basic medical procedures. Always clean off the areas where food will be prepared, and wash your hands after touching any uncooked foods. Do not use the same tools to prepare different foods. Always refrigerate foods before and after they are used. Label stored food to indicate when it was produced. Dispose of any uneaten food that cannot be stored. When performing basic medical procedures, always use sterile bandages and any necessary protective clothing, like masks, gloves, or eyewear. Always make sure any medical waste, like used bandages, is disposed of securely.

Meal Planning and Service

Ethics and Religion

An individual's religious, moral, and ethical beliefs can play a large part in their diet because some beliefs can result in the exclusion of certain foods. Ethical and moral considerations such as preventing animal cruelty or showing disapproval of environmentally unfriendly practices that are used to acquire certain types of food can lead some individuals to reduce the amount of certain foods they consume, such as meat, or eliminate those foods from their diet completely. For example, many individuals who choose to be vegetarians or vegans usually do so to avoid supporting what they believe to be the unethical slaughter of animals.

Religious considerations can also determine a person's dietary choices, as some religions dictate what sort of foods the members of that faith can consume. People practicing Judaism, for instance, can consume only kosher foods, which are foods that conform to a series of guidelines established by the faith and include restrictions related to how an animal was slaughtered, what type of animal was slaughtered, and who prepared the food.

Ethnicity

Ethnicity can play an important role in the foods that an individual includes in their diet because people living in different regions of the world usually have different customs regarding the foods that they eat and have different foods commonly available as well. For example, individuals who live in a country like Japan that has easy access to waters suitable for fishing will typically consume significantly more fish than individuals who live in countries that are landlocked. Individuals who have immigrated to another country or who are descendents of immigrants will often include foods in their diet that are traditional foods from their native countries even if those foods are not easily accessible in their new home. People in some regions may include foods in their diets that are not based on how readily available a particular food is, but rather this diet is based on the culture's customary eating habits, as seen in France, where the population as a whole tends to eat foods that are fresh rather than processed.

Planning a Nutritional Meal for a Group

Individuals or organizations that are planning to prepare a nutritionally-sound meal for a group of people should first decide what the nutritional goals of the meal are. Once these goals have been established, the individual or organization should continue the planning process by researching which foods will best satisfy these goals without exceeding the available time and resource limits. The individual or organization should then put together a written meal plan that details what foods will be included, the average time it takes to prepare and cook each of these meals, and the cost associated with the preparation of these meals. Next, they should determine the best method of preparing food for these meals, including which foods should be prepared first, the best way to handle or prepare the foods to minimize the risk of illness, and what techniques can be used to reduce the cooking time. Finally, the individual or organization can prepare the meal according to the plan that has been established.

Reducing the Amount of Time It Takes to Prepare a Meal

Some of the methods that can be used to reduce the time it takes to prepare a meal include keeping the cooking equipment clean and organized, making sure frozen products are thawed ahead of time, preparing foods that have long cooking times beforehand, and preparing foods in order of their cooking times. By keeping the cooking area and the necessary cooking utensils clean, organized, and easily accessible, individuals or organizations can make sure that the time they have available is used as efficiently as possible. Along with thawing products beforehand, preparing foods that require long cooking times ahead of time and re-heating them later can also greatly reduce the amount of time it takes to prepare a meal. As noted, preparing foods according to their cooking times, from longest to shortest, also greatly reduces preparation time because the individual or organization can prepare other foods for the meal while the foods that take the longest are already cooking.

Choosing What Foods to Prepare for a Meal

An individual or organization that is deciding what foods to prepare for a meal should consider the food's nutritional value, the time it takes to prepare each food, the number of people to be served, and the cost of preparing each food. Each food has its own cooking time and offers different nutrients, so it is important that whoever is preparing the meal chooses to serve foods that satisfy people's nutritional goals without exceeding their time constraints for cooking the meal. Since most individuals or organizations will likely have a budgeted amount of money for the meal, they must consider the number of people to be served and how much each food item costs to prepare. If the cost is too high, some meals may not be practical to serve to large groups of people. For example, if an individual or organization is interested in serving a good source of protein for a meal, steak might be a good option for a small group of people but it would probably be too expensive for a larger group.

Food Found in the Marketplace

The two primary types of food that an individual can find in the marketplace are animal products and plant products. Animal products include any foods that either are a part of an animal or are produced by an animal, such as meat, milk, assorted dairy products, and honey. Plant products are foods that originate from some sort of vegetation and include foods such as fruits, vegetables, syrup, nuts, oils, and rice. It is important for an individual to understand the difference between these two groups, as animal products often have more foodborne illnesses associated with them than do plant products; because of this, there are different methods of storing and preparing each type of food to minimize these risks. Animal products and plant products provide different nutrients that the body requires to continue functioning normally, so a healthy individual would need to eat both animal and plant products to receive enough of the various nutrients they require without the use of vitamin supplements.

Factors That Might Influence What Foods are Available to a Consumer

Some of the major factors that might influence what foods are available to a consumer include the region in which a consumer lives, current weather conditions and seasonal effects, and the demand for a particular type of food. Each geographical region has its own natural resources and different climate, which results in foods unique to the area being more readily available. For example, certain crops that react poorly to sudden temperature drops, such as oranges, are easier to grow in areas that have relatively stable and warm climates. Weather and seasonal conditions also play a large role in whether a particular food is available, as certain foods may not be produced during some times of the year in a particular region, while other crops may die as a result of hurricanes, droughts, and other natural disasters. The demand for a particular type of food can also have a significant impact on the availability of that food. Oftentimes, if the demand for a particular type of food increases suddenly, suppliers may have difficulty in meeting that demand.

Food Distributors

Some of the major types of food distributors a consumer might find in the marketplace are chain supermarkets, independent grocery stores, farmers' markets, restaurants, and local farm stands. Each type of food distribution center has its own distinct advantages and disadvantages. Chain supermarkets are large stores that usually offer a large selection of foods at mid-range prices, but foods are often not as fresh and are sometimes of poorer quality than a consumer might find at a farm stand or farmers' market. Independent grocery stores and farmers markets usually have a smaller selection and are slightly more expensive than chain supermarkets, but many consumers prefer to purchase food from these sources because the food is usually locally grown and more fresh. Even though restaurants are the most expensive distributors of food because the food is prepared by the restaurant for the consumer, many people appreciate the quality and variety of foods a restaurant can offer. Local farm stands frequently offer the freshest, highest-quality foods for the lowest prices, but they are open for shorter periods of time, often seasonally.

Food Consumption Patterns

Food consumption patterns are comprised of an analysis of the eating habits of people belonging to a particular region or area. Food consumption patterns indicate that individuals from different regions have very different diets and therefore receive more or less of certain nutrients than individuals from other regions. Knowing the kinds of nutrients that are common in the everyday diets of individuals native to a particular area is important, as that information allows health care professionals to understand what types of diseases and deficiencies pose a threat to the people who live there. By understanding which diseases and vitamin deficiencies the individuals of a particular area may be suffering from, resources can be allocated for treating and preventing those diseases. Monitoring food consumption patterns also allows researchers to study these patterns and determine the ingredients in certain foods that may be contributing to illnesses that are prevalent in a particular region.

Eating Preferences

Just as every individual is fond of certain foods, her or she will dislike or refuse to eat other types of foods as well. In general, people will find the foods that offer them the most physiological and psychological satisfaction to be the most appealing. Most people who refuse to eat a particular food usually do so for one of four basic reasons: they dislike the taste of the food, the condition of the food, how the food was produced, or they fear that the food will make them ill. Such preferences are important because they serve as one of the body's safety mechanisms to prevent individuals from eating foods that may be contaminated or foods that the individual may be allergic to. In some circumstances, however, an individual's eating preferences may need to be ignored so that the body can receive all of the nutrients it needs.

Protecting Consumers from Unsafe Foods and Help Keeping Food Affordable

A number of government regulations in the United States are intended to protect consumers from unsafe foods and help keep food affordable. Some of the most important regulations include food subsidies, price ceilings, tariffs and import quotas, quality-control inspections, and sanitation regulations. Government regulations can manage and even reduce the price of food in several ways: imposing tariffs on imported foods, limiting the amounts of particular foods that can enter the country, offering American farmers and food production facilities financial incentives, and then limiting how much those subsidized producers can charge for their goods. Ideally, these techniques help keep local food sources in business so that the United States does not have to rely too much on outside food sources. Government regulated quality-control inspections and sanitation regulations, such as the Egg Products Inspection Act, the Federal Meat Inspection Act, and the Sanitary Food Transportation Act, all have the purpose of ensuring that foods are produced, stored, and transported following certain guidelines to prevent the food from being contaminated.

Reducing the Risk of Foodborne Illnesses

Some of the methods that can be used to reduce the risk of foodborne illnesses include thawing food appropriately to prevent the growth of bacteria, storing perishable foods in airtight containers and keeping them refrigerated or frozen, and sanitizing all cooking areas and cooking equipment. Individuals should wash their hands before and after handling raw foods, and they should also wash fruits and vegetables before eating to remove any bacteria and pesticides. In addition, foods, especially meats, should be cooked at a high enough temperature for a long enough period of time to avoid the growth of bacteria that lead to foodborne illnesses. Perishable foods should be stored in temperatures of 40 degrees Fahrenheit or below to prevent the growth of bacteria, and frozen foods should be thawed in the refrigerator rather than left out to thaw at room temperature because bacteria grows most quickly at temperatures between 41 degrees and 140 degrees Fahrenheit.

Cooking Equipment

Some of the factors that a consumer should consider when choosing what cooking equipment to purchase include the materials used in the construction of the cooking equipment, the heat conductivity of the materials used, the energy conservation of the cooking equipment, and how easy the equipment is to use and clean. The materials that are used in the construction of a piece of cooking equipment are important because certain materials conduct heat more effectively, retain heat more efficiently, are more durable, and are less expensive than other materials. Certain materials are also rustproof, stick-resistant, and easy to clean, do not flake, and do not react to certain foods. Both the heat conductivity and energy conservation of a piece of cooking equipment are also relevant because the greater the conductivity of the material used in the construction of the equipment and the more efficiently it can retain the heat, the faster the food will cook. Consumers should also know that some types of cooking equipment are easier to use and clean than others, which can make food preparation and clean-up faster.

Food Irradiation and Shelf Life

Food irradiation is the process of using radioactive materials to disinfect and preserve certain types of food. Shelf life refers to how long food will last before it spoils and begins to breed bacteria. Irradiation is important for food manufacturers because it allows a facility to use varying amounts of radiation to kill any bacteria that might be growing on a particular food item, thereby reducing a consumer's risk of foodborne illness. As a result of irradiation techniques that prevent or slow the growth of bacteria, the shelf life of many foods is significantly lengthened. Studies have shown that irradiation methods are completely safe and pose no noticeable risk to individuals who eat foods that have been treated. Foods that are commonly irradiated include apples, bananas, fish, onions, poultry, potatoes, red meats, and strawberries.

Food Preparation

Menu planning is the first step. The menu is the food service's marketing and planning tool to ensure profit. It takes advantage of seasonal and locally-grown food to keep costs under control, and it includes items that can be prepared without excessive time and labor.

Menu specifications are developed so that exactly the right amount of food is purchased. Standardized recipes result in food items being consistent. They also help managers develop work schedules for the kitchen staff.

Foods are cooked by dry heat, moist heat, frying, or a combination of the three. Foods can also be simmered in broth or stock. Appropriate seasonings are used. Foods are portioned using a portion scale. If the food is not served immediately, then proper holding or storage techniques are used to avoid bacteria growth.

The Hazard Analysis Critical Control Point (HACCP) is followed to prevent food-borne illness. It follows the food from purchasing through serving.

Food Presentation

Customers like to see attractively prepared meals served to them; they become eager to eat. The plate needs to be balanced, nicely garnished, and well arranged. Color, shape, arrangement, and texture all influence a diner's appetite. Potatoes, pasta, and rice can be livened up with herbs sprinkled on top. Many food service facilities opt for neutral dishware so that a diner's attention is drawn to the food, not to designs on the rim of the plate.

When plating the food, grease and moisture must be wiped away. An appetizing picture should be created, with garnishes added to provide contrast. Garnishes can also be added to beverages. Food items should be separated from each other. When foods are served on hot plates, customers should be warned by the server so they will not touch the plate and get burned.

Etiquette and Table Service Appropriate for Specific Occasions

Different food operations have different styles. A fast food chain will offer its customers a different atmosphere than an expensive, up-scale operation will offer, and the servers will perform differently. The concept follows from what the food service operation is and what it has on its menu, and this includes types of food, service, price, target market, and theme.

Types of service in the food service industry include counter service, where a customer orders and receives food at a counter before taking it to a table. At a cafeteria service, customers select food from a serving line with a number of choices and serve themselves. A buffet service is similar, except customers receive assistance at an omelet or meat carving station.

Seated service operations seat customers at a table where orders are taken and served by servers. At a banquet service a set menu is served to a group of customers, similar to a catered event.

USDA Dietary Guidelines

The United States Department of Agriculture began issuing nutrition guidelines in 1894, and in 1943 the department began promoting the Basic 7 food groups. In 1956, Basic 7 was replaced with the Basic Four food groups. These were fruits and vegetables, cereals and breads, milk, and meat. Basic Four lasted until 1992, when it was replaced with the Food Pyramid, which divided food into six groups:

1. Bread, cereal, rice, pasta
2. Fruit
3. Vegetables
4. Meat, poultry, fish, dry beans, eggs, nuts
5. Milk, yogurt, cheese
6. Fats, oils, sweets

The Food Pyramid also provided recommendations for the number of daily servings from each group. In 2011, the Food Pyramid was replaced with MyPlate, which used a plate image to show fruits, vegetables, grains, protein, and dairy in a simpler visual format.

The New Pyramid

For the 2025-2030 Dietary Guidelines for Americans, the federal nutrition guide shifted from MyPlate to realfood.gov's New Pyramid. Unlike MyPlate, which focused mainly on dividing a meal into food groups, The New Pyramid emphasizes eating real, whole foods dense in nutrients. Its central message is to get people to choose foods in their natural or minimally processed forms, including protein, dairy, vegetables, fruits, healthy fats, and whole grains. The New Pyramid also encourages people to limit their intake of highly processed foods, refined carbohydrates, added sugars, sugary drinks, excess sodium, unhealthy fats, and artificial ingredients. This change reflects a much broader approach to healthy eating. Instead of focusing solely on portions or food groups, The New Pyramid focuses on the quality of food and encourages people to build meals around foods that provide essential nutrients and support lifelong health.

Chapter Quiz

Ready to see how well you retained what you just read? Scan the QR code to go directly to the chapter quiz interface for this study guide. If you're using a computer, simply visit the online resources page at **mometrix.com/resources719/nystcefamconsc** and click the Chapter Quizzes link.

Human Development

Affective, Cognitive, and Psychomotor Skills

Affective skill refers to how effectively an individual can recognize, understand, and handle emotions and relationships. Affective skills allow an individual to feel appropriate emotion in response to certain situations or stimuli, and then to respond appropriately.

Cognitive skill refers to an individual's ability to gather and understand information. Cognitive skills allow an individual to comprehend new situations and apply the knowledge that they have gathered elsewhere.

Psychomotor skill refers to an individual's ability to coordinate their physical movements. In other words, psychomotor skills are a person's control over simple and complex motor functions.

It is extremely important for an individual to be able to use a combination of their affective, cognitive, and psychomotor skills together on a day-to-day basis, as each type of skill is essential to the overall functioning of a healthy individual. An individual who has mastered their psychomotor skills may be in excellent physical health, but the individual's emotional and intellectual health will suffer if they are unable to make effective relationships and understand basic and complex concepts. The situation is the same for individuals who can only maintain effective relationships or who can only understand complex concepts, as it will be significantly more difficult for them to perform everyday functions if they have poor control of their psychomotor skills. For an individual to maintain their physical and mental health, along with that of their family, the individual must be able to use a combination of different skills.

Some of the factors that can be used to measure how well-developed an individual's affective skills are include determining how well the individual receives emotional stimuli and how well the individual responds to those stimuli. It is also important to determine how easy it is for the individual to acknowledge the worth of a particular situation, relationship, or individual and whether the individual has an organized and well-conceived value system. An individual's ability to receive and respond to emotional stimuli can be measured by how aware the individual is of a particular stimulus, how willing the individual is to acknowledge that particular stimulus, and how focused the individual is on that stimulus. An individual's ability to assign value to a situation and uphold a value system can be measured by how motivated the individual is, how the individual behaves, and how consistent that individual's behavior is. For example, a student that always comes to class and clearly always pays attention may have well-developed affective skills.

Some of the factors that can be used to measure how well-developed an individual's cognitive skills are include determining the individual's ability to retain knowledge, comprehend knowledge, apply knowledge, and evaluate knowledge. An individual's ability to retain knowledge can be measured by testing the individual's ability to remember certain facts and information through exams or simply asking questions. An individual's ability to comprehend knowledge can be measured by an individual demonstrating a concept in a different form, explaining a concept in more detail or simplifying a concept, or predicting a result based on a particular concept. An individual breaking a concept down into individual parts and demonstrating how those parts make up the whole can also show comprehension of a particular concept. An individual's ability to apply knowledge can be measured by an individual demonstrating that they can use a particular concept for a real-life purpose. Finally, an individual's ability to evaluate a particular piece of knowledge can be indicated by the individual showing the value of that knowledge.

Some of the factors that can be used to measure how well-developed an individual's psychomotor skills are include how well an individual performs physical skills and acts, how precisely the individual can perform those skills or activities, and how natural those activities seem to be for the individual. An individual's ability to use physical skills can be measured simply by how much difficulty the individual has in accomplishing a particular complex physical activity such as climbing a rope or assembling a model. How precisely the individual can perform those skills or activities can be measured by determining the quality of the result of the individual's physical activity and how long it took the individual to reach that result. For example, if the individual has constructed a model plane, does the model look like a plane, are its wings and other parts attached correctly, how long did it take to assemble, etc. Finally, an activity is natural for an individual if the individual can perform it without thinking.

Meeting the Special Needs of a Student

The first step an educator should take when determining the best way to meet the special needs of a student is to identify exactly what that particular child's needs consist of, as each student is unique in their ability to learn and comprehend. If a student is performing poorly, a teacher must determine the cause of the student's poor performance. Once the cause has been identified, the teacher can then determine how much assistance the student needs. If the student's needs can be met through such techniques as one-on-one attention or special project assignments, this is usually the best course of action. However, if the student has needs that require solutions beyond simple changes in curriculum, including potential psychological or physiological disorders, the educator has an obligation to consult with other educational professionals and to discuss other options with the child's parents.

Early Childhood Intervention and Intellectual Giftedness

Early childhood intervention is the process by which children who are experiencing or showing signs of developmental difficulties are diagnosed and treated early to allow them to continue developing in the best manner possible. Early childhood intervention services usually take place before the child reaches school age because studies indicate that the earlier a child who is experiencing difficulties receives special education, the more effective that education will ultimately be.

Intellectual giftedness refers to children who are born with a significantly higher than average IQ and who are capable of learning concepts and information much more quickly than other children their age. Even though intellectual giftedness is an asset to the child, the child often requires education that is adjusted for the speed at which the child can learn. Otherwise, the child will become bored, frustrated, isolated, and may begin to underachieve.

Jean Piaget's Theory of Cognitive Development

Jean Piaget's theory of cognitive development theorizes that children will learn more effectively if they are allowed to actively adapt to the world around them through play and exploration rather than being taught skills and knowledge by others. Piaget's theory suggests that there are four major stages that children will go through as they begin to acquire new skills that will aid their ability to learn and process information independently. The four stages of cognitive development that Piaget identifies are:

- The **sensorimotor stage**, which spans from ages zero to two
- The **preoperational stage**, spanning from ages two to seven
- The **concrete operational stage** for ages seven to 11
- The **formal operational stage** for ages 11 and up

Piaget's theory is important to the study of child development because it was the first theory that recognized that children can actively and effectively learn on their own rather than being dependent on another person for learning to occur.

Review Video: Piaget's Theory of Cognitive Development
Visit mometrix.com/academy and enter code: 100376

THE SENSORIMOTOR STAGE

The first stage of Piaget's theory of cognitive development, the **sensorimotor stage**, lasts from birth to age two. This is the period during which a child uses their senses of sight, hearing, and touch to learn about and explore elements of the world. Using these senses, children are able to discover new ways of solving simple problems such as using their hands to drop a block into a bucket and then remove it from the bucket. Another example is learning to use their eyes to find an object or person that has been hidden. As a result, it is also at this stage that a child begins to develop hand-eye coordination and the ability to reason out a method of achieving goals.

THE PREOPERATIONAL STAGE

The second stage of Piaget's theory of cognitive development is the **preoperational stage**. It spans from ages two to seven. This is the stage in which children begin to use words, symbols, and pictures to describe what they have discovered about particular elements of the world around them. During this stage, children begin to develop an understanding of language, and they can focus their attention on a particular subject or object. Piaget theorized that children at this stage have a faulty sense of logic when attempting to understand certain concepts such as volume, mass, and number when some element is changed. For example, if a liquid is poured into a tall container, and then an equal amount of liquid is poured into a smaller but wider container, the children would believe that the taller container contains more liquid even though this obviously is not the case.

THE CONCRETE OPERATIONAL STAGE

The third stage of Piaget's theory of cognitive development is the **concrete operational stage** occurring between ages seven and 11. It is the stage in which a child's thinking becomes more logical regarding concrete concepts. In this stage, children are capable of understanding concepts of mass, volume, and number. For example, they can understand that two containers of different shapes that each have the same amount of liquid poured into them still contain the same amount of liquid despite their differences in appearance. The child also begins to identify and organize objects according to shape, size, and color. The child will not be able to understand more abstract concepts such as those found in calculus or algebra, however, until they reach the formal operational stage of development.

THE FORMAL OPERATIONAL STAGE

The fourth and final stage of Piaget's theory of cognitive development, the **formal operational stage**, starts at age 11 and continues until the end of an individual's life. During this stage, an individual understands more abstract concepts and develops a logical way of thinking about those concepts. In other words, an individual begins to understand ideas that are less concrete or absolute and that cannot necessarily be backed up by physical evidence or observation such as morality, advanced mathematics, and a person's state of being. It is also within this stage of development that individuals can understand all the variables in a problem and are able to determine most, if not all, the possible solutions to a problem rather than just the most obvious solutions. This stage is never truly completed; it continues throughout a person's life as the individual develops and improves their ability to think abstractly.

CHALLENGES TO PIAGET'S THEORY

Later researchers have challenged Piaget's theory of cognitive development because studies indicate that Piaget may have underestimated the abilities of younger children to learn and understand various concepts. Piaget's theory indicates that younger children are unable to understand certain concrete and abstract thoughts early within their development even if another individual teaches the child. However, this notion has been disproved. Research shows that young children can be taught how to handle and understand problems that Piaget believed only older children would be able to comprehend. Researchers have also challenged Piaget's theory because studies indicate that if a younger child is given a task like one an older child might receive, but the difficulty of the task is adjusted to compensate for age, the younger child would actually understand the concept more effectively. Also, notably, Piaget's theory ignores many of the benefits of adult learning. Piaget's theory is still important, though, because it presents the importance of active learning in a child's development.

ABRAHAM MASLOW'S HIERARCHY OF HUMAN NEEDS

Abraham Maslow theorized that there are five types of human needs that, if arranged in order of importance, form a pyramid. Maslow maintained that individuals would not be able to focus on the upper layers of the hierarchy until they were first able to meet the needs at the lower layers. The first layer of the pyramid represents the **physiological needs**, which are the basic needs required for an individual's survival such as food, water, breathable air, and sleep. The second layer of the pyramid represents the **safety needs**, which are the elements that an individual needs to feel a sense of security such as having a job, good health, and a safe place to live. The third layer of the pyramid corresponds to the **love and belonging needs**, which are needed to form social relationships such as those with friends, family, and intimate loved ones. The fourth layer of Maslow's hierarchy of human needs is the **esteem layer**, which represents the individual's need to respect themself and be respected and accepted by others. The fifth and top layer of the pyramid is the **self-actualization layer**. It represents the individual's need for morality, creativity, and trust. Maslow theorized that individuals could survive without reaching the higher levels of the pyramid but that would feel a sense of anxiousness if these needs were not met. Maslow also believed that individuals who reached the higher levels of the pyramid did not receive any tangible benefit from meeting these needs other than a feeling of fulfillment and the motivation to fulfill needs higher on the pyramid.

Maslow later added two additional layers above the self-actualization layer of the pyramid. These are the **cognitive layer** and the **aesthetic layer**. The cognitive layer is the layer that represents an individual's need to acquire and ultimately understand both abstract and concrete knowledge. The aesthetic layer, which became the final layer in later versions of the pyramid, is the layer that represents the individual's need to discover, create, and experience beauty and art. Maslow later theorized that if an individual was unable to meet the needs of any given layer of the pyramid, those needs could become neurotic needs. Such needs are compulsions that, if satisfied, would not facilitate the individual's health or growth.

Review Video: Maslow's Hierarchy of Needs
Visit mometrix.com/academy and enter code: 461825

ERIK ERIKSON'S THEORY OF PSYCHOSOCIAL DEVELOPMENT

Erik Erikson's theory of psychosocial development breaks the process of human development into eight stages necessary for healthy functioning. The eight stages Erikson identified are infancy, younger years, early childhood, middle childhood, adolescence, early adulthood, middle adulthood, and later adulthood. During each of these stages, individuals must overcome a developmental obstacle, which Erikson called a crisis, to be able to progress and face the crises of later stages. If an individual is not able to overcome one of the crises along the way, later crises will be more difficult for them to overcome. Erikson's theory also maintains that individuals who are unable to successfully pass through a particular crisis will likely encounter that same crisis again.

INFANCY

The first stage of Erikson's theory of psychosocial development is **infancy**, which spans from birth to 12 months. In this stage, a child is presented with the crisis of trust versus mistrust. Although everyone struggles with this crisis throughout their lives, a child needs to be able to realize the concept of trust and the elements of certainty. For example, a child learns that if their parents leave the room, they aren't going to abandon the child forever. If a child is unable to realize the concept of trust because of traumatic life events, such as abandonment, the child may become withdrawn and avoid interaction with the rest of society.

YOUNGER YEARS STAGE

The second stage of Erikson's theory of psychosocial development is the **younger years stage**, which covers ages one to three. In this stage, a child is faced with the crisis of autonomy versus shame and doubt. The child is presented with the need to become independent and learn skills such as using the toilet without assistance. If the child is able to overcome this crisis, they will gain the sense of self-pride necessary to continue fostering the child's growing need for independence. If, however, the child is unable to overcome this crisis and cannot establish their own independence, the child will develop feelings of shame and doubt about their ability to function without assistance.

EARLY CHILDHOOD STAGE

The third stage of Erikson's theory of psychosocial development is the **early childhood stage**, spanning ages three to five. In this stage, a child is faced with the crisis of initiative versus guilt. The child is presented with the need to discover the ambition necessary to continue functioning independently. This stage is strongly linked with the moral development of the child as they begin to use make-believe play to explore the kind of person they want to become in the future. If children are unable to explore their ambitions or if they are expected to function with too much self-control, they will develop feelings of guilt as they begin to see their ambitions, dreams, and goals as unattainable or inappropriate.

MIDDLE CHILDHOOD STAGE

The fourth stage of Erikson's theory of psychosocial development is the **middle childhood stage**, which covers ages six to ten. In this stage, a child is faced with the crisis of industry versus inferiority and is presented with the need to develop the ability to complete productive tasks such as schoolwork and working in groups. If children are unable to learn how to work effectively, either alone or in a group, they will develop a sense of inferiority as a result of their inability to complete the tasks set before them that their peers are capable of completing. For example, if a child is regularly unable to complete their homework because the child does not understand the material while the rest of the child's peers are not having difficulty, this can lead the child to develop a sense of inferiority.

ADOLESCENCE STAGE

The fifth stage of Erikson's theory of psychosocial development is the **adolescence stage**, which covers ages 11 to 18. In this stage, the child is faced with the crisis of identity versus role confusion. During this stage, the child attempts to find their place in society and identify future goals and the skills and values necessary to achieve those goals. At this stage, the child also becomes more aware of how people perceive them and becomes concerned with those perceptions. If the child is unable to determine what future goals they are interested in pursuing, it can lead to confusion about what roles the child will play when they reach adulthood.

EARLY ADULTHOOD STAGE

The sixth stage of Erikson's theory of psychosocial development is the **early adulthood stage**, which covers ages 18 to 34. In this stage, the young adult is concerned with the crisis of intimacy versus isolation in which an individual needs to begin establishing intimate relationships with others. If an adult is unable to form intimate relationships with others, perhaps because of disappointing relationships in the past, this person will become more withdrawn and will isolate themself from others. Isolation can prove to be a perilous problem in the development of a healthy adult, as it prevents the individual from forming lasting relationships. The lack of social interaction can also lead to severe personality flaws, which may hinder the development of future relationships.

MIDDLE ADULTHOOD STAGE

The seventh stage of Erikson's theory of psychosocial development is the **middle adulthood stage**, occurring between the ages of 35 and 60. In this stage, an adult becomes aware of the crisis of generativity versus stagnation in which the individual is concerned with continuing their genetic line before it is too late. Generativity refers to the ability to produce offspring and then nurture, guide, and prepare that offspring for future life. At the same time, however, generativity in this context also refers to any act that gives something of value to the next generation such as teaching children how to read. If an individual is unable to contribute to the next generation in some form, the individual will feel a sense of failure resulting from stagnation, which is simply a lack of accomplishment.

LATER ADULTHOOD STAGE

The last stage of Erikson's eight stages of psychosocial development is the **later adulthood stage**, which is the period that starts at age 60 and extends to the end of one's life. In this stage, an individual is confronted with the crisis of ego integrity versus despair. During this time, an adult begins to examine the course of their life by reflecting on the kind of person that they have been. If the adult feels that they have had a meaningful life and accomplished something during it, this will lead to a strong sense of integrity. However, if the individual is unhappy with the way they have acted, this person will experience despair and will fear death as the absolute end of further achievement.

CHANGING FAMILIAL ROLES OF MEN AND WOMEN

Fifty years ago, women were the primary caretakers of the family's children, and they were in charge of maintaining the household while men worked to provide for the family. This has changed, however, because of the drastic increase in the number of women entering the workforce since that time. This is partially because it has become more difficult for families to subsist on one income alone. Both members of the marital couple are often forced to work to provide for the family, which can make it difficult when trying to balance the responsibilities of caretaker and provider. Men, who were once the primary providers for the family, are still out in the workforce, but their spouses have joined them, and both individuals have to find ways to make the time to care for the family's children.

NATURE VERSUS NURTURE

The concept of nature versus nurture is the idea that of all a person's traits, some result from their genetic heritage, and some result from their environment. In this context, nature refers to any trait that an individual is born with or has acquired through genes. Nurture may be seen as the opposite of nature; it refers to any trait that an individual learns from the environment. Nurture often refers specifically to the environment created by the parents of the child, but it can refer to any environmental condition that affects the development of the child. The concept of nature versus nurture is important because it shows that individuals inherit some of their traits from their parents, but they also develop many of their traits from their environment.

GENETIC AND ENVIRONMENTAL TRAITS

Research has shown that some traits that are almost completely genetic include eye color, blood type, and most diseases. In most cases, genetics also determines one's risk of future diseases, vision, and vision impairments. Religion and language, on the other hand, are examples of traits that researchers have proven to be almost completely environmental. These traits are all linked to specific genes or to specific environmental factors, but most traits are actually a result of both environmental and genetic influences. Traits such as height, weight, and skin color are all examples of traits that are influenced by both an individual's genes and their environment.

ROBERT HAVINGHURST'S DEVELOPMENTAL TASK CONCEPT

The developmental task concept is a theory of human development established by Robert Havinghurst that states that there are certain tasks each individual needs to go through at points during their life to continue developing into a happy and successful adult. These tasks, separated into three groups by their causes, are tasks resulting from physical maturation, personal causes, and societal pressures. A child learning to crawl is an example of a task that becomes necessary as the child matures physically. An individual learning basic first aid because they are interested in becoming an EMT is an example of a personal cause. An example of a task resulting from societal pressure is a child learning to behave appropriately in a store.

1. **Infancy and early childhood**: The period from ages zero to five, and it consists of tasks such as learning to walk, talk, and eat solid foods as well as learning right from wrong.
2. **Middle childhood**: The period of development from ages six to 12 that includes tasks such as learning to get along with others, moral values, and skills and knowledge required for day-to-day living.
3. **Adolescence**: The period from ages 13 to 18, and it requires tasks that include learning how to relate with members of the opposite sex, learning the social role of one's gender in society, and preparing for life after childhood.
4. **Early adulthood**: The period of life from ages 19 to 29, and it is the age range where tasks such as starting a long-term relationship, finding a career, and starting a family are required.
5. **Middle adulthood**: The period from ages 30 to 60 that includes tasks such as finding adult recreational activities, achieving in one's chosen career, and helping one's teenage children become healthy and happy adults.
6. **Later maturity**: The period from ages 61 to the end of a person's life. This period consists of tasks such as adjusting to the death of a spouse, adjusting to the effects of old age, and finding people in one's peer group to interact with.

MULTIPLE INTELLIGENCES IDENTIFIED BY HOWARD GARDNER

Students with high **logical-mathematical intelligence** excel at calculations and reasoning, thinking abstractly and conceptually. They detect and explore patterns and relationships, ask cosmic questions, and enjoy solving puzzles and conducting experiments. Before addressing details of a problem, they must learn and formulate concepts. Compatible teaching strategies include offering mysteries, investigations, and logic games. Students with strong **linguistic intelligence** are effective with words. Their auditory skills are highly developed. They often think in words, not pictures, feelings, or sounds. They enjoy reading, writing, and playing word games. Teaching methods and tools include reading books with them, encouraging them to see and pronounce words, lectures, books, computers, multimedia materials, voice recorders, and spoken-word recordings. Students with high **intrapersonal intelligence** tune into their own feelings and are "loners," avoiding social interaction. They are independent, confident, strong-willed, motivated, opinionated, intuitive, and wise. Introspective reflection and independent study, journals, diaries, books, creative materials, time, and privacy are useful instructional methods and materials. Students with strong **interpersonal intelligence** are social, interactive, empathetic, and "street-smart." Group activities, dialogues, seminars, telephones, audio- and video-conferencing or Skyping, and email are good teaching methods and tools.

Chapter Quiz

Ready to see how well you retained what you just read? Scan the QR code to go directly to the chapter quiz interface for this study guide. If you're using a computer, simply visit the online resources page at **mometrix.com/resources719/nystcefamconsc** and click the Chapter Quizzes link.

Family Studies and Parenting

Stress, Substance Abuse, Crises, and Decision Making

Teenage Suicide

There are a number of factors that increase the risk of teenage suicide, but studies indicate that a teenager's history, emotional and physical health, social pressures, and access to the methods necessary to carry out a suicide are the most influential factors. If a teenager has attempted suicide, has a history of drug or alcohol abuse, a history of depression or other mental illness, or another family member has committed suicide or been abused, the teenager's risk of suicide increases. Physical illness, religious or cultural pressures, and other suicides in the community can also lead to an increased risk of suicide among teenagers. Finally, if the teenager has access to guns, knives, drugs, or any other means of taking their own life, the teenager may be at heightened risk for suicide.

Although teenage suicide can be difficult to prevent, especially when teenagers have easy access to instruments conducive to committing suicide, identifying the risk factors and attempting to minimize their effects before they are allowed to escalate is the most effective way to prevent teenage suicide. Teenagers who have access to both mental and physical health facilities and have strong family, societal, and religious support are much less likely to commit suicide. In addition, teenagers who have been taught methods of solving problems and conflicts in non-violent ways have a lower risk of suicide.

Substance Abuse

Substance abuse is a disorder in which an individual begins to become dependent on or overuse a particular drug or group of drugs that ultimately has a negative impact on their health and human development. Substance abuse, especially when the individual becomes addicted to or dependent on the drug, can affect the individual's ability to interact both socially and physically. Their ability to communicate intelligibly or even to complete relatively simple tasks can be severely hindered. After an individual has become chemically dependent on a particular drug, their body develops a physical need for the drug, and the individual will experience the effects of withdrawal if they are unable to meet that need. However, substance abuse not only affects a person by causing health problems, it also severely hinders an individual's ability for social development, as the individual often has difficulty improving social skills because of their inability to control behavior, actions, or even basic speech.

Smoking Addiction

Nicotine is consistently shown to be far more addictive than alcohol; whereas only one in ten users of alcohol will eventually become alcoholics, approximately eight out of ten heavy smokers will attempt and fail to quit. The method that nicotine uses is similar to that of other addictive substances: it creates an immediate positive feeling when taken, it will cause painful withdrawal symptoms if it is not taken, and it stimulates powerful cravings in the user even after it is removed from the system. Nicotine addiction can become so strong that a heavy smoker will experience withdrawal symptoms a mere two hours after smoking. Persistent tobacco use will also lead to an increased tolerance for nicotine, and so the user will have to consume more and more to achieve the pleasure or avoid the pain.

Alcohol Abuse

There are a few guidelines that alcohol users should know so that they can avoid chronic alcohol abuse. First, never use alcohol as a medicine or as a way to escape personal problems. Always drink slowly, and if possible, alternate alcoholic and non-alcoholic beverages. It is a good idea to eat both before and during drinking so that less alcohol rushes into the bloodstream. Drinking should never be the primary reason for a social function, though individuals should also try to avoid drinking alone. At a party, it is a good idea to avoid mixed drinks, as it is often difficult to tell just how much alcohol they contain. Finally, and most importantly, every person should have the self-control to say "no" to a drink without feeling guilty or rude.

Psychological and Physical Dependence on Drugs

A psychological dependence on drugs may begin as a craving for the pleasurable feelings or relief from anxiety that the drug provides. However, this craving can soon turn into a dependency on the drug in order to perform normal mental operations. A physical dependency, on the other hand, is said to occur when the individual requires increasing amounts of the drug to get the desired effect. Many drugs, like marijuana or hallucinogens, do not cause withdrawal symptoms; others, like heroin or cocaine, may be extremely painful to stop using. Individuals with a severe chemical dependency will eventually use a drug like this simply to avoid experiencing the effects of withdrawal. Typically, an individual with a severe dependency will try to stop many times without success.

Common Causes of Conflict Within a Relationship

The many sources of conflict within a relationship are too numerous to mention, but some of the common problems include the following: setting expectations that are too high, not appreciating or respecting the other person in the relationship, not considering the feelings of the other person, being afraid of showing affection or emotion, being overdependent, being inflexible, expecting the other member of the relationship to change, and lacking effective communication. Preventing conflict can be extremely difficult. Preventing it altogether is virtually impossible, but avoiding some or all of these common sources of conflict can greatly reduce the number of conflicts that take place within any given relationship.

Problem Solving

A well-functioning family would first identify the problem itself and determine the cause of the problem. The family would then develop a list of solutions that could potentially solve the problem, and they would attempt to determine the benefits of each solution. After determining the benefits of each solution, the family would choose the solution that seems to best solve the problem and then, after putting the solution into effect, monitor the solution to make sure that it actually solved the problem. Finally, the family would decide whether the solution worked or not to determine whether it was necessary to try something else. This entire process is important to the functioning of a family because it prevents problems from being misdiagnosed early on and prevents them from getting too far out of control.

Introducing a Model for Responsible Decision-Making to Students

A health educator teaching a responsible decision-making model to middle and high school students can begin with a presentation and student worksheets with term definitions. They discuss definitions with students. Empowerment is feeling control over one's decisions and behavior, resulting in inspiration; teachers tell students they must take responsibility for their decisions to achieve empowerment. Decision-making styles determine responsibility; they explain that teens with inactive decision-making styles cannot or do not make choices, and they lack control, accountability, and the ensuing self-confidence and empowerment. They explain that teens with reactive decision-making styles let others make decisions for them; needing others to like them and being easily influenced by others also impede self-confidence and empowerment. They then identify proactive decision-making styles as those involving analyzing a necessary decision, identifying and evaluating potential actions, choosing one action, and taking responsibility for the consequences of taking that action. Teachers can then introduce students to a model for responsible decision-making as a guide for making proactive decisions.

A model for responsible decision-making is meant to make sure that student decisions result in actions that show good character; that follow guidelines which parents, guardians or other responsible adults have established for them; that demonstrate self-respect and respect for others; and that protect safety, obey the laws, and promote health. A health educator can teach students in grades 6–12 the following seven steps included in a responsible decision-making model:

1. Describe the situation requiring you to make a decision.
2. List all of the decisions you could potentially make.
3. Share this list of potential decisions with an adult you trust.
4. Evaluate what the consequences of each of the decisions could be.
5. Determine which of the potential decisions you identified is the most appropriate and responsible one.
6. Take action on the decision that you have chosen.
7. Evaluate the outcomes of the decision that you have made.

The steps in the responsible decision-making model are describing the situation wherein they need to make a decision, listing the decisions they could potentially make, sharing their list with a parent or other responsible adult, evaluating each decision's potential consequences, deciding which decision is the most suitable and responsible, acting on the chosen decision, and evaluating the outcomes of that decision. When evaluating potential consequences of each decision, students can ask themselves the following five questions:

- Will making this decision lead to taking actions that are lawful or legal?
- Will making this decision lead to taking actions protecting my and others' safety?
- Will making this decision lead to taking actions that agree with the guidelines and advice that my parents and other responsible adults have given me?
- Will making this decision lead to taking actions that demonstrate my respect for myself and for other people?
- Will making this decision lead to taking actions that are demonstrations of good character?

As they learn to make decisions responsibly, students are bound to make mistakes, as with all new learning. Teens may experience anxiety over responsibility for poor decisions with unwelcome consequences. Paralyzed by doubt and indecision, they may avoid taking responsibility and action. In the same way that many teens fear being judged, rejected, disliked, or even viewed as different, they also fear doing the wrong thing. In addition to peer pressure and desiring acceptance, fear of misusing new responsibilities can motivate inaction to avoid unintentionally doing harm and experiencing guilt. Health educators can offer four steps to take after a bad or otherwise wrong decision:

1. Admit it; take responsibility, not trying to hide the mistake, blame others, or make excuses.
2. Immediately consider things done based on the decision; avoid perpetuating actions misguided by a wrong choice.

3. Parents and guardians are responsible for decision-making guidance: inform them of the decision and discuss corrective actions.
4. Apologizing is not always adequate: make restitution for any harm, damage, or loss by paying, replacing something, volunteering time, and/or similar appropriate effort as applies.

Stress Management

Stress is inevitable; however, effective stress management skills and techniques enable healthy coping. According to the Mayo Clinic, individuals begin stress management by understanding how they currently react to stress, and then adopting new stress management techniques or modifying existing ones to keep life stressors from leading to health issues. There are several unhealthy but common reactions to stress.

- Pain: internalized or unresolved stress can trigger headaches, backaches, upset stomachs, shortness of breath, insomnia, and muscular pain from unconsciously tensing the shoulders and neck and/or clenching jaws or fists.
- Eating and/or activity: some people skip eating from stress, thereby losing weight; others overeat or eat when not hungry and/or skip exercise, gaining weight.
- Anger: some people lose their tempers more easily over minor or unrelated things when stressed.
- Crying: some people cry over minor or unrelated things when stressed; experience unexpected, prolonged crying; and/or feel isolated and lonely.
- Depression and anxiety: stress can contribute to depressive and anxiety disorders, including problem avoidance, calling in sick, feeling hopeless, or giving up.
- Negativity: individuals not coping effectively with stress may exaggerate the negative qualities of undesired circumstances and/or always expect the worst.
- Smoking and/or substance use: people may escalate current smoking, drinking, or drug use under stress; those who had previously quit may relapse.

Stress Management Techniques

1. Cut back: when overextended, examine duties and delegate, eliminate, or limit some.
2. Prepare: set realistic goals for major and minor tasks; improve scheduling; allow time for unexpected events like traffic jams, car trouble, minor medical emergencies, extra work, etc. to prevent stress from accumulating.
3. Reach out: revisit lapsed relationships; form new ones; volunteer. Surrounding oneself with supportive friends, relatives, colleagues, and spiritual leaders enhances psychological well-being, boosting capacity for coping with stress.
4. Hobbies: enjoyable activities that do not stimulate competitiveness or anxiety are soothing. These vary between individuals. Some choices include crafts, music, reading, dance classes, gardening, woodworking and carpentry, electronics, fishing, and sailing.
5. Relaxation techniques: these include meditation, yoga, massage therapy, and physical activities. The technique selected is less important than increasing body awareness and refocusing attention onto calmness.
6. Adequate sleep: lack of sleep exacerbates stress. Insufficient sleep impairs judgment and the immune system. Sleep-deprived individuals are more prone to overreacting to minor irritants. Most of us require eight hours of sleep nightly. Interrupted or irregular sleep impedes REM sleep, dreaming, and deep sleep-enabling physical and neurological repairs.
7. Professional help: if stress management techniques are insufficient, see a physician before uncontrolled, ongoing stress causes health problems.

Coping with Common Stressors in Life

Four major life skills that people can apply to cope with common life stressors are values clarification, decision-making, communication skills, and coping skills. The following are typical life stressors in early childhood, adolescence, middle adulthood, and later adulthood, along with coping mechanisms that can be applied from the life skill perspective of values clarification.

- **Early childhood**: a pet's death. According to values clarification, reviewing the pet's positive qualities (similarly to adults' celebrating the life of the deceased) and considering getting another pet can address stressors.
- **Adolescence**: unwanted pregnancy. Discussing feasible alternatives and their ramifications for the teen, unborn baby, family, and society is not only required to make decisions, but also provides positive coping.
- **Middle adulthood**: divorce. Evaluating its impact on the couple and their relatives and friends; and the roles played by marital status, social expectations outside home, and religion inform values clarification coping mechanisms.
- **Later adulthood**: retirement. When people retiring from careers or employment view retirement in terms of their values, this can facilitate their ability to choose feasible options for post-retirement living.

Among life skills that enable coping with the stress of common life events are values clarification, decision-making, communication skills, and coping skills. Common stressors in four life stages follow, accompanied by coping mechanisms utilizing the decision-making life skill.

- **Early childhood**: a pet's death. Helping the child discuss the pros and cons of each alternative for disposing of the pet's remains is a decision-making-oriented way to cope with the loss.
- **Adolescence**: unwanted pregnancy. Careful consideration and evaluation of such alternatives as abortion; carrying the baby to term and surrendering it for adoption (and open or closed, public or private adoption, etc.); carrying to term and keeping the baby, etc. are necessary decisions to make and cope proactively with stressors. Decisions about future birth-control methods are also indicated.
- **Middle adulthood**: divorce. From the decision-making perspective, considering alternatives, risks, and consequences and making choices among career options, life roles, and future social relationships have major impacts on post-divorce living.
- **Later adulthood**: retirement. The decision-making life skill enables the retiree to consider alternatives and their advantages and disadvantages (e.g., not retiring, pursuing leisure activities, embarking on a second career, volunteering, realizing a long-deferred dream).

Four major life skills are values clarification, decision-making, communication skills, and coping skills. Examples of common stressors in each life stage, plus ways to cope using communication skills, follow.

- **Early childhood**: a pet's death. When a child feels sadness and anxiety over the loss, encouraging the child to communicate their feelings and thoughts can mediate psychic distress.
- **Adolescence**: unwanted pregnancy. Teenage mothers need support from various sources including family, friends, counselors, educators, and health professionals. Effectively utilizing communication skills enables them to know how, where, and from whom to solicit help and advice to cope with their situation.

- **Middle adulthood**: divorce. Adults undergoing divorces often have to assume various new life roles, including some that their former spouses may always have addressed. As a part of the process of divorce, adults need to apply communication skills to seek out supportive friends, relatives, and professionals as they establish and adjust to these new roles and experiences.
- **Later adulthood**: retirement. When older adults retire, they may lose some of their autonomy. Using communication skills assertively can help them maintain their independence.

DECREASING TOBACCO USE

WHO recognizes tobacco as "the most widely available harmful product on the market." Therefore it negotiated the first international, legally binding treaty, the WHO Framework Convention on Tobacco Control (FCTC), providing protocols and guidelines for evidence-based interventions to decrease tobacco supply and consumption. Raising tobacco prices and taxes is a documented cost-effective method that substantially increases quitting and decreases starting smoking, particularly among poor and young people. With proper implementation, enforcing smoke-free public place and workplace laws obtains high compliance levels: fewer youths start smoking; smokers are supported in quitting or reducing smoking; and smoke-free policies prevent perpetuating addiction at earlier stages, especially in youth. Informing and educating the public is another cost-effective measure. Studies in multiple countries find graphic health warnings on cigarette and tobacco packaging and creative media campaigns succeed in powerfully decreasing consumer demand, despite opposition from wealthy tobacco companies and health officials' comparatively limited resources. Another cost-effective measure is providing smoking cessation assistance, combining pharmaceutical and behavioral therapies, through primary medical care and public health providers. Though a minority of the global population has received these measures, research finds them affordable in all world nations.

CHARACTERISTICS OF CONFLICT

According to experts, a conflict is not simply a disagreement, but a situation wherein both or either party perceives a real or imagined threat. Because such perceived threats are to people's survival and well-being, conflicts continue; ignoring them does not make them go away. Confronting and resolving conflicts stop them from going on indefinitely (or until the relationship ends). People do not necessarily (or usually) respond to conflicts based on objectively considering the facts, they react to them based on their personal values, beliefs, cultural backgrounds, and life experiences. Hence individual reactions to conflict are according to individual perceptions of the situation. Conflicts naturally provoke strong feelings. Therefore, people who cannot manage their emotions under stress or who are uncomfortable with them will be unable to succeed at resolving conflicts. Another characteristic of conflicts is that they present opportunities for growth. When members of a relationship succeed at resolving interpersonal conflict, they build trust between themselves. They gain direct experience that their relationship can withstand disagreements and challenges. This proof enables them to feel more secure about their relationship's existence and future.

UNHEALTHY VS. HEALTHY WAYS OF RESOLVING CONFLICT

When conflict inevitably arises, one unhealthy reaction is being unable to recognize and respond to things that are most important to the other person. A healthier response is being able to identify and address things that matter most to another. Emotional reactions that are resentful, angry, explosive, or designed to hurt the other person's feelings are unhealthy. Healthier responses involve staying calm, not becoming defensive, and showing respect for the other person. When one person reacts to conflict by rejecting the other, withdrawing their affection, isolating himself or herself, saying or doing things to shame the other, or showing or expressing fears of being abandoned, these are unhealthy reactions. Healthier responses are being willing to forgive the other person; forget undesirable reactions, words, and deeds; and progress beyond the conflict without retaining anger or resentment. Being unable to see the other person's viewpoint or make any compromises is unhealthy; being able to compromise instead of punishing the other person is healthier. Fearing and avoiding conflict due to expected negative outcomes is unhealthy; believing in the mutual benefit of confronting conflict head-on is healthier.

Peer Pressure

Children and teens often have more life experience being cared for, controlled, and told what to do, and relatively less experience being on their own, making independent choices, and taking initiative. Adults should tell them that being pressured is not good for them and is not right. Many children and teens (and even adults) have difficulty resisting pressure. Motivations include because they want to be liked, don't want to alienate friends, are afraid others will reject them, do not want others to make fun of them, do not want to hurt other people's feelings, are afraid others will perceive refusal as rejection, are not sure what they actually want, or do not know how to extricate themselves from the situation. Children and teens must know they have the right to say no without needing to give any reason, and they have the right to walk away from any situation involving pressure. Some brief tips to support refusing and resisting pressure include standing up straight, making eye contact with the other person, stating one's feelings clearly, not making excuses, and standing up for oneself.

Resisting Spoken Pressure

Children and teens (and adults as well) can find it hard to resist pressure that other people exert on them through spoken words. It is normal for most people not to want to hurt other people's feelings or feel responsible for bad feelings in others. However, children and teens especially must be reminded how important it is for them to stand up for themselves in order to prevent others from verbally pressuring them into doing unsafe or unwanted things. Some strategies recommended by experts to help young people refuse to use alcohol (or do other things that they know are not in their best interests and that they do not wish to do) include the "Dos and Don'ts." Dos: do say no assertively. Do abstain from drinking alcohol. Do propose some alternate activity. Do stand up for others being pressured who do not want to drink. Do walk away from the situation. Do look for something else to do with other friends. Don'ts: don't go to a party without being prepared to resist alcohol use. Don't be afraid to say "no." Don't mumble. Don't say "no" in an overly aggressive way. Don't behave like a "know-it-all" when refusing.

Domestic Violence and Abusive Relationships

Domestic violence is domestic abuse or spousal abuse, wherein one relationship partner dominates and controls another in a way that incorporates physical violence. Some violent behaviors include having an unpredictable, bad temper; harming, threatening harm, or threatening to kill the partner; threatening to hurt or take children; threatening suicide if the partner leaves; forcing sex; and destroying the partner's belongings. Manipulative power tactics abusers employ include: dominance, humiliation, isolation, threats, intimidation, denial, and blame. The cycle of domestic violence follows a common pattern: one partner abuses the other with violent behavior to exhibit dominance. The partner appears guilty, but really fears being caught and punished rather than feeling remorse. The abuser avoids responsibility by making excuses for the violent behavior, rationalizing it, and/or blaming the other partner for it. The abuser, trying to keep the victim in the relationship and regain control, behaves contritely, "normally," or with great affection and/or charm, often fooling the victim into hoping they have changed or will change. The abuser fantasizes and plans further abuse to make the victim pay for perceived wrongs. The abuser then places the victim in a situation to justify further abuse, and the cycle repeats all over again.

Domestic violence is domestic abuse including physical violence. Physical force that injures or endangers someone is physical abuse. Physical battery or assault is a crime; police have the authority and power to protect individuals from physical attacks, whether outside or inside a family or home. Sexual abuse is an aggressive, violent act and a type of physical abuse. This includes forced sex, even by a partner with whom one also has consensual sex. Victims of physical and sexual abuse are at greater risk of serious injury and death. Even if incidents seem minor (e.g., being pushed or shoved), they are still abuse and can still cause severe injury or death. Even if incidents have only happened once or twice in a relationship, they are still abuse and are likely to continue and escalate. If physical assaults stop when the victim becomes passive, this is not a solution: the victim has given up their rights to independence, self-expression, and decision-making as a partner and as a person. Even when no physical violence exists, victims may suffer from verbal and emotional assault and abuse.

People who want to determine if they are in an abusive relationship should consider whether they think or feel the following: they feel afraid of their partner often, they avoid mentioning certain subjects for fear of making their partner angry, they feel they cannot do anything right with their partner, they believe being mistreated is what they deserve, they wonder whether they are the member of the relationship who is crazy, and they feel helpless and/or emotionally numb. To consider whether their partner engages in belittling behaviors toward them, they should consider the following: whether their partner yells at them often; whether the partner says or does things to humiliate them; whether the partner insults them or criticizes them regularly; whether the partner treats them so poorly they find it embarrassing for family, friends, or others to witness it; whether the partner dismisses, disparages, or ignores their successes and/or opinions; whether the partner blames them for the partner's abusive behaviors; and whether the partner views and/or treats them as a sexual object or property instead of a human being.

Victims in abusive relationships should consider whether their partner behaves in an overly possessive and jealous manner toward them; whether the partner controls what they do or where they go; whether the partner prevents them from seeing their family or friends; whether the partner limits their access to the car, the phone, and/or money; and whether their partner is continually checking up on what they are doing and where they are going. These are all behaviors intended to control the other person, and they are not normal or healthy. Threats of violence or violent behaviors to watch for in a partner include: the partner has a bad temper, and is unpredictable about losing their temper; the partner threatens to harm or kill them, or actually does harm them; the partner threatens to hurt their children, actually hurts them, or threatens to take them away; the partner threatens that if they leave, the partner will commit suicide; the partner forces them to engage in sex when they do not want to; or the partner takes away or destroys their personal belongings.

People often associate the idea of domestic abuse with physical battery. However, many partners are victims of emotional abuse. Without physical bruises, the victim, abuser, and other people unfortunately overlook or minimize emotional abuse. The intention and result of emotional abuse are to erode the victim's independence, control, and feelings of self-worth. Victims come to feel they have nothing without the abusive partner, or have no way to escape the relationship. Emotional abuse includes verbal abuse like blaming, shaming, name-calling, insulting, and yelling. It also includes controlling behaviors, intimidation, and isolating the victim. Threats of punishment, including physical violence, frequently enter into psychological or emotional abuse. Emotional abuse scars are less visible than physical ones, but are equally or more damaging. Financial or economic abuse is another way to control the victim. It includes withholding money, checkbooks, credit or debit cards; withholding shelter, food, clothing, medications, or other necessities; making victims account for every cent they spend; rigidly controlling the victim's finances; restricting the victim to an allowance; sabotaging the victim's job by constantly calling there and/or causing the victim to miss work frequently; preventing the victim's working or making career choices; and stealing from or taking the victim's money.

Some people observe that abusive individuals lose their tempers and/or apparently have some psychological disorder. Some also abuse substances (though others do not), and, equating their problems with the illness or disease model of substance abuse, mistakenly assume that abusers cannot control their behavior. However, experts point out that abusive behaviors and violence are deliberate choices that the abusers make to control their victims. Evidence that they can control their behavior includes that they do not abuse everybody in their lives, only those they claim to love who are closest to them; that they choose carefully where and when to abuse, controlling themselves in public but attacking the victim once they are alone; that they can stop the abusive behavior when it is to their benefit (e.g., when their employer calls or the police arrive); and that they frequently aim physical attacks to parts of the victim's body where they are hidden by clothing, so others cannot see them.

Tactics Employed by Domestic Abusers

- **Dominance**: abusers, needing to feel in control of victims and relationships, dominate by making decisions for victims and family, giving them orders, and expecting unquestioning compliance. They often treat victims as children, servants, slaves, or possessions.
- **Humiliation**: to keep victims from leaving, abusers make them feel worthless and that nobody else will want them. To make victims feel inadequate, they insult and shame them publicly and privately, making them feel powerless and destroying their self-esteem.
- **Isolation**: abusive partners make victims dependent on them by cutting off their contact with others. They may stop victims from visiting with friends and relatives, or even from going to school or work. Victims may have to ask permission to see anybody, go anywhere, or do anything.
- **Threats**: to frighten victims into dropping charges and/or prevent their leaving, abusers typically threaten to: harm or kill victims, children, other family, or pets; commit suicide; report victims to child services; and file false charges against them.
- **Intimidation**: threatening gestures and looks, property destruction or smashing objects in front of victims, hurting pets, or displaying weapons are tactics signaling violent consequences for noncompliance to frighten victims into submission.
- **Denial and blame**: abusers minimize or deny abuse or blame it on circumstances or, commonly, the victim. "You made/make me do it" is a frequent accusation used by abusers.

Warning Signs of Domestic Abuse

Warning signs of domestic abuse: the person agrees with everything the partner does and says; frequently checks in with the partner, reporting what they are doing and where they are; often receives harassing phone calls or texts from the partner; appears anxious or afraid to please the partner; and/or mentions the partner's jealousy, possessiveness, or temper. Warning signs of physical violence: the person often misses school, work, or social events without explaining; often has injuries, excusing them as "accidents" or "clumsiness"; and/or wears sunglasses indoors, long sleeves in summer, or other means of hiding injuries. Warning signs of isolation: the person never or seldom goes out in public without the partner; is unable to see friends and family; and/or has limited access to the car, money, or credit or debit cards. Psychological warning signs of being abused: someone who used to be confident displays significantly lowered self-esteem; an outgoing person becomes withdrawn; or an individual shows other major personality changes. The person appears anxious, depressed, despondent, or suicidal, verbalizing suicidal ideations or displaying suicidal behaviors.

Advice for People Who Suspect Somebody They Know Is a Victim of Abuse

Abusers are experts at manipulating and controlling victims. Victims are drained, frightened, ashamed, depressed, and confused. They need to escape the situation, but frequently have been isolated from others. Those suspecting abuse should be alert to warning signs, offer support to victims for extricating themselves, getting help, and starting the healing process. Some people may hesitate, thinking they could be mistaken; learning the victim does not want to discuss it or have them interfere; or simply be told that it is none of their business. In these cases, experts advise people to speak up regardless: expressing concern not only informs a victim somebody cares, it moreover could save that person's life. They should speak with the person privately, identifying signs they have observed and explaining why they are concerned, reassure the individual they will keep all conversation confidential, that they are there whenever they are ready to talk, and will help in any way possible. Regarding dos and don'ts, do the following: express concern, ask whether something is wrong, listen, validate the person's communications, offer help, and support the individual's decisions. Don't: wait for the person to approach you, blame or judge the individual, give advice, pressure the person, or attach conditions to your support.

Pregnancy and Childbirth

Teenage Pregnancy

Teenage pregnancy can be defined as the act of a woman expecting a child prior to her twentieth birthday or, in some areas, prior to her being considered a legal adult. Teenage pregnancy can have a significant number of physical, social, economic, and psychological effects. Studies show that women who become pregnant as teenagers have a significantly higher chance of giving birth to the child prematurely, a higher risk of the child being born at an unhealthy weight, and a higher risk of complications during pregnancy (especially when the mother is under the age of 15). It has also been shown that teenage mothers are more likely to drop out of high school and are even more likely never to finish college. This can make it much more difficult for a teenage mother to find a job, especially if she is the sole caretaker of her child. Also, children born to teenage mothers have been shown to be at higher risk for behavioral problems and often have more difficulty functioning in school.

The two primary ways that the risk of teenage pregnancy can be reduced are through the promotion of contraceptive use or abstinence and through the promotion of social interaction between teenagers and their parents. The best way to reduce the risk of teenage pregnancy is to abstain from intercourse, but the use of a contraceptive, even though it does not guarantee that a teenager will not become pregnant, can greatly reduce the chances of pregnancy when used correctly. Studies have also shown that teenagers who have regular, open communication with their parents are more likely to wait to have intercourse until later in their lives. However, regardless of what precautions are used, the risk of teenage pregnancy cannot be eliminated completely, as there is always the risk of contraceptives failing or the risk that a teenager may become a rape victim.

Maintaining a stable and effective support system before and after a child is born is the most important factor for a teenage mother to function and raise her child in a healthy fashion. Studies have shown that most of the physical effects on the children of teenage pregnancy are a result of malnutrition and poor prenatal care. Both of these factors can be greatly reduced or eliminated if the young mother has help from parents or outside resources that teach her what to eat and where to get appropriate care. Because teenage parents almost always lack the resources and the life experience necessary to both supply and care for the child, a strong support system is essential in helping the mother, both financially and in raising the child.

Unprotected Sex and How to Prevent Pregnancy

Some teens may not know how pregnancy occurs; others may believe it can only happen when a male ejaculates inside a female's vagina. However, a few drops of pre-ejaculate released before and during sex, which can be almost undetectable, also contain sperm. Though the probability of conception from this small amount is lower, it is still possible. Though less common, conception can also result from semen on the vulva without penetration. Males cannot control pre-ejaculate release; therefore, Planned Parenthood® advises putting on a condom *before* sex and wearing it continuously during sex. Though the point is not to encourage sex among immature students, educators can inform those harboring misunderstandings regarding kissing, body rubbing, masturbating, and that oral and anal sex cannot cause pregnancy without vaginal or vulvar contact with sperm. Abstaining from sex, or using both a condom and birth control continuously during sex, are the ways of preventing pregnancy. Teen couples contemplating sex should discuss birth control with each other and a parent or trusted adult, visit a Planned Parenthood center, and see a physician, nurse, or healthcare provider. Planned Parenthood's website offers a quiz to help choose a method.

Contraception

Some young (or uninformed older) people assume condoms worn by males are sufficient for contraception. However, condoms can break, leak, or slip off during or following intercourse. Ideally, foam, gel, or other spermicide should accompany condoms. Female contraception includes IUDs, diaphragms, and birth control pills. IUDs are typically inserted by physicians and worn continuously. They can periodically require removal and replacement. While effective, they can have undesirable side-effects for some women including irritation, inflammation, cramping, spotting, tissue damage, or other issues. Diaphragms are typically self-inserted by women before intercourse, often with spermicidal gel applied to the surface, and removed afterward. They are also effective, but some women have difficulty inserting them properly and/or cannot tolerate their presence. They can also sometimes shift position, impeding contraception. Birth control pills are very effective, though a very small percentage of women using them might still get pregnant. Oral hormones cause some women undesirable side effects like weight gain and symptoms resembling pregnancy. Lower-dose pills have fewer side effects; different dosages affect individual women differently. More extreme measures include tubal ligation (often reversible, but not always) and hysterectomy (irreversible) for women, and vasectomy (often reversible, but not always) for men.

STIs

Over half of Americans contract an STI (sexually transmitted infection) during their lives. According to Planned Parenthood®, there are many ways to practice safer sex, such as using condoms. Monogamous sex is generally safer, although many individuals are unaware of being infected, and others are aware but are untruthful about it, hence safer sex includes partners' getting tested regularly together. There are also sexual activities that do not transmit STIs (e.g., masturbating or mutual masturbation, fantasy sharing, cybersex, or phone sex). Other sexual activities considered low-risk include kissing; fondling (manual stimulation); "outercourse" (body rubbing); oral sex with a condom, dental dam, or other barrier; and using sex toys with partners. Vaginal and anal intercourse are high-risk activities. Without condoms, they are likely to transmit chancroid, chlamydia, cytomegalovirus (CMV), genital warts, gonorrhea, hepatitis B, herpes, HIV, human papilloma virus (HPV), molluscum contagiosum virus, pelvic inflammatory disease (PID), pubic lice ("crabs"), scabies, syphilis, and trichomoniasis. Unprotected oral sex is high-risk for transmitting

CMV, gonorrhea, hepatitis B, herpes, syphilis, and HPV. Skin-to-skin contact without intercourse is risky for transmitting CMV, herpes, HPV, molluscum contagiosum, pubic lice, and scabies. Many STIs are often asymptomatic. Planned Parenthood's website has a search engine for finding health centers by ZIP code to schedule testing.

Parental Avoidance in Talking About Procreation with Their Children

Many parents feel squeamish about "The Talk" or discussing "the birds and bees" with their maturing children. This is not just discomfort over an intimate topic; parents frequently fear that discussing sex with preadolescent and adolescent children is akin to giving them permission to engage in it. However, research studies find the opposite is true: teens are more prone to sexual behaviors when their parents have *not* talked about sex with them. When uninformed of possible consequences, they are more likely to act, not knowing of any disadvantages; they may experiment to get knowledge their parents have not imparted; and/or sexual behavior may be a reaction against parental avoidance and lack of openness. Communications researchers say sex is a continuing, two-way conversation that starts when very young children see pregnant women and ask questions. They advise parents to use Socratic questions, such as "What do you think the right time is for having sex?" and sharing their own thoughts after children do. Open, receptive attitudes are critical: if children bring up sex and perceive avoidant or shocked parental reactions, they will stop approaching parents, shutting down this vital conversation.

Conflict in Relationships

Many people try to avoid conflict at all costs because they find it unpleasant and feel threatened by confrontation. However, conflict is normal and integral to healthy relationships. Its source is rooted in differences between and among people, whether major or minor. No two (or more) people can agree about everything 100 percent of the time. Any time that people disagree, conflict results. Though some disagreements seem unimportant, any conflict that evokes strong emotions indicates some deep personal need at its core (e.g., to be valued or respected, to be closer or more intimate, or to feel safety or security). As one example, young children need to explore and take risks to learn and develop normally, while parents need to protect children's safety, and this can present a child-parent conflict. Conflicts in personal relationships can cause discord and even end the relationships when members do not understand each other's different needs. Conflicts in workplaces can ruin deals, lower profits, and end jobs. Acknowledging needs that conflict with a willingness to examine them in understanding, compassionate environments enables team-building and creative problem-solving. Both avoiding and mismanaging conflict can damage relationships, but positive and respectful conflict management can improve them.

Female Reproductive System

Because females do not have a Y-chromosome, during embryonic and fetal development they are not affected by testosterone to develop male reproductive organs. Without testosterone stimulation, reproductive organs develop into ovaries, a uterus, and other female organs. Most internal female organs are formed by the end of the first trimester. Immature eggs (ova) form in the ovaries in utero; all of a female's eggs are produced before birth. Female infants are born with all reproductive organs formed, but these organs are immature and not functional. These do not grow much in childhood, but rapidly mature and grow during puberty. Girls typically start puberty one or two years before boys and take around four years to complete, whereas boys take around six years. The primary female sex hormone is estrogen. In the brain, the hypothalamus stimulates the pituitary gland to secrete luteinizing hormone (LH) and follicle-stimulating hormone (FSH), which stimulate the ovary to produce estrogen. (The same hormones stimulate the testes' testosterone production in males.) Estrogen stimulates uterus and breast growth; pubic hair growth; bone development; the adolescent growth spurt, which begins and ends earlier than in males; and menarche (menstrual cycle onset).

Male Reproductive System

While a male fetus develops in utero, the testes begin to develop. Around two months before birth, the testes begin descending into the scrotal sacs outside of the main body cavity, allowing slightly lower temperatures to aid sperm production. The testes additionally produce hormones enabling development of secondary male sex characteristics. Puberty activates an increase in brain hormones, triggering the pituitary gland's increased production and release into the bloodstream of luteinizing hormone (LH) and follicle-stimulating hormone (FSH). In the bloodstream, LH stimulates testes cells to produce and release testosterone, which enlarges and develops the penis and other sex organs, promotes skeletal and muscular growth, and deepens the voice. Testosterone and FSH stimulate sperm production in seminiferous tubules within the testes. Each sperm cell takes 65-75 days to form; about 300 million are produced daily, stored in the epididymis, wherefrom the vas deferens carries sperm through the prostate gland below the bladder to the urethra. The male urethra releases both sperm and urine. The prostate gland and seminal vesicles—accessory sex glands—produce specialized fluids, mixing with sperm during transport, creating semen which exits from the urethra through the penis during ejaculation.

Adolescent Sexual Attitudes and Behaviors

Various studies find teens' sexual attitudes are influenced by variables including their parents' attitudes regarding teen sex, religiosity, the media, bonding in school relationships, and adolescents' perceptions of social norms among their peers. According to some experts, such research demonstrates the necessity of considering the wide range of sexual attitudes teenagers consider. Warning of negative consequences is insufficient; adults must provide information enabling teens to weigh positive and negative aspects of both engaging in and abstaining from sex to make their own best decisions as they mature and develop physically, intellectually, emotionally, and socially. While many models of teen risk behaviors emphasize perceptions of possible consequences in decision-making, studies also find positive motivations for having sex. Some investigators found teens valued sexual goals and expectations of intimacy, then social status, then pleasure in that order; but then expected sex to result in pleasure, then intimacy, then social status in that order. Male adolescents valued pleasure more; females valued intimacy more. The National Adolescent and Young Adult Health Information Center (NAHIC, 2007) found almost half of high school students reported having sex. CDC's Youth Risk Behavior Surveillance (YRBS, 2008) found sexual intercourse most prevalent in black, then Hispanic, then white, then Asian teens.

Researchers find that, although any age group can be influenced by sexual media content, teens can be especially vulnerable to media messages. Adolescence is a developmental time when individuals are forming their sexual attitudes, behaviors, and gender roles. Teenagers have recently developed the ability to think abstractly and critically; however, their cognitive skills are still not completely developed for critical analysis of media messages and decision-making that takes into account future potential consequences. This places them at higher risk for media influence. Researchers have found (Gruber, 2000) that teens viewed an average of 143 instances of sexual behavior on TV weekly during prime time. Activities between unmarried partners were depicted three to four times more often than between spouses. Network and cable TV channels show movies, an estimated 80 percent of which include sexual content. Researchers' analysis of music videos estimated that 60 percent included sexual impulses and feelings. Sexual TV messages are found to be nearly always presented in positive terms, with scarce treatment of negative consequences or risks of unprotected sex. High school students have reported substantial access to and viewing of TV and video. Over 80 percent of teens report peer discovery about sex from entertainment media.

Stages of Pregnancy

In the first trimester, a zygote transforms into an implanted embryo; organs, hair follicles, nail beds, muscles, white blood cells, and vocal cords form; and the baby starts moving around week eight. While pregnancy does not show externally, mothers awash in pregnancy hormones feel many symptoms. However, every woman and pregnancy is different; no two necessarily have the same symptoms, but most initial symptoms diminish further into pregnancy while others develop. During the second trimester, babies grow hair, begin sucking and swallowing, and their eyes and ears reposition. They have fingerprints and can hiccup and yawn by week 18. Their limbs are coordinated and their senses develop by week 21. Weight gain, capillary formation, and opening eyes occur by six months. By seven months, fetal weight doubles to two pounds. Babies perceive light and dark, taste what mothers eat, and hear their voices by week 31. Transparent skin becomes opaque by week 32; length may increase an inch during week 33. Weight reaches around six pounds by week 36; waxy vernix and hairy lanugo shed in week 38. By week 40, fetal weight is 6-9 pounds and length is 19-22 inches; babies dream, blink, and regulate their body temperatures.

Labor and Childbirth

In late pregnancy, symptoms can mask labor signs, or some contractions can be false labor. If contractions persist, become stronger, last longer, and occur closer together, this usually indicates labor. The "411" method is one way to judge: contractions 4 minutes apart, lasting 1 minute each, continuing for at least 1 hour. Labor's first stage is typically the longest, marked by contractions and gradual cervical dilation. The first stage has three phases: the early phase, usually comfortable, with contractions 20 minutes apart progressing to 5 minutes apart. The second, active phase generally involves 1-minute contractions every 4-5 minutes. The third, transition phase is among the shortest (1-2 hours) but hardest. Contractions are 2-3 minutes apart; some women shake and may vomit. This phase ends with complete dilation. Some women temporarily cease contractions but feel no need to push. Labor's second stage involves a need to push. It can last 3+ hours, but often less. Contractions spread out again to around every 4 minutes. This stage culminates in childbirth. Then the mother must push out the placenta, nursing the newborn aids uterine contractions to expel it. The fourth labor stage is postpartum.

Chapter Quiz

Ready to see how well you retained what you just read? Scan the QR code to go directly to the chapter quiz interface for this study guide. If you're using a computer, simply visit the online resources page at **mometrix.com/resources719/nystcefamconsc** and click the Chapter Quizzes link.

Interpersonal and Family Relationships and Community Connections

ELIMINATING SEXUAL STEREOTYPES

Eliminating sexual stereotypes is a major concern of family and consumer sciences education. It is important for students to disregard sexual stereotypes and recognize that an individual's gender does not necessarily affect the role they play. In the early- and mid-1900s, women were commonly seen as caretakers of the home and men as providers for the family. However, these roles have changed drastically over the past fifty to sixty years, and are not entirely realistic at this point. As the cost of living increases, it becomes more difficult for a single individual to provide for an entire family. As a result, it is more common for men and women to share the caretaker and provider roles to satisfy the physiological, financial, and psychological needs of the family.

DIRECT AND INDIRECT COMMUNICATION

Direct communication occurs when a person who is attempting to convey a given piece of information simply states that information to the person they want to receive the information. **Indirect communication**, on the other hand, is when the person communicating the information states the information, but not to anyone in particular. For example, if a parent says, "Christine, we need to set the table," that is an example of direct communication because the parent is addressing the person they want to talk to directly. However, if the parent instead simply mutters out loud, "We need to set the table," rather than saying it to someone in particular, that would be an example of indirect communication. Direct communication is far more effective in carrying out the day-to-day functions necessary to maintain a family than indirect communication because various tasks can be assigned directly to a particular individual.

MAKING COMMUNICATION MORE EFFECTIVE

Families with individuals who use direct, clear communication are the most effective. These family members listen to one another, spend more time communicating, respect one another's points of view, and pay attention to the more subtle forms of affective communication. By communicating directly and concisely with other family members, each family member creates a much more effective form of communication than that which would be found in any other setting. If the individuals receiving the information listen to and respect their fellow family members and—more importantly—make the time to listen to them in the first place, the communication between family members will become much stronger. Of course, this communication can be strengthened even further if members of the family are careful to take note of emotional indicators that allow them to identify the feelings of another family member without that person having to verbally express their feelings.

CONFLICT RESOLUTION TECHNIQUES

A family can successfully resolve a conflict by following steps very similar to those of the basic problem-solving model. First, the family needs to attempt to identify the problem, making sure to maintain open communication while remaining objective and minimizing hostility. After the problem is identified, the family must strive to recognize the various positions that each member has regarding the conflict while again attempting to minimize hostility. After each person involved in the conflict has made their position clear, the family must move toward a compromise that will work for everyone. Each step of the conflict resolution process requires that the people involved in the conflict remain as patient and as understanding as possible, which can often be extremely difficult when a solution or compromise cannot be determined immediately.

Social Interaction Outside the Family

Outside social interaction is extremely important for all family members, regardless of age, because it offers an opportunity for each individual to improve their social skills, learn about the world around them, and learn more about values that one might not learn from the family alone. This is especially true in the case of children. Research shows that children who have regular outside social interaction through things such as extracurricular activities are less likely to rebel or cause problems and more likely to excel in school and relationships. Outside social interaction is also necessary for the children of a family to eventually leave the household and create families of their own, as they need to seek out their own relationships. Therefore, social interaction with individuals outside of the family is necessary not only for the fulfillment of the members of the family, but also to continue the life cycle of the family.

Divorce

Divorce is the termination of the marriage union before the death of either member of the union. It has a significant impact on the stability of the family unit as a whole, and it affects the relationships and well-being of the individual members of the family. Frequently, when the marital couple decides to divorce, there has already been significant stress placed on the entire family from the difficulties the marital couple has been experiencing. However, divorce can often lead to a great deal more stress being placed on the family, especially when children are involved. As a result, individuals within and outside the marital couple may become more withdrawn or hostile as the structure of the family changes. Divorce also allows both members of the marital couple to later remarry, as their legal obligation to each other no longer exists. This can further alter the family structure by adding stepparents to the mix.

There are many factors that may influence the risk of a marriage ending in divorce, including income, education, religion, pregnancy before marriage, and whether the parents of the married couple are divorced. Couples who make over $50,000 a year are at a much lower risk of divorce than couples who make less than that amount. Couples comprised of well-educated individuals who have graduated from high school and have at least some college background also have a much lower risk of divorce than less educated individuals. Couples with no religious background or drastically different religious backgrounds have a much higher risk of divorce than couples who have religious backgrounds that do not conflict. Couples who have a baby prior to being married also have a higher risk of divorce than couples who have children after they are married. Individuals with parents who are divorced also have a higher risk of divorce than individuals from intact families.

Studies indicate that the age at which a couple marries may have a significant impact on whether they remain married for an extended period. Individuals who marry before either member of the couple is 18 will often separate within a few years of their marriage. Individuals who are in the 18–25 range will separate less frequently than those who marry before 18, but they are still at a very high risk for their marriage ending in divorce rather than death. Individuals who marry after both members of the couple are over 25 have a significantly lower risk of divorce than those who marry at younger ages. Ultimately, statistics show that the risk of divorce decreases as the age of each member of the couple at the time of the marriage increases.

Social and Economic Factors

Social and economic factors affect the overall functioning of a family. In fact, researchers use an index called the **socioeconomic status**, or SES, to measure the ability of the family to function in a healthy fashion. The SES uses the educational background of the members of the family, the family's total income, and the skill (both actual and perceived) required by the occupations of the individuals who act as providers for the family to measure the family's ability to function. Individuals who are well-educated tend to marry later in life, receive jobs with higher incomes, and have careers with a higher social status. These factors all add stability to the marriage and stability to the overall functioning of the family. Families that earn a higher income are also less concerned with obtaining basic necessities because the family consistently has the means to obtain them. As a result, there is often less stress experienced by the family.

Affective and Instrumental Communication

The two primary types of communication used by family members are **affective communication** and **instrumental communication**. Affective communication is communication in which an individual demonstrates their feelings through facial expressions, motions, gestures, or by stating their feelings outright. Instrumental communication is when an individual informs another member of the family of a piece of factual information that is necessary to carry out the normal day-to-day functions of the family. An example of instrumental communication is a mother informing her child where they can find their socks. Families that use both types of communication usually function more effectively than families that use instrumental communication more often than affective communication.

Clear and Masked Communication

Clear communication occurs when an individual explicitly states the information they are trying to convey, and there is no ambiguity as to the meaning of the statement. For example, "I am upset because Daniel is not home from the movies yet" is an example of clear communication because there is no question that the individual making the statement is upset at Daniel for not being home. On the other hand, **masked communication** occurs when an individual states the information they are trying to convey in a vague and somewhat confusing manner. For example, "I am upset" is an example of masked communication because there is no direct indication as to why the person is upset. As these examples illustrate, clear communication is always more effective in conveying a particular piece of information than masked communication.

Family Aid in the Development and Education of Family Members

One of the most important functions a family provides is developing and educating family members. Parents and grandparents pass down their heritage along with teachings of social norms and acceptable behavior to the children of the family through their customs, traditions, and ultimately their actions. Children learn about their heritage through the traditions of the family and also often learn lessons about the manner in which they are expected to behave by using the behavior of their parents and the rest of the household as a model for how they, too, should behave. Children also learn about the manner in which the world around them functions through the interactions of the members of the family with the world outside the household. This allows the child to understand more complex types of social interaction such as what goods the family needs, where the family must go to fulfill those needs, and what is needed to acquire those necessities (e.g., how much money is required to purchase an item).

BEHAVIORAL MODELING, CONSUMER EDUCATION, AND HERITAGE

Behavioral modeling, when related to child development within a family structure, is the manner in which children model their own behavior after the behavior of their parents and other people with whom they interact. Children learn what behavior is socially acceptable by mimicking the behavior of the people around them.

Consumer education is the process of teaching a person about the marketplace and its goods and services, the suppliers, and the various considerations associated with searching for goods and services. These concepts are critical for family members to learn so that they can survive in a consumer society.

Heritage is anything inherited from one's ancestors, including traditions, customs, or physical characteristics. The family conveys the traditions, customs, and social norms of the previous generation to the generations that follow.

ROLES THAT ARE ESSENTIAL TO THE FUNCTIONING OF A HEALTHY FAMILY

There are five major roles that are essential to the functioning of a healthy family. These roles are:

1. Provision of necessities
2. Development and education
3. Emotional support
4. Management of the family
5. Satisfaction of the married couple's needs

Individuals within the family need to provide necessities by creating income so that the family has access to food, clothing, and shelter. Family members need to teach not only customs, but also skills that will help the members of the family achieve academically and professionally. Families must provide emotional support for the family members during times of high stress. In addition, the family needs someone to take a leadership role and handle issues such as managing finances and maintaining the roles essential to the family's survival. The married couple has its own requirements, including basic necessities, sexual needs, and emotional needs that must be met for the family to continue functioning normally.

ROLE, ROLE CONFUSION, AND ROLE STRAIN

A **role** is a collection of social rights, behaviors, and obligations that is assigned to a particular individual. For example, a mother's role might be that of a provider because she is out in the workforce earning an income for the family.

Role confusion occurs when an individual is uncertain of what role or roles they should play in a particular situation. For example, a nurse might run into a patient whom she took care of previously while out grocery shopping and be unsure of whether to act in a formal, nurse-to-patient manner or in an informal, friendly manner.

Role strain occurs when an individual is placed in a situation in which carrying out the duties of a certain role will prevent the individual from fulfilling their obligations of another role. For example, a working mother might be both caregiver and provider. If her child becomes ill, she cannot carry out both roles; she is forced to choose between working and caring for the sick child.

MARRIED COUPLE

The married couple or, in some cases, the couple living together is the core of the family and therefore has a profound effect on the relationships and well-being of the family. If a marital couple is having difficulty in their relationship and the stress of that difficulty becomes apparent, the rest of the family will most likely exhibit signs of stress. For example, if the marital couple is consistently seen fighting, or even if they just become withdrawn after a fight, other family members may react to the stress and become withdrawn, upset, or even hostile. On the other hand, marital couples who are not experiencing marital difficulties and who appear warm and affectionate will foster the same feelings of warmth and affection in the rest of the family.

Marriage

Marriage is a union between two individuals that is often held as a legally binding contract in which the members of the union state their intention to live together and aid each other in maintaining a family. Even though couples who simply live together in the same household can constitute a family under the commonly used definition, the institution of marriage offers a level of stability to the family structure that is not present when an unmarried couple makes up the center of the family. This added stability is primarily a result of the societal, religious, and governmental recognition of the institution of marriage, which creates an expectation that the marriage and, more broadly, the family will remain intact. Although many married couples eventually separate and divorce, it is more difficult for a member of the marital couple to leave the family than it would be for a member of a couple who has no legal or societal obligation to remain together.

Family and Single Individual

A **family** is commonly considered a group of individuals related by birth, adoption, or marriage who reside together, usually for the purpose of raising children. However, a family can refer to any group of people who live together in the same household even if they are not related by blood or legal ties. This means that an unmarried couple who is living together or even a pair of roommates may still be considered a family. A **single** individual, though, is not considered a family because it is a person who lives alone and therefore does not regularly interact with relatives or other individuals within the household.

Family Structures

The four major types of family structures are nuclear, extended, single-parent, and blended. Each of these structures is based on the idea that a family is a group of people who participate in raising the next generation. A **nuclear** family is the traditional concept of a family in which a mother, father, and their children live in the same household. An **extended** family is an expansion of the nuclear family that includes the mother, father, and their children as well as aunts, uncles, cousins, and grandparents. A **single-parent** structure is a family in which one parent is the only one in the home caring for the children. A **blended** family, also known as a stepfamily, is one in which a parent marries or remarries when they already have their own children, and there is a parent, stepparent, and one or more children living in the household.

The typical family structure in the United States has changed dramatically in recent years as the norm moves away from the nuclear family and toward the blended family. As more people divorce and remarry, blended families are becoming much more common. In this family structure, children are cared for by both biological and stepparents. This increase in the number of blended families, which were unheard of 50 years ago, has resulted in two substructures: simple and complex. In a simple stepfamily, only one of the individuals marrying has children before the marriage. In a complex stepfamily, both parents marrying have their own children before the marriage.

Family Life Cycle

There are commonly nine stages in the family life cycle:

1. **Bachelor stage**: The stage in which the individual is yet to be married, and the family has not yet been established.
2. **Newly married couple stage:** The newly married couple stage in which two individuals have just married but do not have children.
3. **Full nest stage I**: The beginning of the three full nest stages, when the parents are beginning to raise children. The youngest child is under six.
4. **Full nest stage II**: The youngest child is six or over.
5. **Full nest stage III**: The stage in which an older married couple has independent children.
6. **Empty nest I stage**: The head of the household is married and still in the labor force, but the couple has no children at home.
7. **Empty nest II stage**: The same as empty nest I stage except that the head of the household has retired.
8. **Solitary survivor in labor force stage**: One member of the couple has passed away, and the survivor must continue to work to support themself.
9. **Retired solitary survivor stage**: The same as the solitary survivor in labor force stage except that the survivor has retired, and there are no longer any individuals living in the household who are still in the labor force.

Purpose of a Family

The primary purpose of a family is to ensure the survival of the family and to nurture the children. Families facilitate survival by sharing the work and tasks such as earning a living and taking care of the home. Family also provides emotional support to one another during stressful times. The family nurtures the children by offering social and emotional interaction, protecting them from potential danger, and educating them in social norms and customs. The family also provides the basic necessities required for the basic physical development of the children in the household, including food, clothing, shelter, and play.

Murray Bowen's Family Systems Theory

Bowen's concept of the nuclear family emotional system consists of four basic relationship patterns that determine where family problems develop. Clinical symptoms or problems typically emerge during times of intensified and protracted tension in a family. Stress levels, family adaptations to stress, and family connections with extended family and social support networks determine tension levels. In the **marital conflict pattern**, spouses project their increasing anxiety into the marital relationship. Each partner becomes preoccupied with the other's shortcomings, tries to control them, and resists being controlled. For example, a couple with a young child conceives a second child. The wife becomes anxious about meeting the needs of two children. The husband questions his wife's ability to cope in order to avoid facing his own anxieties. After the second child's birth, the husband, observing his wife's stress, helps out more at home and is more controlling of her. He starts to feel neglected and disappointed in his wife's inadequate coping. The wife, who used to drink but quit while pregnant, resumes drinking.

In Bowen theory, the relationship **pattern of dysfunction in one spouse** involves one partner pressuring the other to behave in certain ways, and the other acceding to that pressure. While both partners accommodate for maintaining harmony, eventually one does more than the other. Both are comfortable with this interaction for some time; however, if family tensions increase, the subordinate partner gives up enough self-control to become significantly more anxious, yielding to the dominant partner. Combined with other factors, this anxiety contributes to a psychiatric, social, or medical problem. For example, a couple with one young child has a second child. In the relationship pattern of marital conflict, the husband projects his own anxiety into criticizing his wife's coping abilities, taking on more household duties, and controlling her while the wife addresses her anxiety by drinking. The husband accuses her of selfishness and lack of effort. She agrees with but resents his criticism, feeling more dependent on him. Feeling increasingly unable to cope and make decisions, she escalates her drinking. He calls her an alcoholic. The wife becomes increasingly under-functional, the husband increasingly over-functional, functioning for her—all in an effort to avoid direct conflict and maintain harmony.

In the **pattern of impairment of a child or children**, parents project their own anxieties onto their child or children. They view the child unrealistically—either negatively or idealistically. The child reciprocates excessive parental focus by focusing excessively on the parents, overreacting to parental expectations, needs, and attitudes. This undermines the child's differentiation of self from family, increasing their susceptibility to either internalizing or acting out family tensions. Anxiety can disrupt the child's social relationships, school progress, and health. For example, a couple with one young child has another baby. Anxieties over the added stress of raising another child cause marital conflict and a dysfunctional relationship, developing into greater dysfunction in one spouse or parent. This causes emotional distance between spouses, who focus anxiously on the older child. She reacts by regressing, making immature demands of the parents, especially her mother. The mother externalizes her anxiety onto the child, worrying the new baby will displace her, acceding increasingly to her demands. The father avoids conflict with his wife by supporting her focus on the child, relieving her by giving the child attention when he gets home from work. Parents and child unwittingly conspire in seeing and creating dysfunction in the child.

In Bowen's family systems theory, the four basic relationship patterns are marital conflict, spousal dysfunction, child impairment, and emotional distance. Whichever pattern predominates will dictate which family members will manifest familial tensions by developing psychological, social, or medical symptoms. The **pattern of emotional distance** consistently occurs in relation to the other three patterns. When interactions between family members become too intense, they develop emotional distance to decrease intensity. However, the drawbacks of emotional distance are that distanced members can become overly isolated, and they can lose intimacy in their relationship. For example, when a couple with one child has another baby, they first project their anxieties onto each other and experience marital conflict. They then withdraw from one another emotionally to reduce the intensity of the conflict. They react to the emotional distance between them by externalizing their anxieties onto the first child, worrying she will feel left out with the new baby. The child reacts to the obsessive parental emotional over-involvement with her, reciprocating their emotional focus and overreacting to real or imagined parental withdrawal, thus creating impairment of a child. In this manner, emotional distance interacts with the other patterns.

Review Video: Bowen Family Systems Theory
Visit mometrix.com/academy and enter code: 591496

Socioeconomic and Health Variables on Parent-Adult Child Relationships

Some sociological researchers investigating relationships of parents in their mid-50s to mid-70s with their adult children found intergenerational exchanges were characterized by strong reciprocity in both the United States and Great Britain. Contrary to stereotypical views of elderly adults becoming "burdens" on adult children, researchers have seen instead that married parents who gave help and support to at least one adult child were twice as likely to receive support from another adult child as parents who did not provide such support. Investigations showed when researchers controlled for various other parent and child variables, parents who owned homes, had higher incomes, and were married or widowed were more likely to help adult children than divorced parents. Conversely, parents with homes and higher incomes were less likely to receive help from adult children. Parental disability and advanced age correlated positively with adult children's responding to parent needs. Investigators inferred socioeconomic variations in support exchange balances between parents and adult children. Researchers predicted in 2005 that demographic trends would likely increase adult children's demands for support from older parents in the future.

Chapter Quiz

Ready to see how well you retained what you just read? Scan the QR code to go directly to the chapter quiz interface for this study guide. If you're using a computer, simply visit the online resources page at **mometrix.com/resources719/nystcefamconsc** and click the Chapter Quizzes link.

Education and Early Childhood

Studying Moral Development

Most laypeople recognize a good person by unconsciously applying the accepted criteria of their culture. Scientists do not disagree about who is a good person but, depending on their field of study, they may define morality differently. The specific age the scientist is researching will also influence their definition of morality. Taken together, these scientific viewpoints establish a complex picture of what constitutes a "good person" and how involved the lifelong process of moral development really is.

Psychoanalysts study internalized behavior (conscience or superego) and the way a person reacts to stimuli. Behaviorists study outward behavior such as sharing, helping, and lying. Sociocultural scientists focus on how society's values are passed on, personality traits (moral character), and cognitive behavior. Biologists study neuroanatomy, how genetics influence moral characteristics, and the role hormones play. Cognitive psychologists focus on moral reasoning and the decision-making process.

Attachment Bond

Scientists firmly believe that infants must form a secure **attachment bond** with their primary caregivers in the early years to have a healthy social orientation throughout their entire lives. Studies confirm that establishing a secure attachment bond is an accurate predictor of the ability to form successful relationships later in life. This bond is critical in the child's moral development and in learning to interact appropriately in a social setting. Researchers believe that failure to form a secure attachment bond with the primary caregivers is the most consistent cause of antisocial behavior in childhood because the child did not develop a conscience. Conversely, children who did form a healthy attachment bond are more likely to follow family rules and therefore will also comply with rules imposed by outside authority figures and institutions, including teachers and schools.

Self-Control

Some researchers consider **self-control**, or self-discipline, one of the two most critical building blocks of character. The other is empathy. Between the ages of about five and seven, children should learn to resist temptation, suppress impulses, and delay gratification. The primary caregivers, including parents, babysitters, and teachers, should help children develop self-regulation:

- Providing situational management, which protects children from their impulsive actions
- Helping children learn to control emotional outbursts by soothing them until they calm down
- Consistently teaching coping skills when children are confronted with a difficult or unfamiliar situation
- Explaining the possible consequences if children say or do certain things
- Showing self-control when dealing with children in challenging situations

Children are highly influenced by and learn from the behavior of those with whom they interact on a regular basis. For this reason, it is important for children to have good role models to imitate and emulate.

Parenting Styles

Most researchers agree there are three parenting styles: authoritarian, permissive, and authoritative.

- **Authoritarian** parents are controlling, demanding, cold, hostile, and uncommunicative. This style of parenting produces children who have difficulty making decisions, often develop antisocial tendencies, and frequently have trouble making and sustaining relationships.
- **Permissive** parents tend to be loving but distant, and they usually establish few guidelines about anything. They want to communicate with their children, but frequently do not do so effectively. Their children have difficulty developing self-regulating skills and seem to flounder when confronted with too many choices.
- **Authoritative** parents are loving, controlling, communicate effectively, and set high expectations. This parenting style produces positive children with higher moral reasoning ability and who are able to form stronger relationships.

Siblings

Studies have shown that siblings influence one another's development in some areas, most notably in developing aggressive behavior and acquiring conflict resolution skills. Scientists believe, but have not conclusively proven, that firstborn children influence the social development and gender identity of later-born children. The overall emotional climate of the family and the different approach parents take with each child has a strong influence on the relationship between the siblings as well as the power one sibling may hold over another.

Researchers are interested in learning why siblings develop differently even though they are exposed to the same environmental dynamics. The theory is that each child experiences the same factors and stimuli differently based on their relationship to the parents, siblings, and other family members such as grandparents, aunts, uncles, and cousins. By establishing the nature, extent, and impact of various familial influences, scientists hope to better understand childhood development.

Friends

Between the ages of three and five, a child begins to understand that the other children in the sandbox are different from one another and from them. Children realize they like some better than others, even though they do not really know or care to understand why. When children start school, one of their most important social tasks is making friends. They are psychologically ready to develop more complex relationships, and they move their focus from family to friends. School-age children begin spending more time with people outside the family circle. They start confiding in peers and sharing their fears, frustrations, and pleasures with friends. Groups form, and sometimes evolve into cliques based on many things from appearance and personality to athletics and other extracurricular activities. Peer pressure increases and may include dressing, talking, walking, and acting alike; listening to the same music; and visiting the same Internet sites.

Temperament

The American Heritage College Dictionary defines **temperament** as "the manner of thinking, behaving, or reacting typical of a specific person." Studies have shown, and casual observation confirms, that a child's temperament will have a direct influence on how they behave in a given situation or reacts to a particular stimuli. For example, if a child has a short attention span, they will be challenged in any learning environment that requires them to sit still and focus for long periods of time. If a child is shy or easily intimidated by adults, they will have a difficult time relating to the teacher, which will have a direct impact on their educational experiences. As childen age, they will exert more control over their environmental choices, which will affect their interactions. As a result, children usually choose people with whom they are comfortable and situations they perceive to be nonthreatening.

Conflict Resolution

A child's ability to resolve conflicts with their peers strongly influences their acceptance into or rejection from the group. Learning to deal with conflict in a positive manner is critical to developing healthy friendships and has a huge impact on social acceptance. Elementary school children with self-control are better able to find solutions that consider both sides in a dispute, which is the way conflicts should be resolved.

Social acceptance in elementary school is a fairly accurate predictor of how successful a person will be in college and in their professional life. Researchers followed two groups of 8-year-olds into their mid-40s. People whose peers rated their social behavior acceptable in elementary school were more successful than those who had social difficulties. Thus, a compelling reason to deal with aggressive behavior early in life is that, if left unchecked, it can have serious academic and professional consequences later in life.

Child-Centered Kindergarten Environment

One critical factor to remember is that five-year-olds learn differently than older children. The physical space and the teacher's approach to instruction should reflect the unique learning requirements of the kindergarten student. Five-year-olds need an environment that grows and changes as they acquire new skills; a curriculum that addresses their physical, social, emotional, and intellectual development; provides lots of different hands-on activities and materials that encourage active participation; and views play as fundamental to their development. Kindergartners' experiences should include opportunities to try new ideas and concepts as well as introduce and celebrate multicultural differences. The physical area should be inviting, colorful, easy to navigate, and encourage interaction. The room should be arranged from the child's viewpoint, with large and small spaces designed for different activities; all areas should be visible to the teacher. Parental involvement should be strongly encouraged, from helping in the classroom to asking about the kindergartner's day.

Child-Centered Elementary School Environment

Elementary school children between the ages of six and nine have progressed beyond learning just through play, although play remains essential to their development. From first grade through fifth grade, children are honing their problem-solving skills and improving their ability to listen, follow instructions, and make friends. A child-centered elementary school environment provides students with an active atmosphere and a curriculum that focuses on themes built on topics in which they are interested. When the child feels their needs and interests are considered, he or her is more cooperative, happier, less competitive, and involved in fewer conflicts at school and at home. The motivation behind a child-centered learning environment is that children learn by doing as well as by exploring their world in their time and in their way. When the elements that encourage this active learning are present, children's natural curiosity is aroused, and knowledge is acquired.

Chapter Quiz

Ready to see how well you retained what you just read? Scan the QR code to go directly to the chapter quiz interface for this study guide. If you're using a computer, simply visit the online resources page at **mometrix.com/resources719/nystcefamconsc** and click the Chapter Quizzes link.

Textiles and Design

Housing and Home Design

Functions That Any Type of Housing Is Expected to Serve

The primary purpose for any type of housing is to act as a form of shelter. Shelter in this context refers to protecting people from harsh weather such as rain, snow, extreme heat, extreme cold, harsh winds, extensive exposure to UV radiation, or any other conditions that might prove unpleasant or harmful. Housing can also provide security by making it more difficult for harmful things, such as animals, insects, unscrupulous individuals, and other threats, to reach people and their belongings. In some cases, housing can also serve as a location for individuals to conduct business in and work from. A house itself can even act as a symbol of the wealth and status of its owners.

Security can be extremely important for an individual or group that is wealthy, well known, or at high risk of being victimized by thieves or other criminals. A home can provide a wide range of protective measures to help keep people and their belongings safe, including locks on doors and windows, burglar alarms, fire alarms, and carbon monoxide detectors to warn residents of potentially deadly threats. Some homes, especially homes that are located in high-risk areas, might contain a large percentage of an individual's personal assets. Residences that house individuals who are at high risk due to their social status, political rank, or amount of personal assets may also have additional security measures in place. These measures include security features such as strong deadbolts locks, security cameras, gates, and checkpoints.

Running a Business from Home

A number of advantages are associated with running a business from home. Probably the most important advantage of running a home-based business is the fact that individuals or groups can usually significantly reduce their overhead costs as a result of using a single building for both business and living purposes. Overhead costs that can be reduced include expenses related to transportation, business clothing, office furnishings, maintenance, mortgage or rent, taxes, and other similar expenses. Some of the other major advantages of running a home based business are that the individual has a more flexible schedule, has the ability to put most of the time that would be spent commuting to better use, and the individual is readily available to fulfill their domestic responsibilities as well.

For an individual to be able to work successfully and efficiently in any environment, they need a private place to work that is relatively free from distractions. Regardless of what type of business an individual is attempting to run, they will also require time to accomplish the work that needs to be done, as well as the necessary equipment to perform that work. Equipment an individual may require for their home business includes a computer, printer, telephone, and computer programs appropriate to the type of work to be performed. It is also important that an individual is able to find the storage space necessary for any equipment that the business will need to function appropriately.

The single largest problem that home business owners face is the conflict that arises between the needs of the family and the needs of the business. Every business has its own distinct needs, and those needs can be difficult to achieve in a home setting because a conflict can arise between the space, time, and equipment that the family needs and the space, time, and equipment that the business needs. For example, a child or other family member may need the business space or equipment, such as a computer, to complete their homework at the same time that the business owner is using the space and equipment for conducting business. On the other hand, the children of the family may not need to use the computer but instead need the business owner to step into a parental role and feed them or help them with their homework, which distracts the business owner from the tasks they need to complete for work purposes. Any equipment purchased specifically for the business will also require space that the family might have already had dedicated for another purpose in the household.

Using a Home as a Status Symbol

The major reason that a home can act as a status symbol for an individual or family that lives in it is because of the financial investment necessary to own a home. Regardless of the type of home that someone lives in, purchasing or leasing a home is usually the single largest expense that anyone will take on during their life. As a result, the home of an individual or family can act as an indication of the overall wealth that a person or family possesses. This means that the larger and more luxurious a house is, the greater the amount of wealth a person must have had in order to acquire that home. Since wealth is commonly associated with the status of an individual, the type of home that an individual or family lives in acts as an indicator of their social status as well.

Major Types of Housing

The two major types of residential housing are **houses** and **apartments**. A house is an entire building with the primary purpose of providing shelter for the individual or family that resides in it. An apartment is a section of a building that has been split into units, and the primary purpose of each unit is to provide shelter for the individual or family that lives in that unit. The major difference between and house and an apartment is that a building is considered a house if the whole building belongs to one individual, family, or several families that share the entire building or at least most of the building. On the other hand, a building is considered to be an apartment building or a complex if it contains separate sections or units that each allow individuals or families to live on their own without sharing a large portion of the building.

Common Types of Houses and Apartments Found in the United States

The three major types of houses found in the United States are **single-family houses**, **townhouses**, and **semi-detached houses**. A single-family house is any building used for residential use that is separate from any other buildings. Townhouses are a series of buildings where all of the houses share both of their side walls with the buildings on each side (with the exception of the houses at the ends of the row, which only share one wall). Semi-detached houses are two residential buildings that share only a single wall and have empty space on their other side. These three major types of houses are typically determined by how much space is available around the building. A single-family home has space available on all sides, a semi-detached house has space clear in front, behind, and on one side of the house, and townhouses, with the exception of the townhouses on the end of the row, have space only in front and behind the house.

The most common types of apartments found in the United States are single or multi-bedroom apartments and studio apartments. Single or multi-bedroom apartments are units that have one or more bedrooms that are separated from the rest of the unit. Studio apartments are units that have one large room that makes up the entire unit and performs the functions of a bedroom, living room, dining room, kitchen, and any other rooms that the unit's tenants require. Studio apartments and single or multi-bedroom apartments are usually rented, but it is becoming more and more common for apartments to be sold to consumers as condominiums or cooperatives. Regardless of whether an apartment is rented or purchased, studio apartments are almost always less expensive than multi-bedroom apartments; the price of an apartment increases significantly with each extra separate bedroom attached to the unit.

Condominiums vs. Cooperatives

A **condominium**, also known as a condo, is a type of apartment ownership where an individual has purchased complete ownership of a single unit but has shared ownership of certain common areas and common expenses associated with the building. This means that the individual living in the condo owns the unit and is responsible for all of the expenses associated with that unit, but shares the rest of the building and the expenses associated with the remainder of the building. A **cooperative**, also known as a co-op, is a type of apartment where an individual owns shares in a corporation, and that corporation owns the entire building. An individual who owns the shares has the right to live in a particular unit within the building as long as they follow certain guidelines set by the corporation.

The major difference between a condominium and a cooperative is that a condo owner actually owns the unit and shares ownership of the building, while a co-op owner does not actually own the unit or the building, but rather owns part of a corporation and that corporation owns the building. By paying condo fees and discussing problems with a condo association, the owner of a condo directly shares the decisions and expenses related to the upkeep of the building. A co-op owner, on the other hand, is not directly responsible for the expenses and problems of the building as the corporation that owns the building handles these expenses and problems using the funds they gather from the rent or subscription fees paid by the co-op owners.

Methods Used to Pay for Housing

The two most common methods that an individual or family might use to pay for their housing are *renting*, also known as leasing, and *purchasing* a house through a mortgage or loan. When an individual does not actually own a house or apartment where they reside, but rather pays a monthly fee for the use of that house or apartment, that is renting. People who rent a place to live will never own the property no matter how long they live there and how much rent they pay. In contrast, an individual who takes out a mortgage on a particular type of housing actually purchases that house or apartment using the money acquired from a loan.

Advantages and Disadvantages of Renting

The two major advantages of renting housing rather than purchasing housing are that renting is usually less expensive in terms of monthly payments and the individual or family does not have to be concerned with costs associated with maintaining the building. A renter or lessee does not actually own the building and has to pay only whatever fee the building's owner has set for that particular unit, regardless of any work that the rest of the building may require. For example, if a building's plumbing needs work, any cost that is associated with repairing the plumbing is the responsibility of the building's owner and not the responsibility of the apartment's tenant. The major disadvantage of renting is that the individual does not gain any long-term financial advantage from paying rent because each rent payment is not being applied toward the purchase of the property.

Advantages and Disadvantages of Purchasing

The major advantage of purchasing housing rather than renting is that an individual or family actually owns the property and can sell that property or rent it to someone else at a later time. Each monthly payment is applied to paying off the loan that was used to purchase the property, and the owner can decide to sell that property at any point and keep any money that is left over after paying the bank back. An individual who is renting can leave their apartment at any time but will receive no benefit from the money they paid while living there. The two major disadvantages of purchasing a home are that the monthly payments are usually higher than what an individual renting a home pays and the individual or family is responsible for all of the expenses associated with maintaining the home.

An individual who is attempting to decide whether to rent or purchase a particular type of housing should base the decision on their income. This can be done by estimating how much buying a piece of property will cost the individual per month, how much renting will cost the individual per month, and the individual's monthly income. If the individual has the money available to put a reasonable down payment on a piece of property that they are interested in and has the income to make the monthly mortgage payments on the property without a problem, buying is usually the better option. This is because purchasing a piece of property, unlike renting, is an investment that can be sold, usually with some degree of financial return for the original property owner. On the other hand, if an individual cannot afford to make a reasonable down payment and the monthly mortgage payments are more than they can comfortably afford, renting is a better option.

An individual or family that is considering what building to rent or purchase should first determine how much they can afford to spend on housing. Purchasing or even renting housing is always a major investment, and the individual or family needs to make sure that they have the funds available to make the required payments. Next, the individual or family should determine what attributes of the house or apartment are important to them, such as the location of the building, how big the building should be, how much storage space the building has, and how much yard space it includes. Once the individual or family has made a list of all of the things that should be ideal features of their house or apartment, they can then begin looking for houses or apartments that are within their price range and best suit their needs.

Housing Considerations

Factors to Consider When Looking for Housing

Some of the most important factors regarding the surrounding area of a house or apartment that an individual should consider include the current state of the neighborhood, how accessible the property is, and the quality of local schools and recreational facilities. The current state of the neighborhood refers to factors such as the overall appearance of the neighborhood, the traffic and noise level, the number of children living in the area, parking, zoning or other regulations and restrictions, and the level of police, fire, and community involvement in the neighborhood. The accessibility of a piece of property refers to its location and how close it is to stores, public transportation, major roads and highways, and a resident's place of employment. For active individuals and families with children, quality local schools and recreational facilities are important. Considerations include how close the house or apartment is to these facilities, how well maintained these facilities are, and the reputations of these facilities.

Importance of Floor Plans

Some of the factors that an individual should consider when designing a floor plan include what size the room or rooms should be, what furniture needs to go in each room, how often each room will be used, and the traffic patterns of the room. The individual should also consider how many electrical outlets the room requires, how much lighting is necessary for the room, and whether the room has any special requirements to fulfill the purpose of the room. For example, a photographer who is planning to add on a darkroom to his house would need a room that is located away from outside walls and windows, lets in virtually no light, has access to a number of electrical outlets and countertops for developing equipment, and has sinks for rinsing film. A well-designed floor plan is important because it allows an individual to eliminate problems such as not enough storage space, not enough room for furniture and equipment, not enough light, and not enough access to power outlets.

Interior Design

Interior design is the process of planning the best way possible to construct a room, a series of rooms, or an entire house. The primary purpose of interior design is to make each room both as functional and as appealing as possible. Interior designers usually consider seven basic elements of design when deciding how to make a particular room appealing: color, texture, pattern, line, shape, form, and mass. Once the interior designer knows the purpose and functional requirements of a room, they can then create a floor plan of how the room or rooms will fit into the rest of the house and of how the room itself will be organized to fulfill its intended purpose.

Factors to Consider When Analyzing Traffic Patterns

An individual who is analyzing the traffic patterns of a room should consider the purpose of the room, the location of the room in relation to other rooms, the number of people that will be using the room, and the ease of movement in the room. The traffic patterns of a room refer to how many people are moving into, through, and around that room and how easy it is for them to make those movements. For example, a room that is near the center of a house and connects two rooms on different sides should have a clear, straight path entering and exiting each connecting room. This means that people walking through the room should be able to walk straight through without having to walk around couches, tables, chairs, or other furniture that is blocking their path. A room with a well-planned traffic pattern will allow people to access every part of the room without climbing over or walking around furniture.

Clothing and Textiles

Planning a Wardrobe

Individuals who are planning their wardrobes should begin by considering what kinds of clothing they usually wear, along with what kinds of clothing they will need for casual, business, and other environments. For example, the president of a major corporation would need to focus more on purchasing formalwear and business attire as opposed to buying a closetful of very casual clothing. After an individual has established a basic outline of the kinds of clothing that best suit their wardrobe needs, the individual should take an inventory of what clothing they already have in order to determine what types of clothing need to be purchased. Once the individual has determined which types of clothing are lacking in their wardrobe, the individual will decide what factors are important for each of those types of clothing. For example, an individual searching for formalwear that will be worn only occasionally might be more concerned with corresponding colors and overall appearance than how durable the materials are. Finally, the individual can select clothing to build a wardrobe based on the factors they have established.

Selecting Clothing

The four major factors that an individual should consider when selecting a piece of clothing for their wardrobe include:

1. Price
2. Purpose
3. Quality
4. Overall Appearance

A consumer who is considering purchasing a garment would be wise to compare the price of the item that they are interested in to other similar items to see what price range is reasonable. A consumer should also consider the purpose of the piece of clothing to be purchased. Under what conditions the clothing will be worn can dictate not only the style of clothing desired, but also the materials that the clothing is made of. Someone camping at a remote wilderness site, for instance, would not purchase a satin robe to wear during the trip. The quality of the clothing is also significant because garments that are better constructed can be worn for a longer period of time; paying more for a high-quality piece of clothing instead of choosing a less expensive garment may cost the consumer less money on additional clothing or mending later on. The overall appearance of a garment may be the most influential factor in a person's choice because a primary purpose of any garment is to help the individual convey a certain image.

Reducing the Cost of Purchasing Additional Clothing

An individual whose goal is to purchase clothing as cheaply as possible might begin their search by making a detailed list of exactly what types of clothing they are looking for. This list should include what types of clothing are desired, an estimate of how many garments of each type the individual wants, and an estimate of how much they are willing to spend overall. The individual should then decide how much time they are willing to devote to comparing various garments and their prices, where to go shopping, and when to go. Because many retailers offer deep discounts on certain days of the year, such as the day after Thanksgiving, consumers who want to reduce the cost of adding to their wardrobes might consider shopping during those special sales. Consumers also have the option of shopping online and looking through store circulars to get a general idea of how much an item costs, to compare prices, and to see what sales are currently being offered. Less expensive alternatives to department stores are second-hand and discount stores, along with online auction sites that give consumers the opportunity to purchase inexpensive pieces of clothing that might never have been worn.

Well-Constructed Clothing

The three universal concepts that an individual should consider when determining the quality of any garment include:

- **Functional**: A garment is regarded as functional if an individual can wear it and move in it without difficulty or fear of damaging the garment.
- **Inconspicuous**: An inconspicuous garment has no apparent flaws and the garment was assembled using techniques that hide any stitching or seams that should not be showing.
- **Durable**: A garment is considered durable if the garment was constructed with strong, high-quality materials, with the seams and stitching done correctly so that they hold together.

Several factors indicate that a ready-made garment is well-constructed: the fabric is used and seamed together correctly; the various colors, fibers, and designs appear to go well together; the garment appears to have a smooth appearance; and the garment does not have any obvious loose threads. Well-constructed garments should also have a seam allowance of half an inch or more, which means that there should be at least half an inch between the edge of one material and the seam stitching that material to the second material. If any of these basic elements is lacking, it usually indicates that the garment may have been assembled incorrectly. If the garment does not have a smooth appearance or the seam allowances are less than half an inch, it is likely that the garment will not hold together very well.

A consumer can conclude that a belt is well-constructed if it has well-finished ends, is made out of a durable material, and has a buckle that is securely attached and closes the belt appropriately.

A consumer can conclude that a collar is well-constructed if both the right and left sides of the collar appear to be the same shape and size, if the collar has both smoothly curved edges and sharp flat points, and if the collar lays flat or sits correctly on the shirt. It is also important that the underside of the collar does not show and that there does not appear to be an excessive number of seams across the collar.

A consumer can conclude that a neckline is well-constructed if the design is the same on both sides and matches correctly, the neckline does not appear to be bulky, and the facings are flat and have stitches that are not obvious.

A consumer can conclude that the darts of a garment have been constructed correctly if the darts are smooth and pressed in the appropriate direction, if the darts have been placed in positions that improve the overall appearance of the garment, and if each dart is the same size and shape. The direction that a dart should be pressed depends on the type of dart: Vertical darts should be pressed toward the center of the garment, while horizontal darts should be pressed toward the bottom of the garment.

A consumer can conclude that the hem of a garment has been constructed correctly if it is flat, hangs smoothly, and sits parallel to the floor. A properly constructed hem has an edge that is smooth and secure with no loose threads. The seams of the hem should be pressed and concealed as much as possible. It is also important that the hem is the appropriate width and length for the individual who will be wearing the garment.

A consumer can conclude that the buttons of a garment have been well-constructed if the buttons are attached securely to the garment, the buttons are the appropriate size to fit through the button holes and stay secure once they are through the hole, and the buttons are spaced evenly on the garment. The buttons should also be stitched starting and ending at the bottom of the button. A consumer can conclude that the buttonholes of a garment have been well-constructed if the buttonholes are spaced evenly and are even in width and length, the buttonholes are the correct size, they lay flat, and they are stitched correctly. The edge of the garment that has the buttonholes should also be interfaced, and buttonholes should be cut on grain at points of strain and carefully stitched to make sure that the buttonhole is secure and does not cause the garment to come apart.

Importance of Correctly Fitting Garments

Several factors indicate that a garment fits correctly: the garment is comfortable and allows the wearer free movement; each part of the garment, such as the neckline or the waistline, sits properly; and the garment lies flat. Garments that fit correctly should also have a smooth appearance with no wrinkles and should not have any folds in the fabric other than the folds that are part of the garment's design. If a garment does not fit an individual properly, that person will not be able to function normally because they will have difficulty moving in the garment. Additionally, the garment should fulfill its intended purpose while also giving the wearer a certain look. A garment that does not fit correctly and does not look right will usually not convey the image the individual intends to project.

ELEMENTS OF DESIGN

There are four basic elements that make up the design of any garment:

- **Color**: Color refers not only to the shade of the garment, such as red or blue, but also to how bright or dull and how light or dark that shade is.
- **Shape or form**: Shape refers to whether a garment or detail is flat, such as a T-shirt lying on a table, while form refers to the depth that garments have, such as the tiers of a wedding gown.
- **Texture**: Texture refers to how the garment feels to the touch, like rough, soft, coarse, or silky.
- **Line**: Line refers to the seams and lines that are inherent to the fabric, as well as any designs present in the garment.

The principal elements of design are important because they allow an individual who is attempting to construct or select a garment to understand the basic parts that comprise a design. An individual who understands these parts can determine what makes a garment look good and what sorts of garments will complement each other. The elements of design may not be of utmost importance if an individual is not concerned with the garment's overall appearance and is simply looking for a comfortable or useful piece of clothing; however, understanding these elements can be extremely useful when an individual is looking to improve their overall appearance. Ultimately, the elements of design are the basic components that make up a garment and determine whether or not that garment will give the right look when used with other garments.

PRINCIPLES OF DESIGN

Five basic principles are used in the construction of a garment to make its design more appealing:

- **Balance**
- **Emphasis**
- **Proportion**
- **Rhythm**
- **Unity**

BALANCE

A garment is **balanced** if both the left and right sides of the garment appear to be similar and correspond to each other. The emphasis of a garment refers to any designs, details, or parts of the garment that draw people's attention. A design is correctly proportioned if the attributes of the various parts of a garment, such as size, shape, and color, appear to be appropriate when compared to each other or to the garment as a whole. The rhythm of a design refers to any feature that causes an individual to look at one part of a design and then leads that individual's attention to another part of the garment's design. Finally, the unity of a design is when a garment looks appropriate after all of the parts of the design have been put together.

Balance refers to the fact that both the left and ride sides of the garment appear to be similar to each other, but this does not necessarily mean that both sides of the garment are actually the same. In fact, there are two different types of balance that an individual might find when examining a garment: symmetrical balance and asymmetrical balance. In order for a garment to have symmetrical balance, both sides of the garment must sit at the same level, and the parts on one side of the centerline of the garment have to be an exact mirror of the other side. A garment is considered to have asymmetrical balance if both sides are not physically identical, but are similar enough that an individual believes that both sides seem to have the same "weight." Balance is extremely important to the overall appearance of a garment because a garment that is comprised of unevenly positioned parts will not look as appealing.

EMPHASIS

The **emphasis** of a design is important because the overall purpose of using the principles and elements of design is to create a certain appearance that will draw people's attention to the garment. The emphasis of a design can refer to virtually anything from the use of a bright color to a subtle form to an intricate image, such as an ivy vine that wraps its way around the garment. However, any individual attempting to decide whether the emphasis of a garment is effective should consider whether it fulfills its purpose of drawing attention without being too flashy or gaudy because garments that place too much emphasis on flashy and gaudy features are usually unappealing.

PROPORTION

In some ways, **proportion** is similar to the design principle of balance in that it pertains to how the various images, lines, and other attributes of the garment appear to fit the garment when they are compared with one another. For example, a garment that has several roses of a similar size evenly spaced on it would probably be considered correctly proportioned. However, a garment with one enormous rose on it and several other roses of differing sizes placed randomly across the garment would probably be considered incorrectly proportioned, as the roses do not appear to complement or relate to one another. Proportion also refers to how those individual design elements relate to the garment as a whole, so an enormous image of a rose covering an entire garment would not be proportional to the garment and would therefore appear to be overwhelming and unappealing.

RHYTHM

If a garment employs the important design technique of **rhythm**, its overall design will have a basic sense of flow, which means that one part of the design seems to ease into the next, leading the viewer's attention to the next detail in the design. The most common way of accomplishing a sense of rhythm in a design is to repeat patterns or colors within a garment, which draws the viewer's focus first to the pattern and then to the details of the pattern along the entire garment. Some garments may have a rhythmic quality to a part of the design that may not necessarily be the main emphasis of the entire garment.

UNITY

Unity is a design principle that is achieved when all of a garment's individual parts look right on a person after those parts have been brought together. For unity to be achieved, all of the elements of a garment's design, including the design's color, lines, shape or form, and texture, must coordinate in order to create the look that an individual is attempting to achieve. If the elements of the garment, along with any other clothing that the individual is wearing, do not appear to go with each other, the overall garment will not create a sense of unity and will not be able to convey the image that the individual had intended. Ultimately, unity is achieved when all of the other principles and elements of the design are brought together to create the desired image.

REMOVING STAINS FROM A GARMENT

Regardless of what type of garment and what kind of stain an individual is dealing with, it is important to check the garment label for care instructions before attempting to remove a stain. All efforts should be made to remove a stain as soon as possible after it appears. Generally, the best way for an individual to remove a stain from a garment in most cases is to take a clean cloth, wet it with cold water, and blot the stain with the cloth, starting from the outside of the stain and gradually moving towards its center. Using hot water or rubbing the stain can cause it to set into the fabric or to spread. The technique of blotting with cold water is safe for most washable garments, but it should be used sparingly, if at all, on non-washable fabrics.

Cleaning and Washing a Garment

The two primary techniques that an individual can use to clean a garment are **home washing** and **dry cleaning**. Home washing refers to an individual either washing a garment by hand or machine-washing a garment using some combination of water and detergent to remove dirt and stains from the clothing. Dry-cleaning refers to a process by which the garment is cleaned using chemical solvents that are heated, and very little water is used. It is important that an individual determines the appropriate technique to clean a garment because certain materials may shrink or disintegrate if they are washed with water, while other garments may react poorly to the solvents used in dry cleaning. Some types of materials must be washed at specific temperatures, so it is also important for an individual to know if the material might be damaged by the heat involved with dry cleaning or by being washed in hot water.

The best way for an individual to determine which technique to use in washing a garment is to follow the care instructions on the garment's care label. Nearly all garments are tagged with care instructions written by the manufacturer explaining what techniques are best to use in washing the garment. These labels are actually required by law, but in some instances, the care label may have been removed or accidentally left off the garment. If the label is missing, an individual will have to determine what techniques to use based on the materials of the garment. Stronger materials such as cottons, linens, polyesters, and durable silks can usually be machine-washed in warm water without a problem. Garments made out of materials like nylon that can shrink or pick up colors should be washed only in cold water. Garments that contain more delicate materials, such as most acetates, acrylics, and most types of wool, should almost always be dry-cleaned.

Washing Techniques with Specific Care Instructions

- **Machine-washable** garments can be cleaned using any normal method of washing and drying unless the care instructions state otherwise. This means that machine-washable garments can be hand-washed, cleaned using a washing machine and dryer, dry-cleaned, washed by commercial laundry services, or cleaned using any other reasonable method.
- **Home launder** means that a garment can be cleaned by any method except for commercial laundry services because the procedures frequently used in commercial laundering may damage the garment.
- **No chlorine bleach** means that an individual can use only bleaches that do not contain chlorine, such as oxygen bleaches, because chlorine bleaches may damage or discolor the garment. A label indicating no bleach is a warning that no bleach of any kind should be used when washing the garment to avoid permanently damaging it.
- **Cold wash/cold rinse** means that the garment should be washed in cold water; warm wash/warm rinse means that the garment should be washed in warm water; and hot wash means that the garment should be washed in hot water.
- Applicable only if a garment is being machine-washed, **no spin** means that the garment should be removed from the washer before the final spin cycle to avoid being damaged.
- When the care instructions indicate **delicate cycle**, **gentle cycle**, **durable cycle**, or **permanent press cycle**, the instructions refer to the cycle setting on a washing machine that should be used to minimize the chances of damage to a garment. Stronger materials can usually be washed on any setting, but some materials are more delicate and therefore more likely to be damaged during longer cycles when the inside of the washing machine is spinning faster for a longer period of time.

- **Wash separately** means that a garment should not be washed with other garments or should be washed with garments of a similar color. Garments usually need to be washed separately because either the colors in the garment are likely to run and damage other clothing or the garment is likely to pick up colors from other clothing.
- The instruction **hand-wash** means that a garment should not be machine-washed, but it can be washed by hand- or dry-cleaned. Garments that should be hand-washed have this particular instruction because they are extremely delicate. Hand-wash garments are usually washed in warm water. Hand-wash only means that the garment should be washed by hand; any other method, including dry cleaning, should not be used.
- **Dry-clean only** means that the garment should not be cleaned by a commercial laundry service or a home method and should only be dry-cleaned. **No dry clean** means that the garment should never be dry-cleaned.
- **Tumble-dry** means that a garment can be dried using a normal dryer. The temperature that should be used—low, medium, or high—usually follows the "tumble-dry" instruction. Drip-dry means that a garment should be hung while it is still wet and let dry.

YARN, THREAD, AND FABRIC

Yarn is a collection of long lengths of tightly spun fibers that are used in the production of fabric. **Thread** is a collection of long, thin lengths of fibers that are used for sewing two fabrics together. **Fabric** is a material constructed by weaving or knitting yarn together to form a type of cloth. Fabrics come in a wide range of colors, textures, and appearances and can be used to make such items as carpeting, towels, and clothing.

FIBERS

Fibers are thin filaments similar to thread found in plants or the fur of animals. Fibers can also be man-made filaments that are formed by forcing chemicals through small holes called spinnerets. These fibers are used for a number of different purposes including the construction of yarn, thread, and fabric.

The two major types of fibers that are used in the construction of fabrics are **natural fibers** and **synthetic fibers**. Natural fibers are any fibers that are taken from plants or animals, while synthetic fibers are fibers that are created in a laboratory or factory through the use of chemicals. Each type of fiber has its own distinct characteristics. Synthetic fibers are often similar to natural fibers, as researchers will base a synthetic fiber on a natural fiber in order to create a stronger or less expensive alternative to the natural fiber. However, synthetic fibers often react very differently under certain conditions such as heat and sunlight than natural fibers, so it can be extremely important for an individual to understand the differences between synthetic and natural fibers.

Acetate fibers are synthetic fibers that are soft, smooth, dry, weak, lustrous, and heat-sensitive. Acetate fibers are used in the construction of a variety of fabrics including satins and taffetas primarily to give the fabric a shiny, lustrous look. Fabrics that are made from acetate fibers are more resistant to shrinking.

Acrylic fibers are synthetic fibers that are soft, lightweight, resilient, and heat-sensitive. Acrylic fibers are often used as a replacement for wool because they have a very similar feel to wool. Acrylic fibers are also often used as a less expensive alternative to cashmere, as they have a very similar appearance.

Cotton fibers are natural fibers that are relatively strong, soft, light sensitive, elastic, and breathable and can absorb and retain water effectively. Many fabrics are made completely out of cotton fibers or a blend of cotton fibers with other fibers such as rayon and polyester. Fabrics made from cotton fibers are usually both soft and heat resistant, but they are also more likely to shrink.

Similar to cotton fibers, **flax** fibers are natural fibers that are soft, breathable, and strong but lack the elasticity that cotton fibers have. High-quality flax fibers are used primarily in the construction of linens. Fabrics made from flax fibers are usually similar to fabrics made from cotton in that they are soft and heat resistant and also likely to shrink.

Nylon fibers are synthetic fibers that are smooth, strong, lightweight, elastic, and lustrous. Nylon fibers are primarily used as a cheaper alternative to silk. Fabrics made from nylon are relatively inexpensive, strong, and extremely light, but they will melt at high temperatures.

Polyester fibers are synthetic fibers that are strong, lightweight, resilient, and resistant to many of the conditions that might normally harm a fabric, such as mildew, sunlight, harsh weather, and moths. Polyester fibers are used in a wide range of fabrics and are often used in a cotton/polyester blend.

Ramie fibers are natural fibers that are very strong, have a lustrous appearance similar to silk, and absorb and retain water effectively. However, they are also brittle, stiff, inelastic, and not very resilient. Ramie fibers are very difficult work with and are usually used in blends with other fibers, such as wool, to make a variety of fabrics.

Rayon fibers are synthetic fibers that have many of the same characteristics as cotton fibers and are relatively soft, smooth, strong, resistant to moths, and can retain water extremely well. Rayon fibers are used in a variety of fabrics, including most types of velvet because it can imitate the feel of silk and other natural fibers.

Silk fibers are natural fibers that are extremely soft, strong, and lustrous, and they absorb and retain water effectively. They are also resistant to mildew, molds, and moths. Silk fibers are used in the construction of a wide range of fabrics such as chiffon, organza, and taffeta because of the silk's soft feel and extremely lustrous appearance.

Wool fibers are natural fibers that normally are coarse, relatively strong, resilient, and can retain water well. Wool fibers are commonly used in a variety of fabrics such as flannel because wool fibers improve a fabric's ability to retain heat. Most types of wool have a scratchy feel to them, which is why many individuals believe that they are allergic to wool, but some wool fabrics such as cashmere are very soft.

Making Fabric from Natural or Synthetic Fibers

A textile manufacturer making a particular type of fabric would begin by acquiring the appropriate fibers from plant or animal sources or by manufacturing the fibers that are needed for that particular fabric. The manufacturer would then convert those fibers into yarn through a process called spinning in which the fibers are spun together tightly. The yarn is then knitted or woven together by hand or by machine to form fabric. The fabric is then put through a series of treatments that are designed to improve the overall appearance and feel of the fabric. These treatments include processes such as dyeing, which the manufacturer would use to achieve the desired color for the fabric unless the natural or plant fibers are already that color. Finally, the fabric is treated with a series of finishing chemicals that are designed to improve the fabric's resistance to harmful conditions such as weather or sunlight.

Chapter Quiz

Ready to see how well you retained what you just read? Scan the QR code to go directly to the chapter quiz interface for this study guide. If you're using a computer, simply visit the online resources page at **mometrix.com/resources719/nystcefamconsc** and click the Chapter Quizzes link.

Consumer Skills and Resource Management

Economics and Resource Management

Time Management

Time management is the process of using skills, tools, principles, and practices together in order to most efficiently use the time that an individual or group of individuals has available. The efficiency goal of time management is similar to that of work simplification; however, time management itself does not actually make work easier. Instead, time management involves finding the most proficient way to complete a task at hand in the amount of time given. Time management is extremely important in both business and personal settings, as people often do not have enough time available to complete every single task they face. Planning how to complete the greatest number of tasks possible in the amount of time available allows people to get more value out of their time and efforts.

Some of the techniques used in time management include setting goals, planning the best way to complete a task, scheduling, prioritizing tasks, making sure that all necessary equipment is easily accessible, and effectively managing one's workload. A successful time management system successfully incorporates all of these techniques, with the end result of accomplishing the most tasks possible in the amount of time given.

Prioritizing Activities

One of the most important techniques in time management is **prioritizing** so that the most important tasks are completed first and the least important tasks are left for when a person has more time available to do them. This system allows people to rank both goals and the corresponding tasks that lead to achieving those goals based on how essential they are to the individual or the organization. An individual, family, or organization can determine what activities are important by first identifying and defining which goals need to be achieved in order to continue functioning. Once this step is completed, people can then decide what tasks are the most crucial for the individual or organization to continue functioning. These tasks should be given the highest priority, while less important tasks, although they also can lead to goal accomplishment, should be considered a lower priority.

Goals and Decision-Making

A **goal** is a particular purpose that an individual or organization wants to achieve in the near or distant future. In a corporate setting, for example, a goal could be achieving a specified amount of sales in the next quarter. In a family setting, a goal might be for a teenager in the family to find a job before the end of summer.

Decision-making is the process by which an individual or group attempts to determine what would be the best managerial selection from a set of possible options and/or actions from a managerial perspective, usually for the purpose of achieving a particular goal. For instance, a couple looking for a new home may make a list of the advantages and disadvantages of living in each house they view to help them decide which house to buy.

Goal-Setting

Goal-setting is important because it allows individuals and organizations to identify what objectives they seek to accomplish and then determine the best means by which to accomplish those objectives. Goal-setting typically involves establishing a particular timeframe in which a goal should be achieved. Knowing what goals an individual is striving to reach in a set amount of time helps motivate each individual involved to reach that ultimate objective. Goals also provide the individual or organization with a means of measuring the amount of effort—or lack thereof—that each individual puts into obtaining those goals. In a corporate setting, goals can also provide the organization with a way to measure its overall success, which in turn can be important in determining what future actions the organization will need to take.

Creating a Valid Goal

Individuals or organizations attempting to set a goal can follow the common management mnemonic SMART (specific, measurable, achievable, relevant, and time-bound) to make sure that their goal is well-defined, valid, and useful when both measuring success and motivating the organization as a whole. Established goals should be specific and well-defined, have some way of being measured accurately, be attainable, and be relevant to the tasks that need to be completed for the success of the organization. The individual or organization should also decide upon an appropriate amount of time that should be spent in achieving a goal not only to make sure that it is achieved in a timely fashion, but also to ensure that the goal can be compared to other goals in the future.

Explain Whether or Not the Following Goals Are Valid:

A manager of a local retailer that usually does somewhere between $35,000 and $60,000 a week decided that their store should set a goal of making $50,000 in sales a week each week for the month of November.

This example demonstrates a completely valid goal, as the goal is well-defined and quantifiable. It can be measured by examining the amount of sales the store has done each week. In addition, the goal is relevant to the store's ability to make a profit within a set amount of time, as the goal of $50,000 is achievable because it falls within the store's normal sales range.

The mother of a child who is having difficulty in school has decided that her son needs to improve his grades.

While the goal of improving the child's grades may be achievable and relevant to the success of the child, it is not well-defined enough to be considered a valid, effective goal. Although the goal could be measured, no criteria are established as to what would be satisfactory improvement in the boy's grades. Furthermore, the mother has not established a timeframe in which her son is expected to reach the goal.

Working Toward Achieving Any Given Goal

Both internal and external factors can have an effect on whether an individual or organization will be able to achieve a particular goal. However, the most important thing for an individual or organization to keep in mind, regardless of the situation, is that everyone involved in the goal-attaining process should remain focused on the goal and the appropriate ways by which they can achieve that goal. This means that if a goal is important to the success of the individual or the organization as a whole, people must be committed to giving their best efforts to achieve that particular goal. Any less important or irrelevant goals should not be allowed to distract the individual or the organization from the primary goal; any secondary goals should ultimately be put aside until the primary goal is achieved. From a managerial standpoint, it is important that people are regularly encouraged to recognize that the goal is achievable so that no one gives up before the goal is actually reached.

Importance of the Decision-Making Process

The **decision-making process** is important because understanding the process can aid in the discovery of a future rational and reasonable course of action when an individual or organization is presented with a decision that must be made. Each individual has a unique perspective and therefore a different way of reaching a particular decision; through a combination of intuition, knowledge, and an understanding of how the decision-making process works, a decision that is best suited for the goals of a particular individual or group can be made. Effective, knowledgeable decision making consists of identifying the decision that needs to be made, recognizing the benefits of each choice related to that decision, analyzing the potential drawbacks of making each choice related to that decision, and, finally, actually making the choice. By understanding what specifically needs to be identified at each stage of the decision-making process, an individual or organization will be able to make a more informed decision that will be more likely to lead to the achievement of a particular goal.

Attempting to Make a Well-Informed Decision

Some of the most common pitfalls that should be avoided when attempting to make a well-informed decision are entering the decision-making process with a preconceived notion that the individual is unwilling to abandon, allowing peer pressure to influence a decision, and overgeneralizing. Entering the decision-making process with a prejudice either for or against a particular idea, source of information, or choice will often lead to the selection of an option that is not the best or most logical choice available. While outside sources should be used to gather information about the decision that needs to be made, no single source should be allowed to pressure the individuals involved in making the decision into making a particular choice. Furthermore, the overuse of generalizations, stereotypes, and attempts to attribute effects to causes that may not have any logical link will often lead to a decision being made that may not be the best course of action.

Techniques That an Individual Might Use When Making a Decision

An individual who is in the process of making a well-informed decision will often gather as much information as possible from as many reliable sources as possible, list the advantages and disadvantages of each choice, and then compare each choice with the others. In an employment or business situation where finances are involved, an individual may use a mathematical approach and calculate exactly how much money each job choice or each potential new product could offer, as well as how much a poor decision might cost if something goes wrong. A mathematical approach can be an extremely solid strategy when one is attempting to determine what choice might be the most appropriate. Unfortunately, many individuals do not make well-informed decisions because they oftentimes employ faulty methods of decision making. In such instances, they may rely too heavily on the opinions of their peers, gather information from such unreliable sources as erroneous web sites, or even leave the decision to random chance by flipping a coin.

Strategies That a Business or Organization Might Use When Making a Decision

Some of the most common decision-making strategies that a business or other organization might use when making a decision include the **Pareto analysis system**, a cost/benefit analysis strategy, a force field analysis strategy, a grid analysis strategy, and a scenario analysis strategy. Because each strategy has its own advantages and disadvantages, businesses and other types of organizations will usually select the system or systems that best support the kind of decision they are attempting to make. For example, a Pareto analysis system can be useful when an organization is attempting to handle a group of related problems that are discovered to be responsible for most of the difficulties that the organization is experiencing. However, a Pareto analysis system will not work as well, if at all, in situations where a large number of problems are caused by completely unrelated factors.

Pareto Analysis System

Fundamentally, the Pareto analysis system is a decision-making model which assumes that approximately 80% of the benefits that an organization receives from a particular task are the result of 20% of the effort that the various individuals within the organization put into the task. It also assumes that 80% of the problems that the organization faces are produced by approximately 20% of the factors that may be causing them. The first step necessary in using the Pareto analysis system is to list all of the problems that need to be addressed and/or the choices that are available. Next, each of those problems or choices should be grouped so that the choices offering similar benefits and/or the factors leading to larger related problems are grouped together. Each group is then given a score based on how much that particular group affects the overall organization.

Cost/Benefit Analysis

Cost/benefit analysis is a decision-making strategy that examines the total estimated cost of each option that is available alongside the total estimated benefit of each option available and then compares the cost with the benefit to determine if the benefits of the option outweigh their cost. Usually, a cost/benefit analysis refers to the financial cost and benefit of a particular decision, but it can actually be used in any situation in which resources are used. For example, if a corporation has two clothing materials, A and B, that both cost the same but material B can be used more efficiently, the cost/benefit analysis would show that material B is the best choice because it allows for the production of the most clothing using the most efficient amount of material. While cost/benefit analysis can be useful when deciding which option will have the greatest benefit, this method also relies heavily on estimation, which makes it not as accurate as other methods of analysis.

Force Field Analysis

Force field analysis is a decision-making strategy that examines all of the factors that affect a particular situation and identifies those factors as either aiding the organization in achieving a goal or ultimately causing the organization to fall short of reaching its specified goal. Basically, force field analysis is the process of identifying and listing which factors involved with each option help the organization and which ones hurt the organization. The first step of the force field analysis strategy is to make a list of all of the factors involved with a particular option and then identify them as either aiding the organization in moving towards a particular goal or hindering the organization's movement towards that goal. Each factor is then given a rating on a scale of 1 to 5, with 1 being the weakest and 5 being the strongest. If the forces that hinder the organization have higher numbers, indicating that they are stronger overall, the option is probably not a sensible or realistic choice; however, if the forces that aid the organization have higher numbers, then the option may prove beneficial.

Grid Analysis

Grid analysis is a decision-making strategy that takes all of the factors involved with each option, rates each factor, and then gives each factor a weight based on its importance to the overall decision. For example, if the owner of a clothing factory had three materials and was attempting to decide which material would provide the most profit, they might consider each material's cost, how much material is wasted during the manufacturing process, and how difficult each material is to use. The owner would then rate the materials using a set scale—from 0 to 5, for example, with 0 being the most expensive or most wasteful and 5 being the least expensive or least wasteful—and rate the cost, waste, and difficulty of each material's use. By using a similar scale, the owner would then assign the factors of each option a weight based on the effect each factor has on the company's overall profit. Finally, the owner would determine a weighted score by multiplying the weight by the rating that each factor received. The material with the highest total score would be the best option.

Scenario Analysis

The **scenario analysis** strategy is a decision-making method whereby individuals or organizations use their experience, knowledge, and intuition to predict what kind of situations may arise from each option if that particular option were chosen. In other words, decision-makers employing the scenario analysis strategy attempt to determine all of the possible outcomes of a particular choice and what effect each outcome might have on the organization or individual as a whole if that choice were made. In some instances, especially in a business setting, each of these potential outcomes might be assigned a score based on how likely it is that each scenario will actually occur. However, anticipating every possible outcome that might occur and accurately predicting what events are most likely to occur in the future can be impossible.

Resources

A **resource** is anything that can be used to aid either in the daily functioning of an individual or organization or in the achievement of a particular goal. The four primary types of resources are land and natural resources, labor resources, capital and capital goods, and information resources. Land and natural resources consist of anything that comes from the environment, such as water, oil, soil, timber, and the land itself. Labor resources are comprised of the actual effort that various people involved in an organization put into a project, leading to the completion of that project. Capital and capital goods consist of any financial and human-made resources, including money, tools, equipment, buildings, and houses. Information resources are any resources that allow an individual or organization to find, compile, and put to use knowledge that might help in achieving a particular goal.

Determining If Enough Resources Are Available for a Particular Project

An individual or organization that is assessing whether enough resources are available for a particular project might begin by determining exactly what the project consists of and researching how much the project will cost in both time and money. After the individual or organization has developed a basic outline of what the project needs, an inventory of what resources are readily available should be conducted. This inventory would include noting such resources as how much money has been allocated for the project, how many people are available to work on the project, what kind of equipment is available to complete the project, and whether workers have sufficient information regarding the project to complete it. If the individual or organization determines that the resources necessary to complete the project are not available, then the project is not realistic.

Steps a Family Should Take Towards Financial Resources

A family that is attempting to determine the status of its financial resources should first collect all of the financial records from each source of income that it has. The family should then list all of its assets, including the amount of cash the family has on hand, along with the amount of cash it could get by selling any stocks, bonds, mutual funds, and property that it owns. After adding up all of its on-hand assets and potential assets, the family should then list all of its loans, unpaid bills, balances due, and financial obligations and add the numbers together to get the family's total amount of liability. By subtracting its estimated total liability from its estimated total assets, the family will get a good estimation of its financial standing in terms of its net worth.

Non-Financial Resources

Non-financial resources, or resources that are not cash or cannot be sold outright and turned into cash, can be extremely useful to a family that is experiencing financial problems. Non-financial resources can often be used to produce income or reduce costs that the family is experiencing. For example, a family that may not want to sell its house can rent out a room to make additional money. A family member who is a seamstress could lower the family's costs by mending everyone's clothing instead of throwing it away and buying new garments. A carpenter in the family could make necessary repairs to the family home, eliminating the cost of paying anyone else for labor. Any skill that a family member possesses can help cut the family's costs, and any service the family can offer to people outside the home can serve as a way of gathering additional income.

Allocation of Different Resources

Land resources can be used as locations for homes and businesses or as sites for other natural resources located on a piece of land, such as oil, minerals, soil that can be used for planting, and water for drinking and fishing. Examples of people who can be considered labor resources are marketers who determine the best way to sell a product, salespeople who sell the product to the consumer, factory workers who assemble that product, and anyone else who aids in achieving the end goal of those dealing with the product. Capital refers specifically to money, but capital goods include the machinery that turns raw goods into a finished product in a factory. Information resources may be books or online sites that can be used to learn how to construct a better product or how to better manage a particular organization. All of these resources can be used in a variety of ways, and most projects require a combination of different types of resources.

Change Management

Change management is the process by which an organization attempts to modify a particular aspect of how it operates with as little harm to the organization as possible. In most cases, an organization makes these operational changes either to adapt to changes in societal or economic demands or to improve the organization's overall operations. Although everything undergoes change at some point, many individuals have difficulty adapting to social, economic, or other changes despite how important adapting to these changes might be. Organizations that want to continue functioning must respond to changes by using change management techniques that do not place too much unnecessary stress upon the members of the organization.

The three main strategies an organization can use when making changes in its overall functions are the empirical-rational strategy, the normative-reeducative strategy, and the power-coercive strategy. Each strategy has its own advantages and disadvantages, and which strategy an organization chooses is usually based on how much the organization needs to change and what resources are available to relieve problems that may be caused by particular changes. Which strategy an organization uses may also be based heavily on how much time is available to make the changes and how many members of the organization will resist the changes.

The **empirical-rational strategy** of managing change assumes that people are ultimately interested in their own well being and will more quickly accept changes if they believe that those changes offer them some sort of benefit. In other words, the empirical-rational strategy of managing change relies on either offering an incentive to the members of the organization who take part in a change or convincing the members of the organization that the change will benefit them in some way. For example, if a company's board of directors realized that the company's competitors had employees who were performing more effectively because they had more education, the board might decide to use an empirical-rational strategy to encourage its employees to go back to school. By offering to pay for additional schooling and/or offering promotions, raises, or other incentives, the board of directors could encourage some of their employees to seek further education and, as a result, be better trained for their professional lives.

The **normative-reeducative strategy** of managing change revolves around the idea that peer pressure can bring about the changes that an organization needs. Basically, this strategy assumes that people rely heavily on social interaction and therefore will normally behave according to the expectations of society. Using this assumption, an organization can institute new changes by gradually redefining aspects of the organization's structure and purpose, and each individual will then begin to accept the changes as part of the social norm. For example, if the board of directors of a retail chain realizes that customer service is becoming a more important marketing point than the price of goods, the directors may institute a normative-reeducative strategy. The company would then begin emphasizing desirable customer-service behaviors by placing posters in the break room that affirm the importance of customer service, holding meetings and performance reviews that address appropriate ways to treat customers, and training new employees in good customer service tactics.

The **power-coercive strategy** of managing change assumes that people will listen to authority figures and do as they are told. This strategy works by preventing the members of the organization from choosing any option other than the path that the manager wants them to follow, mainly because no other acceptable options are available to them. If an individual still refuses to accept the changes that the organization has implemented, the organization might punish the individual for not complying. In a family situation, if a child is doing poorly in school because he is spending too much time watching television, the child's mother might simply turn off the TV and tell her child to do his homework. If the child turns the television back on, his mother might send him to his room and ground him for a week as punishment for disobeying.

While the empirical-rational strategy is very effective when an organization has enough available resources to offer the incentives necessary to make changes more acceptable to employees, it is much less successful if the organization does not offer substantial enough incentives. The changes must have an obvious benefit to the individuals who need to implement them. The normative-reeducative strategy is useful when the managers and workers of an organization have a strong relationship and have time available to implement the changes; however, this strategy is much less effective when relations between management and staff are strained or when employees feel rushed or obligated to execute the changes. The power-coercive strategy is particularly useful in situations where time is limited and the threat to the organization or individual is more crucial; however, this method can often promote unrest among members of the organization, especially in organizations that have traditionally allowed more individual freedoms.

Review Video: Organizational Change Management Theories
Visit mometrix.com/academy and enter code: 404217

Identifying and Defining Goals and Values Before Making a Decision

Identifying and defining the goals that a family or other organization needs to meet and the moral values that the family or organization wants to uphold can be extremely important prior to any decision because doing so offers a guide as to what options are unacceptable before an incorrect choice is made. By setting well-defined goals to achieve in the future, a family or organization can choose the options that appear to move it closer to the achievement of those goals. Defining the family's or organization's moral values is also important, because doing so aids in eliminating choices that might be directly opposed to what the family or organization considers correct and ethical.

Consumerism

Consumer Rights

Consumer rights consist of a series of protections, usually guaranteed by law, that seek to prevent individuals from being taken advantage of in the marketplace. In the United States, a large number of state and federal laws establish the rights of consumers, rights that are enforced by the consumer affairs departments of each state, the Federal Trade Commission, and the US Justice Department. Some examples of federal acts that have guaranteed certain rights to consumers are the Equal Credit Opportunity Act, the Fair Housing Act, the Fair Credit Reporting Act, the Fair Debt Collection Practices Act, and the Truth in Lending Act. All of these federal acts and state laws are important because they help prevent consumers from wasting their finances by spending them on products or services that have been sold to them under unethical business practices. Some of these acts also protect the consumer from being discriminated against by businesses or individuals that harbor prejudices against certain consumers.

Consumer Laws

The overall purpose of any **consumer law** is to uphold the three basic rights of the consumer: the right to safety, the right to be informed, and the right to be treated fairly. Federal and state laws are usually designed to protect one or more of these basic rights and may include protections against products that are dangerous, protections against deceptive business tactics or hidden costs associated with a transaction, and protections against certain types of discrimination within the marketplace. Ultimately, state and federal laws are designed to hold businesses accountable for the manner in which they conduct business.

Equal Credit Opportunity Act and the Fair Housing Act

The **Equal Credit Opportunity Act** is a federal act prohibiting any organization that issues credit to consumers from denying credit to a consumer on the basis of race, gender, age, marital status, religion, national origin, or skin color. The act also prohibits any organization from denying a consumer credit if they are receiving federal aid or has previously used another of their rights granted to them by federal law so long as the consumer used that right without malicious intent. If a consumer is denied credit, the organization issuing the denial is required by law to send the denial notification in writing, and the consumer has 60 days to request that the organization send the reason for the denial in writing as well. The **Fair Housing Act** is a similar anti-discrimination act that prevents a seller or organization offering financing for a home from denying to sell, rent, or finance a residence on the basis of race, color, gender, religion, family status, national origin, or handicap.

Fair Credit Reporting Act

The **Fair Credit Reporting Act** states that consumer reporting agencies collecting and distributing information about consumers for credit related purposes are required to follow certain guidelines concerning how they maintain and distribute the information they collect. This act requires consumer reporting agencies to follow a series of procedures established by law to verify and correct mistakes on a consumer's credit record if a consumer makes a dispute. Agencies must also keep records confidential and release them only to businesses that have a legitimate need for those records. This act also sets limits as to how long certain negative information can be kept on record. If a negative piece of information is removed through a dispute, that information cannot be added back onto a consumer's record without notifying the consumer in writing within 5 days. This act was later amended by the Fair and Accurate Credit Transactions Act to allow consumers the right to receive one free copy of their credit report from the three major credit reporting agencies each year.

Fair Debt Collection Practices Act

The **Fair Debt Collection Practices Act** requires third party debt collectors, businesses that collect debts due to other individuals or businesses, to refrain from using abusive or deceptive practices in collecting those debts. This act prohibits such actions as calling consumers at times other than in between 8:00 a.m. and 9:00 p.m. local time and contacting consumers in any manner other than filing a lawsuit if the consumer has given written notice not to contact them regarding the debt. This act also prohibits the collection agency from such practices as adding extra fees and charges to the original balance unless allowed by law, threatening consumers with arrest or legal action that is not permissible by law, or reporting false information on a consumer's credit report. This act also requires third party debt collectors to identify themselves as a debt collector to the consumer during every communication and to provide verification of the original debt upon request.

Truth in Lending Act

The **Truth in Lending Act** requires any organization issuing credit to a consumer to disclose the full terms of the lending arrangement and all costs associated with entering into that arrangement. This means that when a consumer applies for a loan, a credit card, or any other type of credit, the organization must provide the consumer with information about finance charges, the annual percentage rate for the loan, and any additional fees associated with the loan arrangement. In addition to establishing a procedure for the fair and timely handling of billing disputes related to credit transactions, this act also limits the amount of money that a consumer can be held liable for if their credit card is lost or stolen.

Responsible Consumer

Even though state and federal laws exist to protect consumers from unethical business practices, preventing every type of unscrupulous tactic from being used is not always possible. As a result, consumers should be knowledgeable about their rights to avoid being scammed. Many businesses adhere to legal standards and do not employ tactics that are illegal or unethical. However, some businesses choose to do what is profitable instead of what is ethical. Finding loopholes in regulations allows businesses to make claims about their products that may not necessarily be true without being held legally accountable for those claims. Unethical business operations have also been known to find ways to charge consumers additional fees that are legally questionable. In spite of the number of laws designed to protect them, consumers must be diligent about protecting their own interests when making transactions in the marketplace.

Caveat Emptor

The Latin phrase "**caveat emptor**" literally means "let the buyer beware." This expression suggests that a buyer needs to be aware of products or services that may be defective or not as useful as the buyer had anticipated. Some states have laws that create implied warranties regarding certain types of products and allow a consumer the right to return a product that is defective. However, even implied warranties do not protect the consumer from some kinds of defects and only protect the consumer from defects that show up before a certain period of time has passed. If the product or service is not what the consumer thought it was and the seller made no deliberate attempt to defraud the consumer, the seller is typically under no legal obligation to take the product back or refund the consumer's money.

Before making any purchase that requires a financial investment, a consumer should gather as much information as possible about the product or service they plan to buy. By finding out what other consumers have said about a particular product and discovering exactly what the product is and is not capable of doing, a consumer can avoid purchasing a product that is defective or less useful than they originally thought. A consumer can also research what kinds of problems other consumers have had with the product, as well as compare the quality and uses of similar products to determine if another product would be a better match for the needs of the consumer. Because the seller of a product is not under any obligation to inform a consumer about how the product compares in price, quality, and usefulness to other products, it is the consumer's responsibility to know exactly what they are getting when making a purchase.

Wants and Needs

A **want** is anything that a person desires, as opposed to a **need**, which is anything that a person practically requires to continue functioning. A plasma television, for example, is a want because it is not necessary to an individual's continued survival. Examples of needs would be food and water, both of which are things an individual requires to survive. Because people are inherently different, wants or desires vary from person to person. Typically, a person has more desires than their resources can fulfill. Needs, however, are universal because they are everyone's basic necessities and must be met for the continued existence of an individual.

Decision Process Before Making a Purchase

The first step of the decision process for any consumer planning to make a purchase is recognizing that they have a need or a want that to fulfill. After the want or need has been identified, the consumer typically gathers information about products or services that will fulfill that need or want by searching online, examining magazines and advertisements, or talking with other people. The consumer will then evaluate the various product or service choices available in order to determine which option will best fulfill that need or want. Once the consumer's options have been evaluated, they will decide which product or service is most suitable and make the purchase. After the purchase is complete, the consumer will be able to decide whether or not that product or service really satisfied the initial want or need that initiated the decision process.

Marketing

Marketing is the process of informing as many consumers as possible of the existence of a particular product or service and the benefits of that product or service with the intent of influencing a consumer's purchasing decisions. In other words, marketing is a combination of tactics that includes many different forms of advertising that individuals, businesses, and other organizations use to convince consumers to purchase their products. Marketing is important because it allows businesses to play a large role in what consumers actually purchase. Consumers may have the final say in what products or services they decide to use, but marketing can make certain products seem more appealing, more useful, and of a higher quality than a consumer would normally believe them to be. Marketing can also be useful to consumers by informing them about various useful products within the marketplace; however, consumers should be wary of claims and advertisements made by marketers that may make products seem better than they really are.

Marketing can influence almost every stage of the consumer's purchase decision process, but it has the greatest direct effect on the first three stages of the process. The first stage of the process can be triggered by an advertisement marketing a certain product that the consumer may not normally consider to be necessary. By creating the idea or image that a product or service is something necessary to the consumer, a business can make something the consumer wants appear to be something the consumer needs. Marketing can also directly influence the second and third stages of the decision making process by making a product appear better or more useful than competing products, even though this may not necessarily be true. The marketing process can even indirectly influence the fourth stage of the process; consumers actually purchase the product because they have the preconceived notion that a certain product is better than other similar products as a result of the advertisements that they have seen.

State of the Economy

The economy plays an important role in how careful consumers are when using their resources and what they perceive as needs as opposed to what they perceive as wants. When the economy is doing well, unemployment figures are low, which means that people can easily attain their basic necessities. As a result, consumers are typically more willing to spend their financial resources. Consumers will also be more willing to spend their resources on products and services that are not necessary to their survival, but are instead products and services that consumers enjoy having and which they believe increase their quality of life. On the other hand, when the economy is in a slump, consumers are much more likely to cut back on their spending because they perceive a significantly higher risk of being unable to acquire basic necessities due to a lack of financial resources.

Environmental Concerns and Economics

The condition of the natural environment can affect the purchasing decisions of a consumer in two major ways. First, most consumers, due to their own personal values or the values of society, are at least somewhat concerned with the state of the environment around them and will seek ways to prevent unnecessary waste. However, while hardly anyone will always purchase the most environmentally-friendly products and conserve every possible resource at all times, consumers will often choose to purchase products that are recycled or less wasteful when they are available and are not significantly more expensive. The second major way that the environment can affect the purchasing decisions of a consumer involves a consumer's decision to conserve a particular resource because that resource has become more expensive due to a shortage. For example, if an area experiences a gas shortage, the price of gas will rise significantly, and many consumers will conserve gas to avoid paying higher prices.

The primary way that consumers can help protect the environment is by conserving natural resources and finding ways to reduce pollution and waste. Some of the best ways to conserve natural resources include reducing the amount of resources that a household uses, finding ways to use resources more efficiently, and reusing resources rather than simply discarding them. For example, a household can reduce the amount of resources it consumes by turning off the lights and heat in an unused room or by insulating exterior walls to reduce the amount of heat that is lost in a room. A household can also participate in area recycling programs or find new uses for items, such as using a cardboard box that a product came in to store other household items.

Environmental economics is the study of the effects that businesses and consumers have on the overall financial and natural environment when operating within set limits. In other words, environmental economics studies how much pollution actually costs based on the costs or savings associated with pollution and the amount of environmental resources lost due to that pollution. Environmental economics is important to businesses and consumers because it can influence what products are available and what processes can be used in manufacturing those products. Based on environmental economists' recommendations, laws and regulations are made to reduce the amount of damage done to financial and natural environments due to the inefficient or irresponsible use of natural resources. Even though these laws ultimately exist to prevent the waste of natural resources, these regulations can result in the elimination of some products from the marketplace, as well as significant cost increases to the end consumer as businesses incur additional costs in meeting those regulations.

Agencies That Provide Resources to Consumers

A number of agencies can provide resources that help inform consumers about the advantages, disadvantages, and even the scams related to certain products and services. Some of the government agencies that are most useful to consumers are the Federal Citizen Information Center, the Consumer Product Safety Commission, the National Fraud Information Center, and the Federal Trade Commission. All of these agencies have extensive information online, as well as available print publications, about many of the most common products on the market. Probably the most well known and useful private agencies to consumers are Consumer's Research, a non-profit agency that publishes the magazine *Consumer Reports*, and the Better Business Bureau, which is a private organization made up of businesses that sets certain standards which its members are expected to follow.

Health Care Services

A consumer who is in need of health care services might take into account the number of complaints and the types of complaints a facility or specific doctor has received and consequently examine the qualifications of the doctors who practice in that facility. These factors are important to a consumer for any health care decision ranging from choosing a physician for a simple examination to choosing a surgeon for a complex surgery because they give the consumer a basic idea of the overall quality and reliability of the doctor and medical facility. By determining the number of complaints and the types of complaints that have been filed against a doctor or facility, a consumer can get an idea of what kinds of mistakes and how many of those mistakes the facility or doctor has made. Experience can also be a key factor in how reliable a particular doctor is and can greatly affect the quality of their care, as more experienced doctors are usually better capable of providing more effective care.

Unfortunately, determining the exact number of complaints a physician or facility has had filed against them is difficult because no federal law exists that requires physicians or facilities to disclose or even report information regarding complaints. However, the United States Department of Health and Human Services does keep track of reported complaints and is a good source of information for a consumer who is attempting to gather information about a specific doctor or medical facility. Despite the lack of federal laws, many states have laws that do require medical facilities to report the number of complaints and the nature of those complaints filed against the facility or doctors employed by the facility. In many of these states, the facility may not be obligated to disclose the information directly to patients, but a consumer can oftentimes access a state database containing the information online.

Child Care Services

A consumer should consider many factors when attempting to decide which child care service to use. Some of the most important factors include how many children each teacher or caregiver is in charge of, what qualifications the teachers or caregivers have, how long those teachers or caregivers have worked for the facility, and whether the facility is appropriately licensed and accredited. The number of children that a particular caregiver has to care for at one time, as well as how many children attend the facility, can play a large role in how much time a caregiver can devote to each child. A consumer should also verify that not only the facility itself is accredited and licensed, but also that the teachers or caregivers who work with the children have the knowledge and experience necessary to care for them.

While many resources are available to consumers seeking the best child care in their area, one of the best sources of information is usually the child care facility itself. By visiting child care centers under consideration, consumers can gather firsthand information about a particular facility, such as how many children the facility cares for at one time. A consumer should also be able to find information regarding the facility's accreditation while visiting the facility and should later verify that the accreditation is valid and accurate. The Child Care Bureau, which is a subdivision of the United States Department of Health and Human Services, has services available to help consumers locate local organizations that will verify the accreditation of a child care provider. The Child Care Bureau can also be a useful resource for finding additional information about local child care programs.

Elder Care Services

The first step in the process of choosing a facility to care for an elderly family member is recognizing that the family member needs assistance beyond what the rest of the family can provide. After the family realizes that the elderly individual needs additional care, the second step is to evaluate the needs of the family member. By having a basic idea of what the elderly individual is capable of doing on their own and what they need assistance with, a consumer will more effectively be able to research facilities that best suit the needs of the individual. The next step of the process involves gathering information regarding the appropriate facilities for the elderly individual. Finally, the family should choose the facility that appears to best suit those needs.

Knowing the needs of an elderly person and finding the elder care facility that best suits those needs is important because each elderly individual functions at a different level of ability. Because each person has different capabilities and needs, facilities should be evaluated on how well they are able to take care of the individual needs of each patient. Ensuring that an elderly individual is placed in the environment that allows them the most freedom and is the closest match to their current level of functioning is of utmost importance. For example, a woman who is capable of performing normal activities such as bathing, eating, and moving around on her own should not be placed in a nursing home. However, for a woman who has a high risk of injuring herself due to medical conditions, an assisted living home may be an appropriate option.

A consumer who is examining possibilities for the appropriate care facility for an elderly family member has the option of using resources available from the Administration on Aging. The Administration on Aging is a division of the Department of Health and Human Services that offers resources for locating local care facilities, as well as state and local agencies that monitor those facilities, so that consumers can get a better idea of what kinds of facilities are available. Another source of information available to consumers is the National Institute of Aging, an organization that provides a variety of publications regarding the needs and health concerns of elderly individuals. The National Institute of Aging also offers an online database for finding local care facilities. Regardless of which resources a consumer chooses to use, the best resource is often visiting the facilities in person to see what kind of services they can offer and what problems the facility might have.

Consumer Advocacy Groups

Consumer advocacy groups such as the Consumer's Union, the Better Business Bureau, the Consumer Federation of America, the Center for Science in the Public Interest, and Consumer Alert are organizations that attempt to protect consumers from unsafe products and unethical business practices. Many of these groups conduct research on various products and offer the results of their research to consumers either online or through their publications to warn consumers about safety concerns, defects, or scams associated with certain products or services. Consumer advocacy groups also organize and fund campaigns targeted at encouraging support for legislation that promotes fair and ethical business practices, as well as any other legislation that protects the rights of consumers. In addition to being a good source of information for consumers who are making a decision about which product to buy or service to use, consumer advocacy groups are an important ally for consumers who have had problems with a particular product or service and need assistance.

Repair Services

A consumer who is looking for a nearby repair service can find information about local repair shops, garages, and other repair services providers from the local Better Business Bureau. Each Better Business Bureau is comprised of a number of area businesses that are expected to uphold a certain standard of operation. In return, the Better Business Bureau suggests member businesses in good standing to consumers. If a consumer is considering using a repair service that belongs to a larger chain of stores, they might consult a publication such as *Consumer Reports* to discover if the chain has experienced problems or had complaints filed against them in the past. Even if these publications make the chain appear to be a good option, the consumer may still want to check with the local Better Business Bureau, as each store within a chain can often have its own problems and complaints that are separate from the chain itself.

Determining Whether or Not a Product Is Safe

The best resources that a consumer can use when attempting to determine if a product is safe are *Consumer Reports* magazine, the Consumer Product Safety Commission, and the National Fraud Information Center. In addition to offering a variety of reviews and information regarding the quality of most common products, *Consumer Reports* documents common defects and complaints that consumers have reported about those products. The Consumer Product Safety Commission offers consumers access to a number of publications regarding what to look for when inspecting products for defects. The Consumer Product Safety Commission also features listings of products that have already been recalled or have been shown to have potentially dangerous defects. The National Fraud Information Center can also be an important resource for evaluating the safety of a product, as it provides consumers information about products that businesses may have deliberately hidden or lied about in an attempt to make their products more appealing to consumers.

Product Labels

Product labels are important because they inform a consumer about the ingredients in a product, the materials used in the construction of a product, the appropriate way to use a product, and the hazards that can result from using a product incorrectly. This information can be useful for determining not only which products suit the needs of a consumer, but also if products are safe to use around children and other family members. As examples, a label allows a consumer to determine if a particular piece of clothing is made out of a strong enough material for the consumer's intended use or if the material could trigger an allergic reaction in the consumer.

Warranty

A **warranty**, also known as a guarantee, is a promise made by the seller of a product or service that the product or service will function as advertised or else the seller will attempt to repair or replace the product or perform the service again. Warranties usually apply only if the product or service fails to function when the consumer is using the product properly, and there are often many other conditions that must be met for the seller to carry out the terms of the warranty. Warranties are important to consumers because they offer a certain amount of protection against products that fail immediately or shortly after being purchased. However, because many warranties limit the types of repairs the seller is required to perform, consumers should be aware of the terms and conditions of a warranty before making a purchase.

Unit Pricing

Unit pricing is the practice of indicating the price of a product based on the cost per piece or unit included in that product. In other words, unit pricing is a method of determining how much an item costs per unit of measurement. For example, a 12-pack of 12-ounce cans of soda might be $2.99 and have a unit price of $0.70 per liter. Unit pricing is important because it can be extremely useful to a consumer who is attempting to compare two similar products of different sizes to determine which product is less expensive. If, for instance, an individual is trying to decide between a 12-pack of soda that costs $2.99 and has a unit price of $0.70 per liter and a six pack that retails for $1.99 and has a unit price of $0.93 per liter, they can easily compare unit prices and see that the 12 pack is the better buy.

Creating a Family Budget

A family that has decided to create a family budget should begin by calculating how much money it has on hand and how much income it receives annually. Next, the family should determine what expenses it has and which of those expenses are necessary and which expenses are for luxuries. Necessary expenses might include housing, food, utilities, child care, health care, transportation, and insurance. Luxuries might include eating at restaurants, going to movies, buying a bigger television, getting manicures and pedicures, and other activities that are not necessary to the family's continued survival. The third step that a family should take when making a budget is to add up all of the total necessary expenses and subtract that total from the family's total annual income to find its total annual income after necessary expenses. Next, the family should decide how much of that money will be applied to the family's savings. Any remaining money can then be budgeted for less necessary items and activities.

Checking and Savings Account

An individual or family should consider several factors when opening a checking or savings account: What are the bank's minimum balance requirements? What bank fees are associated with the account? What is the annual interest rate earned by the account? Most banks charge account holders if they have less than the minimum balance required in their accounts. Banks often charge additional fees for ATM use and other services, which makes an account more expensive to the consumer than they might realize. If the financial institution charges a significant number of fees without offering a high interest rate on the account, the consumer should move their accounts to a different institution. Consumers should also verify that a bank, credit union, or any other institution that they are considering placing money into is insured by the federal government through the Federal Deposit Insurance Corporation (FDIC) or the National Credit Union Administration (NCUA).

Credit

Credit is the ability of a consumer to purchase a product or service now and pay for that product or service at a later time, either in full or in installments. Credit can be useful for consumers because it offers a way for handling larger expenses, such as the purchase of a house, when the consumer does not have enough funds on hand to make the purchase. However, consumers must keep track of the purchases they make with credit and realize that purchases made using credit must be paid back, usually with interest. If consumers either fail to pay back the bank or credit card company that loaned them the money for the purchase or do not pay installments on time, their ability to get credit in the future is greatly impacted. Some tactics that might be useful to consumers attempting to manage their credit more carefully include paying bills on time, avoiding purchases that they cannot afford, keeping track of how much debt they have, and carefully monitoring their credit report. Consumers who avoid making purchases that they cannot afford are much more likely to pay off loans on time, which will help keep their credit in good standing. If consumers make too many purchases, accumulate too much debt, or take out too many loans, they will most likely struggle to pay their bills. Extensive debt often indicates that consumers cannot manage their credit, which adversely affects their credit scores. Consumers should also closely monitor their credit reports so that they can dispute erroneous claims that may be negatively influencing their credit.

Investments and Retirement Plans

Investment is the process of committing an individual's resources to a particular activity, organization, or fund, with the hope that such a commitment will provide additional resources for the individual in the future. Investing and saving for retirement early in a person's career is important because careful investment planning guarantees that a person's financial resources have the opportunity to grow as much as possible. Individuals may have difficulty maintaining their customary standard of living if they do not have sufficient funds set aside when they retire because living expenses increase yearly. Individuals who do not have enough money set aside when they retire could become a burden to family members, as they may depend on the family to help support them financially. Some of the factors that an individual or family might consider when making investment decisions are the risk of the investment, the potential return of the investment, and how difficult liquidating the investment would be. The risk of the investment refers to how likely it is that the individual or family will gain some benefit from the investment versus how likely it is that the individual or family will lose the resources that they have invested. The potential return of the investment refers to how much money the individual or family will likely earn from the investment's interest or dividends over time. The degree of difficulty in cashing-out the investment is an important factor because different investments have different costs, taxes, lengths of time to mature, and stipulations regarding the access of the money associated with them.

Investments such as checking accounts, savings accounts, and CDs are considered low-risk investments, but they also offer a lower return. These investments are safe because banks guarantee that these accounts will earn a certain amount of interest; however, the rate of interest is relatively low in comparison with other investment options. While CDs are low-risk investments, they do offer slightly higher rates of interest than checking or savings accounts, but they can be liquidated only after they mature over a length of time set by the bank. Mutual funds are usually considered low-risk to mid-risk investments, as people have the potential to lose the resources they have invested, but mutual funds also have the potential to yield a higher return, though not as high as high-risk stocks. Because the stock portfolios that mutual funds are invested in are typically diversified and comprised of many different types of relatively stable stocks, mutual funds are generally regarded to be safe investments.

Families that are selecting what investments to make should first consider the financial goals that they hope to attain from these investments. For example, if a family is investing its resources to send family members to college, the family should estimate how much money it will need to pay for each member who plans to attend college. After a family has determined its financial needs, it can begin researching investment options to determine which investments are likely to yield enough financial gain for the family to reach its goals. Once it has identified which investments best suit its goals, the family should assess how much risk each investment carries. Finally, the family should choose the investment that has the lowest risk but will still meet its financial goals.

An individual who is attempting to determine how much money they need to invest or put aside for retirement should start by adding up how much they spend monthly on living expenses, with the exception of health care. That number is then multiplied by 1.5, while health care expenses are multiplied by 2 to determine how much those expenses will increase in ten years. The individual then needs to estimate how many years they have before retirement; for every ten years, the health care expenses once again are multiplied by 2 and all other expenses by 1.5. Finally, adding these two results together equals an individual's estimated monthly expenses adjusted for inflation, thereby providing the individual with a rough estimate of how much they will need each month to maintain the same standard of living after retirement.

INSURANCE

The major types of insurance that an individual or family might need are health insurance, homeowner's insurance, life insurance, and car insurance. The reason that a family should have these types of insurance is that a problem in any of these areas can have a significant impact on the financial security of the individual or the family as a whole. Health problems, fire, theft, the death of a provider in the family, or a car accident can all lead to additional expenses that the individual or family may not be able to afford. Having these types of insurance offers individuals and families a way to pay unexpected expenses without significantly impacting their overall financial well-being.

Chapter Quiz

Ready to see how well you retained what you just read? Scan the QR code to go directly to the chapter quiz interface for this study guide. If you're using a computer, simply visit the online resources page at **mometrix.com/resources719/nystcefamconsc** and click the Chapter Quizzes link.

Workplace Skills and Careers

Careers

Family and consumer science skills are useful in food management, financial management, human resources, public relations, tailoring, dress-making, etc. Indeed, regardless of career, an individual always finds a use for these skills in life. An individual in food management needs to know about nutrition and the proper handling and preparation of food. Financial advisors need to know how to assess resources, cut costs, and determine how much an individual needs to save before retirement. Human resource and public relations managers need social skills and training in time and resource management, human development, and psychology. Finally, tailors and dressmakers use their knowledge of textiles and textile design to create better garments.

In order to help students determine their interests and develop their skills, teachers should give them some example descriptions of various careers. Some of these examples may be family and consumer science careers, though it is not necessary for them all to be so. The class should examine a diverse sampling of different careers, especially since family and consumer science skills can be applied to virtually any setting. For example, a construction worker might not need to know about food, textiles, or housing design, but they still need to know various problem-solving techniques. It can also be extremely useful for students to get some hands-on experience applying family and consumer science concepts to the tasks associated with different careers.

Family and Consumer Education

Family and consumer education aims to improve a variety of skills that are essential for the day-to-day functioning of an individual and their family. Family and consumer education includes specific topics such as family interaction, human development, nutrition, consumer economics, types of housing and housing design, textiles, parenting, and the appropriate cooking and handling of foods. Family and consumer education covers both the physical and the psychological needs of the individual, and emphasizes appropriate social interaction between the individual and the rest of society.

Work Simplification

Work simplification is the process of discovering and implementing a series of procedures allowing an individual or a group of individuals to complete a task more easily and efficiently. Based on the particular type of task being performed, work can be simplified in a number of ways by determining the best possible way to complete a task without significantly impacting the overall quality of the work. Some of the basic methods used to make any task easier and more efficient include ensuring that individuals have access to necessary equipment, that work areas are organized, and that any steps in the work process that do not directly affect the outcome of the work are eliminated.

Goals of Family and Consumer Sciences Education

The Association for Career and Technical Education has identified nine goals commonly associated with family and consumer sciences education. These nine goals include:

1. Improving the overall quality of life for individuals and families
2. Helping individuals and families become responsible members of society
3. Encouraging healthy eating habits, nutrition, and lifestyles
4. Improving how individuals and families manage their resources

5. Helping individuals and families balance their personal, family, and work lives
6. Teaching individuals better problem-solving techniques
7. Encouraging personal and career development
8. Teaching individuals to successfully function as both consumers and providers
9. Recognizing human worth and taking responsibility for one's own actions

The first of the nine goals established for family and consumer sciences education is to improve the overall quality of life for individuals and families, which is also the primary mission of all the goals. Family and consumer sciences education teaches people about how individuals, families, and the rest of society interact with each other, along with methods for improving those interactions. These methods include problem-solving techniques, common scams and problems to avoid, methods to stay healthy both physically and psychologically, and the distribution of a variety of other information regarding how the individual, family, and the rest of society function. Ultimately, family and consumer sciences education strives to improve the quality of life by educating individuals and families in the best manner to function on a day-to-day basis. However, this goal is truly accomplished only when the other eight goals of family and consumer sciences education are met as well.

Basic Concepts of Family and Consumer Education

There are several concepts at the core of family and consumer education, but one of the most important concepts is that families form the basic unit of society. Another important concept of family and consumer education is that individuals need to be life-long learners in order to develop and function successfully. Finally, family and consumer education promotes the idea that individuals and families need to have an understanding of the advantages of experimenting with different decision-making methods and diverse ways of thinking in order to solve any given problem.

Occupational Family and Consumer Sciences Education

Occupational family and consumer sciences education is a teaching discipline that is similar to the standard discipline of family and consumer education but focuses less on the skills for day-to-day living and more on how those skills can be used in the workplace. Occupational family and consumer sciences education covers information regarding skills that can commonly be applied in fields such as health services, food service, child care, hospitality, fashion design, interior design, and many other similar fields. Occupational family and consumer sciences education places more emphasis on family and consumer skills that directly relate to a career, such as management techniques and ethical businesses practices, than the standard family and consumer education discipline. The occupational family and consumer sciences education discipline ultimately takes the skills that an individual has learned from the standard discipline and shows how those skills can be applied to a career.

Community Advisory Committees

Community advisory committees can be extremely useful to an education professional who is attempting to determine what areas of the family and consumer science discipline a teaching plan should emphasize because the committees offer insight into the concerns and demographics of the students. Each community has its own problems, concerns, and level of diversity, and it is important that a family and consumer science teacher can recognize and focus on areas of concern in the school's community. For example, a community that is having problems with widespread teenage drug abuse and teenage suicide may want the community's family and consumer science teachers to focus more on the topics of avoiding substance abuse and handling depression. The goal of a family and consumer sciences educator is to improve the overall quality of life for the students and their families, and the educator cannot do that if they do not know what problems need to be addressed.

Some of the functions that community advisory committees perform, other than offering advice to education professionals, include assessing the performance of family and consumer science programs; assessing the performance of students with special needs; and providing equipment, technology, and resources for family and consumer science programs. These resources may include raw materials, textile samples, charts and diagrams, library books, and access to computers and design software. Community advisory committees also help students improve their chances of finding better jobs and careers and act as a public relations liaisons for local family and consumer science programs. Ultimately, the primary purpose of a family and consumer sciences community advisory committee is to ensure that a family and consumer sciences program has all of the resources and training necessary to achieve the program's goals.

Laboratory Settings

A **laboratory setting** is important for a family and consumer sciences educator because it offers students an opportunity to gain hands-on experience using a variety of skills and techniques. Many important areas of the family and consumer sciences discipline center around using a combination of various skills to achieve a certain end result, and sometimes the best way to teach the appropriate way to integrate these skills is through experience. A laboratory setting offers students a place to demonstrate and improve their skills related to the family and consumer science field with the advantage of having a teacher present to answer questions and correct mistakes. Some examples of useful laboratory settings for the family and consumer sciences field include kitchens or food science laboratories, day care centers, and testing laboratories for textiles and consumer products.

Demonstrating Family and Consumer Science Concepts

There are a large number of methods that an educator can use to demonstrate concepts related to family and consumer sciences, but the best methods always involve promoting students' active participation. Some examples of active participation include allowing students to use a sewing machine; having students test the qualities of various textiles to see how soft, lustrous, resilient, absorbent, etc. each material is; and requiring students to prepare a meal. Students can also demonstrate active participation with the following activities: comparing advertisements to find the best offer for a particular product, examining common marketing tactics, visiting or working in a local daycare center, and being involved in local community service activities. Many of these activities serve not only as effective ways of teaching students about the important concepts of family and consumer sciences, but also as a means of testing the students' ability to apply the techniques, skills, and information that they have learned.

Usually, the best method an educator can use to verify whether a student understands a particular concept is to see if the student can actively apply the information they have learned to such everyday tasks as cooking, sewing, and time management; however, a student may not be able to demonstrate their understanding of certain concepts if a laboratory setting is not available. Alternative methods by which an educator can evaluate a student's level of comprehension include administering written tests, assigning projects and research papers, teaching students to design charts and diagrams, involving students in the evaluation of case studies and scenarios, and requiring students to keep a journal of their activities and eating habits. Which evaluation method an educator should use depends primarily on the curriculum being covered and the abilities of the students who are taking the class.

Professional Organizations

Professional organizations such as the American Association of Family and Consumer Sciences, also known as the AAFCS, play an important role in influencing the education of individuals in the methodology and knowledge associated with family and consumer sciences. Many of these local and national professional organizations offer seminars, courses, and publications on a wide range of topics directly to individuals and families to teach them about essential career and management skills, how to be smart consumers, the importance of following nutritional guidelines, and information about a wide range of other topics. These professional organizations also provide publications, advice, and curriculum guides to educational professionals that help these professionals teach and stay informed regarding important changes to the curriculum that result from changes in legislation, society, and the education system itself. These organizations also have a profound effect on family and consumer science education by influencing public policy and gathering support for programs that help educate and protect individuals and families from unsafe habits, business practices, products, and lifestyles.

FCCLA

The **FCCLA**, which stands for the **Family, Career, and Community Leaders of America**, is a youth organization for students in family and consumer science education. The FCCLA offers a variety of publications and programs designed to educate people about parenting, relationships, substance abuse, teen pregnancy, and teen violence, among other concerns. By focusing public attention to the problems that young people face, the FCCLA gains support for programs and laws that help protect young people and their families. The FCCLA also shows students how they can improve their family and consumer science skills and apply those skills later in life.

The FCCLA and other similar youth organizations play an important role in influencing national policy related to protecting families and consumers. Additionally, these organizations are important because they support family and consumer science educational programs, which strive to improve the overall quality of life for individuals and families by teaching people skills that will enable them to live better lives.

New Acts of Legislation

When a new act of legislation is passed, it can often have a profound impact on the types of materials used in family and consumer sciences classrooms, as well as the issues that should be addressed by family and consumer sciences education. It is important that individuals understand the legal protections and rights granted to them by the various acts put into place by state and federal governments. Since laws are constantly changing, family and consumer science educators must be able to adapt quickly and add information regarding new legislation to their curriculum.

Balancing Home and Work Roles

It is important that an individual can balance their work and home roles because it is becoming more and more common for individuals to have to act as both caregiver and provider for the family. The increasingly common presence of dual roles in society can be extremely difficult for an individual to balance, as there may be instances where work-related responsibilities and family-related responsibilities conflict with one another. Family and consumer sciences education attempts to teach individuals how to avoid and handle these conflicts through the use of successful life management tactics such as time and resources management, problem-solving and decision-making techniques, and effective communication techniques. Family and consumer sciences education also attempts to give individuals a basic understanding of what responsibilities and qualities are necessary for the successful completion of each role so that individuals can set better priorities and find better ways to plan their lives.

Chapter Quiz

Ready to see how well you retained what you just read? Scan the QR code to go directly to the chapter quiz interface for this study guide. If you're using a computer, simply visit the online resources page at **mometrix.com/resources719/nystcefamconsc** and click the Chapter Quizzes link.

NYSTCE Practice Test

Want to take this practice test in an online interactive format?
Check out the online resources page, which includes interactive practice questions and much more: **mometrix.com/resources719/nystcefamconsc**

1. In Piaget's theory of cognitive development, the thinking of children in the later part of the preoperational stage becomes less egocentric but still remains animistic and magical. This corresponds to which tasks in Duvall's family development theory?

a. Encouraging the child to fit into the community and to participate in education
b. Helping the child find career interests and a balance of freedom and responsibility
c. Adapting to the child's needs and coping with a lack of privacy and depleted energy
d. Stages of establishment, expectancy, and integration of a child into the family

2. Which of the following is true regarding critical evaluation of information in modern media?

a. Methods used to capture attention are irrelevant.
b. Various potential interpretations must be considered.
c. The receiver must consider the medium over the message.
d. Who is sending the message matters more than the content.

3. In his developmental theory, what did Erikson identify as the positive outcome of successfully resolving the nuclear conflict of basic trust versus mistrust?

a. Will
b. Hope
c. Purpose
d. Competence

4. Which of the following solutions would be most practical in housing for a family?

a. Moving to other houses as children grow older
b. Remodeling the house as family needs change
c. A house having some rooms with flexible uses
d. Parents get an apartment when children move

5. What do interpreter-sensitive values mean relative to communication styles?

a. The listener is expected to be responsible for interpreting meaning.
b. The speaker is expected to be responsible for giving a clear message.
c. The speaker avoids nonverbal behaviors for the listener to interpret.
d. The listener need not "read between the lines" as decoding is simple.

6. According to wardrobe experts, which is most accurate about women's wearing habits?

a. Most women tend to wear fewer than half the clothes they buy.
b. Most women tend to wear nearly all of the clothes that they buy.
c. Most women tend to wear over half of the clothes that they buy.
d. Most women tend to wear varying amounts of clothes they buy.

7. Which of the following is true about purchasing a home, according to realtors?

a. To buy a house with a mortgage, some down payment is always necessary.
b. When purchasing a home, the buyer is always responsible for closing costs.
c. Some loan programs give buyers no money down and few/no closing costs.
d. Monthly mortgage payments are not affected by the down payment made.

8. Which of the following most accurately represents a concept of Bandura's social learning theory?

a. Children can learn vicariously by observing and imitating others' behaviors.
b. Children only learn directly through consequences of their own behaviors.
c. Children observe and imitate others' behaviors but do not learn from this.
d. Children learn better from positive reinforcement than from punishment.

9. Which is *most* accurate today about type 1 and type 2 diabetes?

a. Type 1 diabetes is only inherited, while type 2 diabetes only develops from lifestyle.
b. Type 1 diabetes is from lack of insulin; type 2 diabetes is from insensitivity to insulin.
c. Type 1 diabetes occurs in childhood, while type 2 diabetes occurs during adulthood.
d. Type 1 diabetes accounts for half of all cases and type 2 diabetes for the other half.

10. For conflict prevention, which of these is an example of cooperative communication rather than of person-centered expressions that put others on the defensive?

a. "You always interrupt me before I can finish what I'm saying."
b. "It will help me to finish, and then I want to hear your ideas."
c. "Can't you just be quiet and listen to me for even a minute?"
d. "You don't know what you're talking about. You don't listen."

11. Which of these is generally accepted as indicating possible delayed or atypical intellectual development in a child?

a. A standardized IQ test score that is 10 points lower than the mean
b. A standardized IQ test score one standard deviation below the mean
c. A standardized IQ test score two standard deviations below the mean
d. A standardized IQ test score is never used for indicating this possibility

12. In the process of finishing knitted or woven fabrics, which of these reflects the correct sequence?

a. Bleaching or brightening, cleaning, dyeing, singeing, Mercerizing
b. Cleaning, singeing, bleaching or brightening, Mercerizing, dyeing
c. Mercerizing, bleaching or brightening, dyeing, cleaning, singeing
d. Bleaching or brightening, dyeing, Mercerizing, singeing, cleaning

13. Some color analysts divide people's coloring into the four seasons for choosing the most flattering palette of colors in clothing and makeup. Others use adjectives associated with temperaments for the same purpose. Which of the following correctly equates these two systems?

a. "Passionate" = "Autumn"; "Dramatic" = "Winter"; "Vibrant" = "Spring"; "Romantic" = "Summer"
b. "Dramatic" = "Autumn"; "Passionate" = "Winter"; "Romantic" = "Spring"; "Vibrant" = "Summer"
c. "Vibrant" = "Autumn"; "Romantic" = "Winter"; "Passionate" = "Spring"; "Dramatic" = "Summer"
d. "Romantic" = "Autumn"; "Vibrant" = "Winter"; "Dramatic" = "Spring"; "Passionate" = "Summer"

14. When reorganizing clothes, which is the best advice regarding clothing colors?

a. We should discard any items in colors outside of our most flattering color group.
b. We should keep a few items in colors outside our color group to ensure variety.
c. We should coordinate all the colors of our clothes for maximum outfit potential.
d. We should do (A) and (C) to look our best and make creating outfits the easiest.

15. Which of the following events decreases metabolism?

a. Rapid weight loss
b. Increase in muscle mass
c. Slow weight gain
d. Moderate workout

16. Baumrind and other researchers applying her theory of parenting styles have found that children who function at low levels in multiple areas of life are most likely to have had parents with which style?

a. Permissive
b. Authoritarian
c. Uninvolved
d. Authoritative

17. The certified dietary manager (CDM) is monitoring foodservice and notices a delay in plating. When randomly checking the temperature of pieces of the roast chicken that is to be served, the CDM finds that temperatures range from 108-120 °F. The most appropriate intervention is to:

a. authorize serving the chicken as is.
b. reheat the meat to 165 °F.
c. reheat the meat to 140 °F.
d. pull the meat and discard it.

18. Which of these correctly relates a stage in each theory to the same age periods and family stages?

a. Freud's Oedipal; Erikson's Autonomy vs. Shame, Doubt; Piaget's Preoperational; Duvall's School Age
b. Freud's Anal; Erikson's Industry vs. Inferiority; Piaget's Formal Operations; Duvall's with Preschoolers
c. Freud's Genital; Erikson's Initiative vs. Guilt; Piaget's Concrete Operations; Duvall's with Teenagers
d. Freud's Oral; Erikson's Basic Trust vs. Mistrust; Piaget's Sensorimotor; Duvall's Families with Infants

19. Obesity is correlated with which of the following health conditions?

a. Diabetes
b. Hypertension
c. All these and more
d. Hypercholesterolemia

20. When a consumer hires a realtor to help in buying a home, which information that the realtor gives the consumer is important for the realtor to update regularly?

a. The current market conditions
b. Various options for financing
c. All these should be updated
d. Specific negotiating methods

21. According to Robert Havighurst, in which stage do an individual's developmental tasks include learning to relate the self emotionally to other members of the family?

a. Middle Childhood (6 to 12 years)
b. Pre-Adolescence, Adolescence (12 to 18 years)
c. Infancy and Early Childhood (0 to 6 years)
d. Early Adulthood (18 to 35 years)

22. Piaget's first stage of cognitive development involves:

a. Operations with concrete things
b. Sensory input and motor output
c. Operations with abstract things
d. Intuition and animism, not logic

23. Some home construction companies design houses based on certain principles. Which of the following is a general rule reflecting good design principles?

a. There should be only one way to get to the kitchen.
b. It is better to have several ways to get to any room.
c. Traffic patterns going through rooms disrupt activity.
d. Separate rooms look bigger than in open floor plans.

24. Which of the following statements is true?

I. Bulimia can lead to tooth decay.
II. Anorexics tend to have a distorted self-image.
III. Bulimia does not always include purging.

a. I only
b. II only
c. I and II only
d. I, II, and III

25. Which of the following forms of insurance related to owning a home covers a loss of personal property in the home?

a. Title insurance
b. Flood insurance
c. Home warranties
d. Mortgage insurance

26. Of the following, which best reflects a principle of effective classroom management?

a. Classroom management should address only disruptive, not off-task behaviors.
b. Classroom management should teach students to manage their own behaviors.
c. Classroom management is only needed if things take on-task students off-task.
d. Classroom management need not teach students to be on-task, which is normal.

27. A consumer reads an over-the-counter, FDA-approved medication's instructions, dosage, and side effects before taking it. He takes the proper dosage over the correct time frame to control his symptoms. This consumer is demonstrating a high level of:

a. Organizational health literacy
b. Personal health literacy
c. Critical thinking skills
d. Evaluating claims

28. Which provision of the Wall Street Reform and Consumer Protection Act of 2010 fulfills the consumer rights and responsibilities regarding redress?

a. Brokers have advisors' duties if advising on investments.
b. Advisors must give information to the SEC upon request.
c. Whistleblowers who disclose wrongdoing are protected.
d. Consumers can sue credit rating agencies for negligence.

29. Which of these cooking methods is the most energy-efficient?

a. A microwave oven
b. A convection oven
c. An electric oven
d. A gas oven

30. Which program focuses on understanding the economic behavior of groups of families, individuals, or consumers?

a. Consumer economics
b. Home economics
c. Consumer science
d. Financial science

31. Which of these do experts identify as the most accurate definition of a conflict?

a. The most accurate definition of a conflict is simply a disagreement.
b. A conflict is a situation wherein somebody perceives some threat.
c. One central characteristic of a conflict is that it undermines growth.
d. A conflict is a temporary upset that will go away if people ignore it.

32. Research finds that a large proportion of adults working in demanding fields like politics and medicine most often had which birth order in their families?

a. Middle children
b. Second children
c. Youngest children
d. First-born children

33. Which of the following food additives is the safest to consume?

a. Sodium pectinate
b. Sodium bisulfite
c. Sodium nitrate
d. Sodium nitrite

34. An ovo-lacto-vegetarian is a person who eats

a. Fruits, vegetables, and grains
b. Fruits, vegetables, grains, and poultry
c. Fruits, vegetables, grains, and dairy products
d. Fruits, vegetables, grains, dairy products, and eggs

35. Regarding the essential human right to housing, which of the following UN events took place the earliest in history?

a. The United Nations appointed its first Special Rapporteur on Adequate Housing.
b. The United Nations held its first Conference on Human Settlements, or Habitat I.
c. The United Nations declared the International Year of Shelter for the Homeless.
d. The United Nations' Universal Declaration of Human Rights, including the right to housing.

36. Which of the following best represents good advice to job applicants for successful interviews?

a. It is good to back up statements about oneself with specific examples.
b. Direct eye contact with interviewers is intimidating and to be avoided.
c. Be prepared to answer interviewer questions but not to ask questions.
d. If one does not understand a question, do not let on and seem foolish.

37. When children become part of a remarried family with other children, which of these is true?

a. A child's rank in the family never changes.
b. The role each child plays remains distinct.
c. All these factors are most likely to change.
d. Incest taboos are the same for all siblings.

38. Business experts find the most important element of total quality management to be effective communication. Which of the following is true about business communication?

a. A company can maintain high quality without good communication.
b. Poor communication leads to interpersonal mistrust in a company.
c. Communication quality has no effect on productivity in a company.
d. Poor communication causes misunderstandings rather than anger.

39. The nutritional requirements of women:

a. Differ from the requirements of men.
b. Are accurately described by all these.
c. Vary throughout the menstrual cycle.
d. Differ when pregnant and/or nursing.

40. For which pair would sibling rivalry likely be greatest?

a. Sister and brother, ages 5 and 10, respectively
b. Sisters, ages 10 and 5
c. Brother and sister, ages 8 and 10, respectively
d. Brothers, ages 3 and 5

41. Vegetarians can get non-heme iron from plant sources, but to improve absorption of these, they should eat them together with foods rich in:

a. Calcium
b. Vitamin C
c. Vitamin D
d. Vitamin E

42. Freud's Latency stage corresponds most closely in terms of child development with

a. Kohlberg's Pre-Conventional stage in his theory of moral development.
b. Erikson's psychosocial development stage, Identity vs. Role Confusion.
c. Piaget's stage of cognitive development he termed Formal Operations.
d. Duvall's Families with School-Age Children stage of family development.

43. In management decision-making, managers may evaluate alternatives according to four parameters. Determining whether a company's performance goals can maintain a particular alternative or not reflects which of these parameters?

a. Whether an alternative is legal
b. Whether an alternative is ethical
c. Whether an alternative is practical
d. Whether an alternative is economical

44. How does effective marketing benefit society?

a. It utilizes technology, increases product support, and decreases consumer waste.
b. It eliminates unnecessary products, increases customer value, and improves sales.
c. It decreases competition, improves customer service, and increases product choices.
d. It increases competition, improves product quality, and lowers product prices.

45. Housing meets human physical, psychological, and social and cultural needs. Which of the following represents how housing meets social needs?

a. By providing a sense of privacy and of personal space
b. By providing a communal space for the human family
c. By providing shelter from weather and giving security
d. By providing all these, which all represent social needs

46. Historically, family and consumer sciences began in:

a. 1909
b. 1910
c. 1899
d. 1926

47. Among the things parents provide for their children, which would be at the bottom of the pyramid in Maslow's hierarchy of needs?

a. Giving love, ensuring they feel they belong
b. Ensuring they get adequate food and sleep
c. Making sure they have shelter and security
d. Building self-esteem and feelings of worth

48. In textile manufacturing, what is the most accurate definition of the term "gray goods"?

a. Fabrics that have not been dyed
b. Unfinished knit or woven fabrics
c. Fabrics that are not bleached yet
d. Any textile that is gray in its color

49. Schaefer (1959) conceptualized parenting styles along continua across two dimensions:

a. Love vs. control and autonomy vs. hostility
b. Neglect-punishment, dependence-demand
c. Love vs. hostility and autonomy vs. control
d. Strict vs. accepting and permissive vs. rejecting

50. According to psychologists, the level of Safety needs in Maslow's hierarchy would typically be a priority for which developmental period?

a. Infancy
b. Adulthood
c. Adolescence
d. Toddlerhood

51. What does the word *carded* mean when it appears on a clothing label?

a. The garment has been evaluated by a licensed inspector.
b. The garment is made of short and thick cotton fibers.
c. The garment was not created in a sweat shop.
d. The garment only contains one type of fiber.

52. What is the name for wool that has been spun into a fine yarn from parallel fibers?

a. Worsted
b. Cashmere
c. Angora
d. Polyester

53. Of the following fabrics, which one is NOT made using a plain weave?

a. Denim
b. Muslin
c. Percale
d. Burlap

54. Which of these is true about the %DV (Daily Value) the FDA requires on food labels?

a. They make it easier for consumers to know in numbers how much they need of nutrients in a day.
b. They make it easier for consumers to know how much of a day's allowance of nutrients a food has.
c. They make it harder for consumers to comparison shop for foods by the relative nutrient amounts.
d. They were developed by the FDA to replace RDAs because the RDAs were found to be inaccurate.

55. A family wherein the parents, children, and grandmother live together is defined as a(n):

a. Nuclear family
b. Extended family
c. Blended family
d. Combined family

56. As adults get older, they are *most* likely to have poorer absorption from foods of which vitamin?

a. Vitamin A
b. Vitamin C
c. Vitamin B_{12}
d. Vitamin E

57. Where can a consumer obtain a mortgage loan to buy a house?

a. Consumers can acquire loans from any and all of these sources today.
b. Mortgage bankers or mortgage brokers are the only sources for loans.
c. Savings and loans, credit unions, various banks, or insurance companies
d. Increasing numbers of realtors can arrange mortgage financing today.

58. Of the following, which is generally a good practice for writing a résumé?

a. Students with no work history should place education first on a résumé.
b. Education or work history should start with the earliest and go forward.
c. As employers may request personal references, put them in a résumé.
d. In work histories, it is best to include reasons for leaving previous jobs.

59. Which of the following fabric care symbols indicates a garment should be line-dried or hang-dried?

a. A square with diagonal lines in a corner
b. A square with one horizontal line inside
c. A square with three vertical lines inside
d. A square with a horizontal arc at the top

60. Lenders generally require mortgages to be guaranteed by outside third parties (e.g., the FHA, VA, or a private mortgage insurer [PMI]) if the home buyer makes a less than __ down payment.

a. 20%
b. 10%
c. 50%
d. 30%

61. Lightweight, usually unlined fabric panels hung directly on a rod that cover either the extreme ends of the window or the entire window are called

a. Curtain
b. Louvered shutter
c. Drapery
d. Grille

62. When a consumer purchases a new mattress from a manufacturer, they have the right to expect that mattress to meet safety standards and to have the features the manufacturer claims it has, even if there is no explicit promise made. What form of contract does this represent?

a. Express contract
b. Written contract
c. Implied in-law contract
d. Implied in-fact contract

63. According to Bowen Family Systems Theory, when both partners in a couple project their expanding anxieties into their relationship, this reflects which basic relationship pattern identified by Bowen?

a. Emotional distance
b. Impairment of child(ren)
c. Dysfunction in one spouse
d. The pattern of marital conflict

64. The FTC does NOT mandate that clothing labels include

a. The country of origin
b. Whether the garment contains mink or rabbit
c. An indication of whether wool is new or recycled
d. The Registered Identification Number or name of the manufacturer

65. Which of the following is NOT a typical developmental task for children at the earliest school ages?

a. Conservation of amount
b. Identifying with sex roles
c. Developing early morality
d. Learning to play in groups

66. Which of the following is NOT a way the FDA protects consumers?

a. Regulating drugs for humans
b. Recalling products that have been deemed unsafe
c. Regulating tobacco products
d. Approving dietary supplements

67. The law requires food labels to include which of the following information?

a. Product name, form, amount, name and address, and ingredients are required.
b. The product name is required, but not the address of the company.
c. The weight or fluid ounces must be listed, but not every ingredient.
d. All ingredients must be listed, but weight or fluid ounces is optional.

68. Which of the following represents a discretionary expense?

a. Textbook
b. Rent
c. DVD
d. Groceries

69. Banks require ____ when issuing a secured loan, giving them more security should the customer default on their payments.

a. Insurance
b. Cosigners
c. Tier 1 credit scores
d. Collateral

70. If a menu item is a green salad made with lettuce, tomatoes, cucumbers, green onions, and carrots, the most appealing name to list it on the menu as is:

a. GREEN SALAD (in all-capital letters).
b. tossed green salad.
c. green salad with mixed vegetables.
d. fresh garden salad.

71. Regarding financial institutions, what is the current status of careers for FCS graduates?

a. Brokerage firms want to hire qualified financial planners, who are among FCS graduates.
b. Banks and savings and loan associations are not presently accepting many job applicants.
c. FCS financial planners are needed at insurance companies but not at counseling agencies.
d. FCS financial planners need not understand community relationship and family dynamics.

72. Among the following developmental theories, what is correct relative to development across the life span?

a. Freud and Piaget had theories that cover the life span, while Erikson's ends at adolescence.
b. Piaget's and Erikson's theories do not go beyond adolescence while Freud's goes to death.
c. Freud's and Erikson's theories cover all of life while Piaget's theory stops with adolescence.
d. Erikson's theory has developmental stages across the life span; Freud's and Piaget's do not.

73. In which of Erikson's stages of development do individuals measure their success by what they contribute to their families and society?

a. Intimacy vs. Isolation
b. Ego Integrity vs. Despair
c. Identity vs. Role Confusion
d. Generativity vs. Stagnation

74. Which of the following represents good dining etiquette at a dinner party?

a. Only giving an RSVP if one will not attend
b. Asking what food the hosts will be serving
c. Asking what dress is suitable when invited
d. Beginning to eat as soon as one sits down

75. According to Urie Bronfenbrenner's ecological systems theory of development, in which system does an individual experience the most interpersonal and social interactions?

a. The exosystem
b. The mesosystem
c. The macrosystem
d. The microsystem

76. Which of the following best reflects a disadvantage of stage theories regarding families?

a. The stages express typical family concerns in each stage.
b. Stage theories provide convenient common vocabularies.
c. They focus on dynamics the same as systems theories do.
d. Many diverse families today are not normative or typical.

77. Which of the following is NOT true of supply and demand?

a. At higher prices, demand is lower and sellers will supply more goods.
b. Supply and demand is a theory explaining the interaction between the amount buyers are willing to pay for an item (demand) and the amount sellers will provide of the commodity at a given price (supply).
c. If supply is constant and demand decreases, the equilibrium price will be lower.
d. The relationship between supply and demand is shown on a graph with a positive slope.

78. In making good consumer decisions, which of the following should smart shoppers do first?

a. Narrow the field of potential choices
b. List attributes of products or services
c. Determine their needs as consumers
d. The order of doing these is irrelevant.

79. According to personal finance experts, what is the maximum percentage of income a family should spend on housing?

a. 5%
b. 50%
c. 10%
d. 25%

80. When describing moral development, Piaget characterized two types of adult-child relationships. In the _____ relationship, the adult _____ the child; in the ______ relation, the adult _____ the child.

a. Heteronomous, "co-operates" with; autonomous, coerces
b. Unilateral, respects; reciprocal, controls and/or constrains
c. Interactive, constrains; heteronomous, "co-operates" with
d. Heteronomous, coerces; autonomous, "co-operates" with

81. Among these food preparation factors, which can cause food poisoning or other food-borne illness?

a. All of these can cause it with certain foods.
b. Cooking foods for the wrong lengths of time
c. Cooking foods at the wrong temperatures
d. Not pasteurizing or refrigerating some foods

82. Which of the following websites is best for finding free information about energy-efficient home appliances?

a. www.sears.com/
b. http://products.construction.com/
c. www.consumerreports.org
d. www.energystar.gov

83. Of the following, which food preparation(s) is/are LEAST likely to cause food-borne illnesses?

a. Improperly canned or fermented foods
b. Uncooked meats/produce
c. Undercooked meats/produce
d. Overcooked meats and produce

84. According to Evelyn Duvall's description of the Family Life Cycle, which of these accurately represents two consecutive stages of the family life cycle?

a. Married couples without children; families with children from birth to 6 years
b. Families with children from birth to 6 years; families with children 6-13 years
c. Families with children 0–30 months; families with children 24 months-6 years
d. Families with teen children 13–20 years; "empty nest" couples to retirement

85. We are advised to analyze our financial goals and values periodically to aid in financial planning. What is true about this process?

a. The reason for analysis is to distinguish between wants and needs.
b. Analyzing our financial values excludes how we feel about money.
c. Financial values analysis omits why we feel as we do about money.
d. Once we analyze financial goals and values, results will not change.

86. Which of these reflects proper dining etiquette when attending dinner parties?

a. When passing dishes, they should be passed clockwise.
b. Bread only should be passed around the table clockwise.
c. Guests should pass all dishes including bread to the right.
d. It is up to the individual guests whether to cut up foods.

87. Which of the following is the most important component of preparation for inspection?

a. Review of compliance issues.
b. Network with similar organizations.
c. Prepare an alert system so the staff is aware of an upcoming inspection.
d. Conduct self-inspections.

88. The research of Walter Toman (also adopted by Murray Bowen) found that in the workplace, which relationship is likely to be most harmonious and effective?

a. A boss and an assistant who were both oldest children working together
b. A boss and assistant who were both youngest children working together
c. A boss who was an oldest child and an assistant who was a youngest child
d. A boss who was a youngest child and an assistant who was an oldest child

89. For many first-time homebuyer programs in the U.S., a 'first-time buyer' is someone who:

a. Anyone who has never owned real estate property before.
b. Anyone who has only owned property less than six months.
c. Anyone who has not owned a principal residence in the last three years.
d. Anyone who did own, but does not currently own, property.

90. What is the best way to sort clothing in the closet to find items and assemble outfits easily?

a. Sort first by colors, and then sort second by category.
b. Sort by placing favorite items to be most within reach.
c. Sort by placing item types wherever they will fit best.
d. Sort first by category, and then sort second by colors.

91. A person who is 41 to 100% heavier than his or her ideal weight is likely

a. Mildly obese
b. Hypertensive
c. Diabetic
d. Moderately obese

92. One factor that influences consumers to consider prices more in their health care decisions is:

a. When they have no prior ideas of provider quality.
b. When their health insurance plan is a PPO or HMO.
c. When they have a severe and/or urgent condition.
d. When they have health care practitioners they like.

93. Many researchers have found that family recreation affords benefits both to the family unit and to its individual members. Of the following, which reflects a benefit to individual family members?

a. Improvements in communication
b. The development of lifelong skills
c. Increased stability and interaction
d. The maintenance of relationships

94. Which of the following foods is a source of the most vitamin A?

a. Sweet potatoes
b. Animal livers
c. Carrots
d. Kale

95. Of the following types of fat, which is considered the *most* harmful?

a. Partially hydrogenated vegetable oil
b. Fully hydrogenated vegetable oil
c. Monounsaturated fat
d. Polyunsaturated fat

96. Erikson's theory of development focuses MOST on a person's relationship with which other aspect?

a. Self
b. Society
c. Other individuals
d. The parents exclusively

97. What is true about information on clothing labels, tags, or packages?

a. Manufacturers are required by law to provide only registered ID number identification.
b. Manufacturers are required by law to show ID, fiber content, country, and care instructions.
c. Manufacturers are required by law to indicate only the country where clothing is made.
d. Manufacturers are required by law to show fiber content; care instructions are optional.

98. Which special resource(s) would most likely be needed by someone with spina bifida?

a. A communication board
b. Text-to-speech software
c. A wheelchair or crutches
d. Cochlear implantations

99. In planning for buying a house, what do realtors recommend the buyer should do first?

a. Determine if they can afford down payment, closing costs, monthly payment
b. Determine in advance that their credit will be good enough to get a good loan
c. Determine what they need and want, and when, in their real estate purchase
d. Determine all of these things at the same time; the sequence does not matter

100. First-in, first-out (FIFO) refers to:

a. employee schedules.
b. sanitation steps.
c. regulatory compliance.
d. product storage.

Answer Key and Explanations

1. C: Piaget's later preoperational stage, when children's thinking becomes less egocentric but still retains animistic and magical characteristics, takes place during the preschool years (ages 3–6 years). This corresponds to Duvall's family development stage of families with preschoolers, when parents must adapt to the needs of young children and cope with young children's intrusions on their privacy and the energy drain of caring for and supervising preschoolers. Duvall described answer choice A as tasks of her families with school-age children stage, answer choice B as tasks of her families with teenagers stage, and answer choice D as tasks of her families with infants stage.

2. B: For critically evaluating information delivered through any of today's many media channels, consumers should consider who is delivering the message, what the message is, why they are delivering it, what medium they are using, how they are getting attention, and how the message can be interpreted. All of these are crucial elements, so no particular one can be ignored, and no particular one is more important than the others. Choices A, C, and D all state that one or more of these elements is on a different level of importance.

3. B: Erikson described the nuclear conflict of infancy as basic trust versus mistrust: A baby whose needs are met fully and consistently develops trust in the world, while a baby whose needs are inadequately or inconsistently met develops mistrust. Erikson found that the positive outcome of this stage was hope. He identified will (A) as the positive outcome of successfully resolving the nuclear conflict of autonomy versus shame and self-doubt during toddlerhood. He identified purpose (C) as the positive outcome of successfully resolving the nuclear conflict of initiative versus guilt during the preschool years. He identified competence (D) as the positive outcome of successfully resolving the nuclear conflict of industry versus Inferiority during the elementary school years.

4. C: A design innovation in home construction is including some rooms planned to be flexible in purposes and use. This allows homes to change along with families. For example, when a grown child moves out, that child's bedroom can easily be converted to a home gym, home theater, craft room, etc. As children grow older, a playroom can become a game room, homework/studying room, hobby room, etc. This eliminates having to move to another house (A), which takes more money, time, and effort; and many families love their homes, neighbors, and neighborhoods and do not want to move. Remodeling (B) also costs more, and ongoing work inconveniences home living. While some "empty nest" parents may want to downsize to an apartment (D), this again involves more effort and time, even if proceeds from a house sale cover moving expenses. And some parents want to keep the space in their house for grown children, their families, and others to visit.

5. A: Interpreter-sensitive values are characteristic of high-context communication and mean the listener is expected to take responsibility for interpreting the speaker's meaning, much of which is conveyed through nonverbal behaviors, which the listener must "read between the lines" to infer. Conversely, low-context communication uses sender-oriented values, meaning the speaker is expected to take responsibility for communicating clearly and directly to make decoding simple for the listener.

6. A: Experts find that the majority of women tend to wear a small proportion of all the clothes they buy, from less than half to 20% or less. Few women wear over half of the clothes they buy (C), and fewer still wear most of them (B). It is also less accurate to say that women vary that much in how many of the clothes they buy that they actually wear (D), because the most common pattern among women is to buy far more clothes than they end up wearing.

7. C: When people buy houses with mortgages, they usually make a down payment in some amount; however, this is not always required (A). Buyers usually pay closing costs as well, but also not always (B). There are some loan programs that allow the borrower to purchase a house with no money down; and in buyers' markets (i.e., when the housing market affords the buyer more leverage), realtors can help buyers negotiate deals wherein the owner or seller pays some or all of the closing costs. While some buyers want to eliminate a down payment, many others prefer to pay something down to lower their subsequent monthly mortgage payment: paying nothing down results in higher monthly payments (D).

8. A: Bandura proposed that children learn not only through the direct consequences of their own behaviors but also through observational learning, in which they watch others' behaviors and the consequences that follow and then imitate those behaviors. Therefore, children can learn vicariously by observing and imitating others (A). Choice B is incorrect because Bandura argued that learning can occur without direct experience. Choice C contradicts the theory by claiming that observation does not lead to learning. Choice D describes a behaviorist principle regarding reinforcement but does not represent the central concept of Bandura's social learning theory.

9. B: In type 1 diabetes, the pancreas does not produce insulin, the hormone necessary for converting sugars, starches, and other foods to energy. In type 2 diabetes, the pancreas does produce insulin, but the body does not respond properly to the hormone; this is called insulin insensitivity. Both type 1 and type 2 diabetes have both genetic and environmental factors, so (A) is incorrect. While type 1 diabetes was previously called "juvenile diabetes," it can develop in childhood or young adulthood; and though most cases of type 2 diabetes used to develop during adulthood, in recent years many children and adolescents have been diagnosed with type 2 diabetes, so (C) is incorrect. Type 1 accounts for only 5% of diabetes cases while the rest are type 2, so (D) is incorrect.

10. B: Cooperative communication prevents conflict by suggesting rather than accusing; using "I" rather than "You"; and focusing on solving problems rather than focusing on the other person. Example (B) has these qualities. The examples in (A), (C), and (D) are all person-centered by accusing the other person of interrupting, not listening, etc.; whereas the example in (B) expresses the speaker's desires both to finish, and also to hear what the other person has to say. It also positively communicates the speaker's need to complete a message instead of negatively accusing the other person of not listening to it.

11. C: Scoring two or more standard deviations (SDs) below the mean (average) on a standardized IQ test is commonly accepted as indicating that a child may have delayed or atypical intellectual development. Thus, one SD (B) is incorrect. On standardized IQ tests used today, one SD = 15 points. Hence, 10 points (A) would not be enough to indicate potentially delayed or atypical intellectual development. Since IQ scores are used to indicate possible delayed/atypical intellectual development, answer choice D is incorrect.

12. B: Unfinished knitted or woven fabrics are first cleaned to remove dirt and oils from the manufacturing process. Then many fabrics are singed with heat to eliminate protruding ends of fibers, which prevents fabric pilling and promotes even color when dyeing. After singeing, cotton and other natural fibers are bleached to get rid of impurities in their natural color and appearance. Fabrics that do not respond well to bleach are treated with optical brighteners instead. Manufacturers may then Mercerize certain linens, cottons, and rayons using alkali to make them stronger, softer, more lustrous, and more readily accepting of dyes. Fabrics are then dyed to add colors.

13. A: Many color analysts use the four seasons to identify the main categories of color palettes. In this system, "Autumn" represents warm, yellow-based earth tones; "Winter" represents cool, blue-based colors and black and white; "Spring" represents bright, vibrant, clear colors; and "Summer" represents soft, light pastel tints of colors. Some color analysts use adjectives descriptive of temperaments for the same groups. In this system, "Passionate" equals "Autumn"; "Dramatic" equals "Winter"; "Vibrant" equals "Spring"; and "Romantic" equals "Summer."

14. D: Everybody has a certain group or family of colors that are most flattering to them based on their skin tones. Experts advise getting rid of clothes with colors outside of this group as we do not look as well in them (A). They also advise keeping and buying clothes whose colors all coordinate, which makes it easiest to mix and match items into different outfits and gives the largest potential numbers of outfits we can create (C). Keeping items in less flattering colors just to provide more variety or a change of pace (B) is not the best advice, because we do not look as well wearing colors we may like to see but which don't flatter us. Others respond less favorably to us when we wear unflattering colors, and we are likely not to feel as good about how we look when we wear them.

15. A: Losing weight quickly decreases the metabolism. Nutritionists and doctors believe that this is a form of self-defense by the body, which senses that food is not as available and therefore tries to limit its use of calories. All of the other answer choices are events that increase metabolism. Weight gain always raises metabolism, in part because there is more muscle or fat to provide with nutrients. Muscle burns more calories than fat, so an increase in muscle mass will correlate with an increase in metabolism. Any exercise tends to increase metabolism.

16. C: Baumrind and others after her who have applied her theory in research have found that children who function at low levels in multiple life areas are likely to have had parents with the uninvolved parenting style. This style makes few demands of children, but also demonstrates little warmth toward them. The children thus lack both parental discipline and parental nurturing. Extremes of the uninvolved parenting style include rejecting and/or neglecting children. As a result, children perform poorly and are likely to be depressed and engage in delinquent behaviors. Children with permissive (A) parents are likely to be impulsive, seem immature, lack self-control, and avoid responsibility. Children with authoritarian (B) parents are likely to behave well, but also to lack initiative, avoid leadership roles, and are moody. Children with authoritative (D) parents are likely to be well-behaved but also independent; self-reliant, socially responsible, achievement-oriented, and to have high self-esteem.

17. B: If the CDM is monitoring foodservice and notices a delay in plating and, when randomly checking the temperature of pieces of the roast chicken that is to be served, the CDM finds that temperatures range from 108-120 °F, the most appropriate intervention is to reheat the meat to 165 °F. Food should be served at a temperature of at least 140 °F, but safe reheating of food requires that it be heated to 165 °F to ensure that all pathogens are destroyed.

18. D: Freud's Oral stage corresponds to infancy, as does Erikson's stage of Basic Trust vs. Mistrust, Piaget's Sensorimotor stage, and Duvall's Families with Infants stage. Freud's Oedipal stage (A) corresponds to preschool; Erikson's corresponding stage is Initiative vs. Guilt, rather than toddlerhood's Autonomy vs. Shame and Doubt; Piaget's Preoperational stage corresponds to preschool, but Duvall's corresponding stage is Families with Preschoolers, not School Age. Freud's Anal (B) stage corresponds to toddlerhood; Erikson's corresponding stage is Autonomy vs. Shame and Doubt, not Industry vs. Inferiority, which occurs during elementary/middle school ages.

Piaget's stages corresponding to toddlerhood are the end of the sensorimotor and beginning of the preoperational, not formal operations, which develops around adolescence. Toddlerhood falls between Duvall's Families with Infants and Families with Preschoolers stages. Freud's Genital (C) stage is in adolescence, as is Duvall's Families with Teenagers, but Erikson's corresponding stage is Identity vs. Role Confusion, not early childhood's Initiative vs. Guilt; Piaget's is Formal Operations, not the elementary/middle school years' Concrete Operations.

19. C: Obesity is correlated with diabetes (A); hypertension, i.e., high blood pressure (B); hypercholesterolemia, i.e., high cholesterol (D); heart disease; certain cancers; autoimmune diseases and other inflammatory conditions; and many other diseases and adverse health conditions.

20. C: The realtor should regularly update information s/he gives the consumer about the conditions of the current housing market (A), available financing options (B), and situation-specific negotiating tactics (D). Buying a house can be a lengthy process, and market conditions can change, sometimes in relatively short periods. So can financing options: lenders can offer new products; different providers may offer different financing plans, and the realtor can recommend some that may suit the consumer better than others; the buyer's credit score and financial resources can change, etc. Also, some strategies for negotiating can apply to some situations, but not others wherein different techniques are more appropriate.

21. C: Havighurst identified developmental tasks in each of the six stages of human development he defined. Learning to walk, talk, eat, eliminate, stabilize physically; sexual modesty and differences, simple physical and social reality concepts, right and wrong; developing a conscience, and learning to relate the self emotionally to parents and siblings are tasks he assigned to the period from birth to 6 years. He identified learning of basic reading, writing, and calculation skills; physical game skills, getting along with peers; developing everyday living concepts, morality, values, personal independence, a gender role, healthy self-attitudes, and attitudes toward institutions and social groups as tasks for those from 6 to 12 years (A). He included tasks in pre-teen and teen years (B) as maturing peer relations; emotional independence from adults; career preparation and choice; marriage and family life preparation; developing concepts and skills for civic competence; developing social responsibility and an ethical system, etc. Among tasks of early adulthood (D), Havighurst included marrying, starting families, raising children, managing households, beginning careers, etc.

22. B: Piaget's first stage of cognitive development is called the sensorimotor stage. This is when infants respond to input they receive from the environment through their sensory organs by engaging in motor actions. When they realize how the environment then reacts to some of these actions, they respond again; this is called circular reactions. Operations with concrete things (A) occur during Piaget's third stage called concrete operations. Operations with abstract things (C) occur during Piaget's fourth and final stage called formal operations. Intuition and animism but not logic (D) occur during Piaget's second stage, which he called preoperational.

23. B: One design principle embraced by some home design companies is that there should be at least three ways to get to a room in the house. They find this especially important for getting to the kitchen, which is the center of many family homes; therefore (A) is incorrect. Floor plans can be designed wherein people get to different rooms by passing through other rooms in an open floor plan, yet without disrupting how the rooms are used (C). These open floor plans make the rooms look bigger than if they were separated by halls (D) used as passageways. They also make it easier to see farther through the house.

24. D: All three of the statements are true. Bulimia can lead to tooth decay, due to a combination of malnutrition and corrosion by stomach acid. Anorexics often have a distorted self-image, believing themselves to be much heavier than they actually are. Finally, bulimia does not always include purging (induced vomiting or defecation). Bulimics may obsessively exercise or abstain from food in order to lose weight. Both anorexia and bulimia are extremely dangerous and should be discussed at great length in the nutrition component of a family and consumer science class. These conditions are especially common among middle-school and high-school students.

25. B: Flood insurance not only covers the loss of or damage to a home due to flooding; it also covers the loss or damage of personal property and other contents within the home. Title insurance (A) only protects home buyers up to the real estate's mortgage value ("lenders" policies), and protects homeowners up to the purchase price of the home including down payments ("owners" policies) if the title to the real property turns out to be invalid. It does not cover personal property. Home warranties (C) cover workmanship in a new home, usually for the first year; wiring, plumbing, and other mechanical issues for the first two years; and structural defects in the building for up to ten years. They do not cover personal property in the home. Mortgage insurance (D) covers the lender, not homeowner property.

26. B: One basic principle of effective classroom management is that it should teach the students to manage their own behaviors, rather than teachers' always having to manage them. Though classroom management techniques are necessary to address disruptive behaviors when they do happen, they should also focus on reducing nondisruptive behaviors that are nevertheless off-task (A). Students who are off-task are not engaged in learning. Students are not simply taken off-task by external distractions (C); it is more normal and natural for them to be off-task than on-task (D). Therefore, classroom management is necessary for students to learn to be engaged in learning activities and stay on-task.

27. B: Personal health literacy is the ability to find, understand, and use information to make health-related decisions. By reading the information associated with the medication and adhering to the manufacturer instructions, the consumer is demonstrating the ability to make safe health-related decisions. Organizational health literacy is how organizations enable individuals to make health-related decisions. This scenario does not require critical thinking skills, as there is no need for the consumer to make inferences, problem solve, or communicate in order to properly take the medication. There is also no need to evaluate claims in this scenario, as they are taking an over-the-counter, FDA-approved medication that has been approved for the usage on the label.

28. D: The provision of the Dodd–Frank Wall Street Reform and Consumer Protection Act of 2010 (Dodd–Frank Act) that consumers can sue credit rating agencies for negligence fulfills the consumer's right and responsibility concerning redress, i.e., to request compensation for an agency's wrongdoing. This law's provision that brokers have the same fiduciary duties as advisors if they give investment advice to consumers (A) fulfills the consumer's right to be given accurate product information, and the responsibility to analyze and apply that information judiciously; and the consumer's right to have access to education to inform purchasing decisions, and the responsibility to pursue consumer education about products as they change. The law's provision that advisors disclose information to the SEC on request (B) also fulfills the consumer's right and responsibility to information [see (A) above]. The law's provision of protection to whistleblowers (C) fulfills the consumer right and responsibility to be heard.

29. A: Microwave ovens are by far more energy-efficient than the others named, in both cooking efficiency and energy factor. (Cooking efficiency equals the fraction of the total energy the oven consumes that is used to cook food. Energy factor equals the ratio of energy used for cooking food to the total energy consumed.) Convection ovens (B) powered by electricity are more energy-efficient than convection ovens powered by gas; and both kinds of convection ovens are more energy-efficient than traditional electric or gas ovens; but a microwave oven is about 7–8 times more energy-efficient than electric or gas convection ovens, about 5 times more efficient than standard electric ovens, and about 9–10 times more efficient than regular gas ovens. (Note that efficiency refers to energy used, not cost in money, which depends on local rates charged for electricity and gas.)

30. A: Traditional branches of economics focus on governments and businesses. Consumer economics looks at the buying choices made in a particular economy. These economists observe consumer patterns and then identify the needs and problems of the observed groups.

31. B: Whether it is real or imagined, when a threat is perceived by one or more persons in a situation, this defines a conflict, which experts say is not simply a disagreement (A). An additional characteristic of conflicts is that they present opportunities for the people involved to experience growth (C) when they succeed in resolving them, which builds interpersonal trust. Conflicts will not go away if people ignore them (D) because the threats people perceive that trigger conflicts are to their survival and welfare. Hence, they will continue indefinitely or until the relationship ends if they are ignored.

32. D: First-born children tend to grow up being responsible and dependable because parents tend to have higher expectations of their first child and give them more responsibility. Middle children (A) tend to feel less pressure as their parents have more experience with parenting by the time they have them. Parents also tend to expect less from their second children (B) and focus less attention on them than first-borns. Parents often give more special attention to their youngest children (C), but also expect less of them.

33. A: Sodium pectinate, like pectin, is a safe carbohydrate added to fruits and vegetables to strengthen their cell walls and to jellies, jams, sauces, yogurts, and frostings as a gelling agent to thicken them. Sodium bisulfite (B) is safe for some people, though it destroys vitamin B_1; however, for individuals sensitive to it, particularly those with asthma, it can cause severe reactions and even death. It is used to prevent bacteria from growing in wines and keep certain foods from discoloring. Sodium nitrate (C) and sodium nitrite (D) are used in cured meats like hot dogs and bacon to preserve color and flavor and prevent bacterial growth, but are also associated with formation of carcinogenic (cancer-causing) nitrosamines. (Today, the addition of ascorbic acid or erythorbic acid mitigates nitrosamine formation, but nitrates and nitrites still present some risk. Also, these additives are mainly used in fatty, salty foods—another reason to avoid them.)

34. D: An ovo-lacto-vegetarian is a person who eats fruits, vegetables, grains, dairy products, and eggs. These people get most of their proteins from beans, eggs, milk, and cheese. There are several other kinds of vegetarians. A vegan is someone who eats only plant foods; vegans do not eat any meat or animal product, including honey. Lacto-vegetarians eat fruits, vegetables, grains, and dairy products.

35. D: The UN issued its Universal Declaration of Human Rights, which includes the right to adequate housing, in 1948. The UN appointed its first Special Rapporteur on Adequate Housing (A) in 2000. The UN held its first Conference on Human Settlements, which it called Habitat I (B), in 1976. (Its second Conference on Human Settlements, called Habitat II, was held in 1996.) The UN declared the International Year of Shelter for the Homeless (C) in 1987.

36. A: One good piece of advice for job applicants preparing for interviews is, when answering questions about themselves, they should support statements they make about their own positive attributes with specific examples to illustrate those qualities whenever they can. However, it is not good advice to avoid eye contact with interviewers (B). This would be good advice in Japan, where direct eye contact is found intimidating and is avoided; but in America, it is a sign that one is paying attention and is interested in the conversation. Avoiding eye contact in job interviews in America can be interpreted as a lack of confidence or as dishonesty. Applicants should be prepared not only to answer questions, but also to ask them (C). Applicants can ask interviewers what the company is looking for in an employee; interviewers' responses can provide applicants with opportunities to explain how they meet those needs. If applicants do not understand an interviewer question, they should not try to hide it (D), but rather should request clarification.

37. C: When adults remarry and their respective children are blended into one family, a child's family rank often changes (A); e.g., a child who was formerly the eldest may now be the second or third oldest child, and is treated as such by the rest of family. The roles played by each child also often become less clear (B) than they were in their previous family's dynamics. Additionally, because stepsiblings have no blood relation, incest taboos among them are also less clear-cut (D) than among biological siblings.

38. B: Research into business communication has demonstrated that poor communication in an organization eventually causes individual employees to mistrust each other. This research also shows that poor communication undermines quality (A); compromises productivity (C); and causes not only lack of understanding among members, but also development of anger (D) among individuals in an organization. Researchers conclude that the difference between profit and loss, or between success and failure, in a business is most often attributable to whether communication in the business is effective or not. These findings are the reasons that experts identify effective communication as the most important element of total quality management in business.

39. B: All of these accurately describe women's nutritional requirements. Women differ from men not only in numbers of calories, but also in the amounts they need of various nutrients. And even among women alone, their nutritional needs will not be the same at different times during their menstrual cycles (C), or when they are pregnant, or when they are breastfeeding (nursing) infants (D).

40. D: Of the given pairs, sibling rivalry would likely be greatest for brothers aged 3 and 5. In general, sibling rivalry is most pronounced in same-sex siblings within three years of age. In the first 8–10 years of life, siblings tend to alternate between cooperation and competition. As they grow older, they will often spend little time together for a few years, but during adolescence will gradually develop empathy for one another. Most research suggests that adult relationships between siblings simply exaggerate the tone of the relationship of youth; that is, good relationships get better and bad relationships get worse.

41. B: Vitamin C increases the body's absorption of non-heme iron, i.e., iron from plant sources such as beans, tomatoes, prunes, spinach, pumpkins, etc. Calcium (A), vitamin D (C), and vitamin E (D) are not known to increase the absorption of iron from vegetables, fruits, and legumes.

42. D: Freud's Latency stage of psychosexual development corresponds with the elementary and middle school years; therefore, Duvall's family development stage of Families with School-Age Children corresponds most closely to it. Kohlberg's Pre-Conventional stage of moral development (A) corresponds to the preschool years; Freud's corresponding stage is the Oedipal. Erikson's psychosocial stage of Identity vs. Role Confusion (B) and Piaget's Formal Operations stage of cognitive development (C) both correspond to adolescence; Freud's corresponding stage is the Genital.

43. D: Whether a company's performance goals can support an alternative reflects whether the alternative is economically feasible. Whether an alternative is legal (A) is reflected by whether an alternative is lawful in this country, and in others for companies that export goods or services. Whether it is ethical (B) is reflected if the alternative will not cause undue harm to stakeholders and is morally acceptable. Whether an alternative is practical (C) is reflected by whether the organization's management has the resources and abilities to implement it.

44. D: The best answer is choice D because marketing forces firms to compete for business, which in turn forces improvements in quality and lowers product prices. Choice A is incorrect because marketing does not necessarily use technology or relate to consumer waste. Choice B is wrong because improved sales are not necessarily beneficial to society. Choice C is incorrect because competition increases with marketing.

45. B: Housing meets human social needs most by providing a communal space where the essential unit of society, the family, can live. By providing a sense of privacy and personal space (A), housing meets human psychological needs. By providing shelter from the weather and giving people security (C), housing meets human physical needs. Since each of these represents a different type of human need, (D) is incorrect.

46. C: In 1899, eleven people convened a conference in Lake Placid, New York, to form a new discipline originally called home economics, later renamed family and consumer sciences. After a total of ten Lake Placid Conferences, a national organization originally called the American Home Economics Association (AHEA) was formed in 1909 (A). This organization's charter was enacted in 1910 (B). The AHEA adopted the Betty Lamp as its emblem in 1926 (D).

47. B: In Maslow's hierarchy of needs, the bottom of the pyramid represents needs that take priority because they are required for survival. Hence making sure that children get enough food and sleep is ranked by Maslow among his first level, Physiological needs. Maslow's hierarchy is progressive: each needs level must be met before a person can ascend to the next. After meeting physiological needs, the second level is Security needs; for parents this includes ensuring their children have adequate shelter and safety (C). The third level is Social needs; for parents, this includes giving children love, affection, and a sense of belonging (A). The fourth level is Esteem needs; to meet these, parents build high self-esteem and feelings of personal worth (D) in their children. (The fifth level at the top of the pyramid is Self-Actualization Needs, i.e., to fulfill one's fullest potential, after meeting all other needs.)

48. B: In textile manufacturing, any knitted or woven fabric that has just been produced and has not yet been finished is called 'gray goods. This includes all fabrics that have not been singed, bleached (C); optically brightened, mercerized, dyed (A); printed, glazed, napped, stonewashed or tumbled; distressed; treated with anti-staining or anti-wrinkling finishes, etc. It does not refer only to gray-colored textiles (D).

49. C: Schaefer conceived of parenting styles as existing across two dimensions: (1) along a continuum from love to hostility, and along a continuum from autonomy to control. For example, parents who give much love and much autonomy tend to be permissive and produce impulsive children; parents who give more love but also more control tend to produce children who are well-behaved but not very independent; parents who are hostile and controlling produce fearful and/or rebellious children; parents with high hostility and low control reject and/or neglect children, producing dysfunctional individuals.

50. D: In infancy (A), Maslow's first level of Physiological needs takes priority. In adulthood (B), people may give priority to any or several of his needs levels depending on their circumstances. However, assuming they have met all the other levels, adults are most likely to be concerned with the highest level of self-actualization needs. In adolescence (C), the third and fourth levels of need, for love and belonging and for esteem, are likely to have priority. Whereas infants are most concerned with meeting their needs to sleep, be fed, changed, etc., in toddlerhood the emphasis typically progresses to meeting their needs for safety and security.

51. B: When it appears on a clothing label, the word *carded* means that the garment was made from short, thick cotton fibers. The use of carded fibers creates a fabric that is soft and strong. When the garment is made of long, straight cotton fibers, it is said to be combed. A combed fabric is smoother and shinier. A garment that only contains one type of fiber is considered pure. Garments that have been subjected to a permanent or durable press are more resistant to wrinkles. These processes are usually noted on the clothing label. A label may also indicate whether a garment has been inspected and that it was not created in a sweat shop.

52. A: Wool that has been combed into parallel fibers and then spun into a fine yarn is known as worsted. Renowned for its strength, worsted is used in dresses and suits. Cashmere is an especially soft form of wool that is created from the hair of a specific Indian goat. Angora is another high-end wool made from the long hairs of the angora rabbit. Polyester is a synthetic textile, meaning that it is not made from plants or animals. It is often blended with other fibers in the creation of clothing. Spandex is a synthetic textile with amazing flexibility.

53. A: Denim, as we commonly see in blue jeans, is made using a twill weave rather than a plain weave. Plain-weave fabrics are made by weaving one yarn over the other and then under it. Twill-weave fabrics are made by weaving the weft yarn under and then over two or more warp yarns at regular intervals. This creates a diagonal "twill line" or wale. Muslin (B), percale (C), and burlap (D) are woven using the plain weave, which is the least expensive and simplest way to weave fabrics.

54. B: %Daily Values (DVs) make it easier for consumers to know how much of what they need daily of certain nutrients a food supplies. For example, if a food contains 33%DV of sodium, the consumer knows that food supplies 1/3 of the sodium s/he should consume in a day. This means consumers need *not* know the actual numerical amounts of nutrients they need daily, or how much of that number a food has (A); e.g., they need not know that 2300 mg of sodium is how much to consume daily, or that a food with 800 mg of sodium has 1/3 the DV. %DVs also make it *easier* for consumers to comparison shop, not harder (C); e.g., they can pick a food lower in sodium instead of one with too much. The FDA developed DVs *not* because the RDAs were inaccurate (D), but because certain nutrients the FDA wanted to require on labels did not have RDAs established for them.

55. B: This is defined as an extended family because a grandparent lives with the parents and children. A nuclear family (A) is defined as only the parents and children living together. A blended family (C) is formed when two parents, each with children from a previous marriage or relationship, marry each other and both sets of children live together with both parents. A combined family (D) is not a commonly used term, but may be used as a synonym for a blended family.

56. C: Aging adults are most likely to have poorer absorption of vitamin B_{12} from foods because their stomachs produce less acid with aging, and stomach acid extracts this vitamin from the proteins containing it. Vitamins A (A), C (B), and E (D) are important to older adults for their antioxidant properties (antioxidants can prevent heart disease and some cancers, and may mitigate the process of aging), but aging is not known to decrease absorption of these from foods as it does with vitamin B_{12}.

57. A: Today, consumers can apply for mortgage loans from diverse sources including mortgage bankers and mortgage brokers, but these are not the only sources (B); they can also apply at savings and loan associations, credit unions, commercial banks, mutual savings banks, and insurance companies (C); and today, more and more realtors are also able to arrange mortgage financing for home buyers (D).

58. A: In résumés, those with work experience should place their job histories first; students with no work history should place their educational histories first. When writing one's educational or work history in a résumé, one should list the most recent item first and work backward, not vice versa (B). One should NOT include personal references in the résumé itself (C). For employers who request personal references, the applicant should submit these separately. Résumés should NOT include reasons for leaving previous jobs (D). If these are relevant, they can be addressed during job interviews.

59. D: The fabric care symbol of a square with an arc resembling a slightly slack clothesline hanging from between the top corners indicates the garment should be line-dried or hang-dried. The symbol of a square with diagonal lines in the upper left corner (A) indicates the garment should be dried in the shade (i.e., not in direct sunlight if this would fade the dye). A square with one horizontal line inside (B) indicates the garment should be dried flat. A square with three vertical lines inside (C) indicates the garment should be drip-dried.

60. A: In general, mortgage lenders require an outside third-party guarantee when the home buyer pays less than 20% of a house's list price as a down payment. Thus, they would definitely require such a guarantee if the down payment were less than 10% (B), but between 10% and 20% would still not be enough to waive this requirement. They do not require as much as 50% (C) down, which would more than double the millions of guaranteed mortgages generated annually. Lenders do not usually require 30% (D) down to waive the guarantee either.

61. A: Curtains are lightweight, usually unlined fabric panels hung directly on a rod. They may cover the entire window or be positioned at the sides of the window for decoration, privacy, or light control. Draperies (c) are typically heavier and often lined, while louvered shutters (b) are rigid window coverings with adjustable slates. A grille (d) is a decorative or structural framework within a window rather than a fabric window treatment.

62. D: An implied in-fact contract exists when two parties enter into an agreement, such as the purchase of a mattress. The manufacturer is expected to produce a mattress that meets all advertised expectations, and the customer is expected to pay the price the manufacturer charges and to use the product as it is intended to be used.

63. D: As described by Dr. Murray Bowen in his Family Systems Theory, the pattern of marital conflict involves both spouses' projecting their escalating anxieties into their relationship. The pattern of emotional distance (A) occurs in relation to the other three patterns, as family members seek to escape the excessive intensity of their interactions by withdrawing emotionally. The pattern of impairment of one or more children (B) involves the parents' projecting their anxiety by focusing excessively on the child(ren). Dysfunction in one spouse (C) results when one partner becomes overly dominant and hyperfunctional, while the other becomes overly dependent and dysfunctional in response. This pattern can emerge out of the pattern of marital conflict.

64. B: The FTC does not require clothing labels to indicate whether a garment contains mink or rabbit. FTC textile labeling rules require disclosure of fiber content using approved generic names, generally listing fibers that make up a significant portion of the product. In addition, imported textile and wool products must disclose country of origin, and labels must include the manufacturer's name or Registered Identification Number (RN). Wool products must also specify whether the wool is new or recycled. Fur content is regulated under separate fur-labeling rules, but mink or rabbit content is not a standard required disclosure on general clothing labels.

65. A: Conservation of amount, i.e., understanding that there is the same amount of a substance even if its shape, appearance, or arrangement is changed, is a typical developmental task for children at the middle school ages, e.g., around six to twelve years old. This is a part of what Piaget called Concrete Operations, which children at the earliest school ages (e.g., around four to six years old) typically cannot yet understand or perform. Typical developmental tasks for these younger school-age children include identifying with female or male sex roles (B), developing early concepts of basic morality (C), and learning to play in groups (D) with other children.

66. D: The FDA does not approve dietary supplements or their claims. However, the FDA does regulate supplements and will pull ones they've found to be dangerous off the market. The FDA also regulates drugs for humans and animals; recalls unsafe medical products, foods, and drugs; and regulates the growth, manufacturing, and consumption of tobacco.

67. A: By law, food labels must include the name of the product (e.g. "chunk light tuna"), its form (e.g., "in spring water" or "in soybean oil"); its amount (i.e., weight in ounces, fluid ounces, pounds, grams, milligrams, etc.); the name and address of the company that packed, processed, or distributed the food; and every ingredient included in the food.

68. C: Purchasing a DVD is a discretionary expense because it is based on personal desire rather than need. In other words, it is an expense made at the discretion of the consumer. Discretionary expenses are those over which a consumer has the most control. A comprehensive budget must include discretionary expenses as well as fixed and variable expenses. Fixed expenses, such as rent, are the same every month. Variable expenses, including groceries, school supplies, and heating oil, are always present but vary in amount over the course of a year.

69. D: Collateral is an asset owned by the borrower. With a secured loan, the borrower uses this asset to guarantee the lender that they will repay the loan. If they default on the loan, the bank will sell the asset to recover funds that were not repaid. For example, with a mortgage loan, the property is the collateral.

70. D: If a menu item is a green salad made with lettuce, tomatoes, cucumbers, green onions, and carrots, the most appealing name to list it on the menu as is "fresh garden salad." Menu items should not be listed in all caps, and "tossed green salad" may be interpreted as only being made with greens. "Green salad with mixed vegetables" is not the usual way that salads are described, so consumers may be unclear about what to expect. "Fresh garden salad" suggests a salad made with different fresh ingredients from the garden, an appealing option.

71. A: Within the wide range of specialties available in FCS education, financial planning is one that is currently needed by many financial institutions. This includes brokerage firms; banks and savings and loan associations, which *are* also looking for financial planners (B); and insurance companies and also counseling agencies (C). Qualified financial planners *do* need to understand both the relationship with community and also family dynamics (D) to serve these financial institutions best.

72. D: Erikson's theory of psychosocial development is the only one of the three named whose stages include young adulthood, middle adulthood, and old age until death. Freud's and Piaget's theories both have stages that end with adolescence. Freud's theory of psychosexual development ended with adolescence because he believed the personality was essentially formed by then. Piaget's theory of cognitive development ended at adolescence because he believed his highest stage of Formal Operations was attained by then. (Later researchers have found some adults never attain it.) Of the three, only Erikson included adult developmental stages in his theory.

73. D: Erikson's stage of Generativity vs. Stagnation occurs in middle adulthood, when people focus on creating legacies to leave for future generations, such as children, businesses, homes, inventions, and other contributions to family and society. Those who stagnate rather than generate become self-absorbed. Intimacy vs. Isolation (A) occurs in young adulthood, when people either succeed at forming intimate relationships with others or become isolated from them. Ego Integrity vs. Despair (B) occurs during old age, when people review their lives and feel either satisfaction or regret. Identity vs. Role Confusion (C) occurs during adolescence, when teens either succeed at establishing a personal identity or become confused about what their role is.

74. C: It is considered acceptable etiquette when invited to a dinner party to ask what kind of dress is expected; however, it is *not* acceptable to ask what will be served (B). If a guest has dietary restrictions, it is politer to inform the hosts of these rather than to ask what foods they are serving. Etiquette dictates that it is courteous to RSVP to dinner party invitations both if attending and if not attending (A). Another rule of dining etiquette is that guests only begin to eat when the host/ess raises his/her fork (or spoon if the first course is soup), not as soon as they sit down to the table (D).

75. D: What Bronfenbrenner termed the microsystem is a person's immediate environment, including family, friends, communities, religious groups, and others with which the person has direct contact and regular interactions. The exosystem (A) is what Bronfenbrenner named the wider social system of events and experiences that directly affect a person's microsystems but which the person does not construct; e.g., getting or losing a job. The mesosystem (B) is what Bronfenbrenner called the system of connections between elements of the microsystem; e.g., between a child's parents and teachers, friends and relatives, etc. The macrosystem (C) is what Bronfenbrenner labeled the cultural beliefs, values, laws, rules, and customs that influence the person. (Bronfenbrenner also identified the chronosystem, a system in the dimension of time that includes processes and events like biological maturation, parental death, etc.)

76. D: American society today encompasses so many and diverse versions of families that stage theories of family development often do not describe them adequately. Families may progress through stages out of their usual sequence, or revisit some stages when parents remarry after being widowed or divorced. This reflects a disadvantage of stage theories, which describe more normative or typical family stages. That the stages in these theories express the typical foremost concerns of families in each stage (A) is an advantage of stage theories (for example, referring to an "infant and toddler" stage evokes health, safety, and protection concerns; labeling periods of childhood as "teething", "toileting," or "tantrum" stages instantly evokes the family's main focus). Providing convenient common vocabularies (B) for describing family development is another advantage of stage theories. Systems theories focus more on less linear family dynamics and family responses to change, whereas stage theories focus more on sequential phases of family development (C).

77. D: Supply and demand theory is a microeconomic theory of the relationship between the amount of a good that is available (supply) to the need or want for that good (demand). A good example of this is in natural disasters, such as a hurricane, where the demand for a product is exaggerated as consumers try to purchase extra supplies. As a result, the supply is heavily reduced temporarily, which may drive prices up until the demand is fully met, at which point the supply, demand, and price will equalize. Equilibrium price is where the supply of goods matches its demand. If price is above equilibrium, the quantity supplied is greater than the quantity demanded, which results in a surplus of the good.

78. C: The first thing consumers should do before making a decision to purchase goods or services is to identify their needs, e.g., how they will use the product or service; how often; where to store a product; the location of a service. The second thing they should do is to list the attributes they want the product or service to have (B); e.g., a doctor has long enough office visits, short enough patient waiting times, and a good bedside manner; an insurance company settles claims promptly, subrogates effectively, and charges low premiums; or a power tool is cordless, lightweight, and powerful. The third thing is to narrow the field of possible choices (A); e.g., which are available for sale, which have prices the consumer can afford; product support and customer service; and how each choice meets the consumer's needs and desired product/service attributes. Thus the order of these steps is not irrelevant (D).

79. D: It is generally agreed that a family should spend no more than 25% of its income on housing. Although some lenders are willing to give money to homebuyers who will spend up to 40% of their income on housing, this is considered a risky loan. Such a loan is especially risky when the borrower has other long-term debt besides housing costs. As a consumer, it is wise to create a detailed budget before committing any funds to housing costs.

80. D: Piaget named a unilateral (B) or one-sided morality and adult-child relationship, based on obedience to authority, heteronomous or controlled by others. He named an independently constructed morality, and an adult-child relationship of reciprocal respect, as autonomous. The adult coerces the child in the heteronomous relation and "co-operates" (i.e., collaborates in performing operations) with the child in the autonomous one, rather than vice versa (A). The autonomous relation involves interaction and cooperation whereas the heteronomous involves adult constraint of the child rather than the opposite (C).

81. A: Food poisoning can be caused by all of these preparation factors with certain foods. For example, cooking for the wrong lengths of time (B) and/or at the wrong temperatures (C) can cause perfringens food poisoning due to the microorganism *Clostridium perfringens*. Unpasteurized milk can cause illness from the bacteria *Campylobacter jejuni; Salmonella; E. coli* 0157:H7 infection; and/or *Listeria monocytogenes;* and unrefrigerated (or improperly refrigerated) meats, cream pastries, and egg or potato salads with mayonnaise can cause food poisoning from the bacterium *Staphylococcus aureus.*

82. D: The government's Energy Star website is best because it lists all home appliances and equipment with Energy Star labels for meeting EPA-set energy-efficiency specifications, and includes annual electricity and water use, free of charge. The Sears website (A) is good for consumers who want to buy specifically from Sears, because they can type "Energy Star appliances" into the site's search bar and it will display all Energy Star products sold by Sears. The Energy Star.gov site is better by not restricting customers to one store for buying energy-efficient home equipment and appliances. McGraw-Hill's Sweets Network site at http://products.construction.com/ (B) is an excellent site, but only for locating construction materials and building products and equipment; it does not sell appliances. The Consumer Reports website (C) rates and recommends appliances among many other products, including whether they meet Energy Star requirements; however, while consumers can read its buying guides online, they must pay for a subscription to view the actual ratings, including Energy Star information.

83. D: Cooking food for too long can burn it or dry it out, causing poor taste and texture and removing nutrients. Grilling or charring foods at high temperatures can produce carcinogens (cancer-promoting agents), as can burning them; however, cancers are not food-borne illnesses, which are caused by viral, bacterial, or parasitic microorganisms present in foods. Improperly canned and fermented foods can cause botulism, which can be deadly. Uncooked or raw meats and produce can cause many food-borne illnesses, as can undercooked foods.

84. C: Duvall's Stages of the Family Life Cycle are: (1) childless married couples; (2) families with children 0–30 months; (3) families with children 24 months to 6 years; (4) families with children 6–13 years; (5) families with children 13–20 years; (6) families launching children, from the first child gone to the last child leaving home; (7) middle-age parents, from "empty nest" to retirement; and (8) aging family members, from retirement to both spouses' deaths. The second stage in (A) incorrectly ends with 6 years instead of 30 months. The first stage in (B) incorrectly represents Stage 2 as ending at 6 years instead of 30 months, and the second stage named in (B) represents Stage 4, skipping Stage 3; thus these two are not consecutive. The two stages in (D) are also not consecutive: they name Stages 5, families with teenagers; and Stage 7, middle-age couples from "empty nest" to retirement, skipping Stage 6, families launching children.

85. A: The reason we are advised to analyze our values regarding money and our financial goals is to help us distinguish between what we want and what we need. We may not have enough income for everything we want, but giving our true needs priority before spending on wants can help us stay within our budgets. Analyzing our financial values does include defining how we feel about money (B) and also why we feel as we do about it (C). The reason we are advised to conduct such analyses periodically is because once we have analyzed our financial goals and values, the results we get can still change over time (D): not only can the things we need and want change, but also the ways we feel about money and the reasons for those feelings can change with changes in life circumstances, personal maturity, etc.

86. B: Dining etiquette dictates that hosts and guests should pass dishes to the right, not clockwise (A) with the exception of bread, which should be passed clockwise; hence (C) is incorrect. The rule for cutting up one's food is to cut up anything larger than one's thumb at the second joint rather than being up to the individual guest (D).

87. D: The most important component of preparation for inspection is to conduct self-inspections using the checklists that the inspectors will use so that any noncompliance can be identified before the inspection and can be corrected. Self-inspections should be carried out periodically even if an inspection is not anticipated. All regulations should be reviewed before the inspection. Networking with similar organizations can help identify resources and strategies. The training and education of staff should be ongoing.

88. C: Toman found in his research that an oldest child, who grew up being comfortable with a leadership role, will have a complementary relationship in the workplace with an assistant who grew up as a youngest child and is more comfortable with following the leader. (Youngest children may also like being in charge, but usually have different leadership styles than oldest children.) A boss and assistant who both grew up with the same sibling positions {(A), (B)} are more likely to clash by being too similar in motivations and styles. A boss who was a youngest child and an assistant who was an oldest child (D) are less likely to have as effective a relationship, as their respective roles are more likely mismatched to their interactional personality characteristics. (Murray Bowen also incorporated Toman's findings into his Family Systems Theory, making it better known.)

89. C: One might assume that the term "first-time buyer" refers to anybody who has never owned any real property before (A), but this is not true in the realty market. In most US states, this term actually refers to anyone who has not owned property within the past three years. It does not refer to anyone who has owned real estate property for less than six months (B), or to anyone who once owned but does not currently own any real estate property (D).

90. D: The most efficient way to sort clothes in the closet for finding them easily is first to sort them by category; e.g., pants all together, shirts all together; for women, skirts all together and dresses all together, etc. After sorting clothing categories, within each category they should then be sorted by color. It is not as easy to find individual items and assemble outfits by sorting into colors first and categories second (A). Putting favorite items most within reach (B) sounds like a good idea if we wear these the most, but is not as efficient as (D). Simply putting things wherever they can most easily be fitted in the closet (C) may be quicker and easier when putting clothes away, but will take longer and be harder to find things when getting dressed.

91. D: A person who is 41 to 100% heavier than his or her ideal weight is moderately obese. Health professionals have divided obesity into three degrees: mild, moderate, and severe. A person who is less than 20% heavier than his or her ideal weight is considered merely overweight, but a person who is 20 to 40% heavier is considered mildly obese. People who are more than 100% heavier than their ideal weight are severely obese. Moderately obese people are much more likely to have diabetes or hypertension, but do not necessarily suffer from these conditions.

92. A: According to research, consumers who have not formed any preconceived notions about the quality of various providers through what they have heard from others, through advertising they have seen/heard, or through their own prior experiences are more interested in price as a factor in their health care decisions. However, when consumers have traditional health insurance plans, like PPOs or HMOs (B), they are less interested in price because these plans control price. When consumers have severe or urgent medical conditions (C), they are less interested in price because obtaining immediate care takes priority. And when they like their current health care practitioners (D), they are less interested in price because they want to see the same provider(s) regardless.

93. B: One benefit of family recreation to individual family members is that it can teach members of the family skills that they will use for the rest of their lives. Benefits of family recreation to the family unit as a whole include improved communication within the family (A), increased stability of the family and of interactions within it (C), and a way to maintain family relationships (D), among others.

94. B: Liver from any animal has the highest amount of vitamin A, with turkey liver being the highest, providing over 1500% of the Daily Value (DV) per 100-gram (3½-ounce) serving. Sweet potatoes (A) provide 384% of the DV of vitamin A per 100-gram serving. Carrots contain beta-carotene, which is converted by the body to vitamin A, providing 334% of the DV for a 100-gram (raw) serving. Kale (D) provides 308% of the DV of vitamin A per 100-gram serving via its carotenes.

95. A: Partially hydrogenated vegetable oil is produced through a chemical reaction of liquid vegetable oil with hydrogen to make it semi-solid, as in shortening. This process creates trans fats, which contribute to heart disease. The US FDA has found trans fats even more dangerous than saturated fats. These fats raise LDL (low-density lipoproteins) or "bad" cholesterol, which clogs arteries, and lower HDL (high-density lipoproteins) or "good" cholesterol, which helps remove "bad" cholesterol from the arteries. They also promote inflammation. Fully hydrogenated vegetable oil (B) does not contain trans fat and seems harmless, as its saturated fat is converted to monounsaturated fat by the body. Monounsaturated fats (C), like olive oil, canola oil, peanut oil and peanut butter, sunflower oil, sesame oil, avocados, and many other seeds and nuts, lower LDL, can raise HDL when replacing saturated fats, decrease inflammation, and supply antioxidants that combat diseases. Polyunsaturated fats (D) like regular, nonhydrogenated vegetable oils, lower total cholesterol and LDL, and can raise HDL when replacing saturated fats.

96. B: Erikson's is a theory of psychosocial development, and his most famous book is titled *Childhood and Society*. His developmental theory focuses most on an individual's relationship with society, not with self (A) or other individuals (C). Erikson did not focus as primarily on the child–parent relationship as Freud did. While he used the child's relationship with parents in earlier stages of development as a basis for the individual's subsequent relationship with society, he did not focus on the relationship with parents exclusively (D) but on the developing individual's increasing relationship to society.

97. B: By law, clothing manufacturers are required to include all of this information on the labels, tags, packaging, or printed on the inside of the fabric: a registered ID number identifying the manufacturer (A); the country where the clothing was made (C); the fiber content of the garment; and the care instructions, which are also required and not optional (D).

98. C: Certain types of spina bifida cause paralysis. The vertical location of the defect in spinal column closure dictates how high the paralysis occurs: in some patients the bladder and bowels are affected, while in others it may be limited to the feet and lower legs. A common symptom is inability or difficulty in walking. Communication boards (A) are for people who cannot speak for cognitive (e.g., intellectual disability) or neuromuscular (e.g., cerebral palsy) reasons or vocal system disorders. Text-to-speech software (B) is also for people who cannot speak normally, including those with autistic disorders, deafness, ALS, etc. Cochlear implantations (D) are to restore hearing for those with sensorineural hearing loss.

99. C: The first step realtors recommend is for future home buyers to determine if they are ready to buy a home by identifying what they will need and want; e.g., whether buying is required or optional; whether they have a schedule for home buying; whether they are relocating; whether their lifestyle is changing, etc. The next step is to know whether potential buyers have the money for a down payment, closing costs, and monthly mortgage payments (A). The third step is to assure their credit is good enough to get a loan with the best terms (B): all debts (car notes, revolving credit card bills, lines of credit, monthly rent payments, etc.) are paid on time and otherwise as agreed. Realtors advise doing this for at least a year before buying a home. (Despite this time frame, maintaining or establishing good credit is not the first step realtors recommend.) Therefore, (D) is incorrect.

100. D: FIFO refers to product storage and is an inventory control method that is commonly used to save costs. New items received should be placed behind older items so that the older items are taken out of storage and are used before the new supplies in order to avoid having outdated or expired products that result in food waste. FIFO is especially useful for products with a short shelf life or those that spoil easily.

How to Overcome Test Anxiety

Just the thought of taking a test is enough to make most people a little nervous. A test is an important event that can have a long-term impact on your future, so it's important to take it seriously and it's natural to feel anxious about performing well. But just because anxiety is normal, that doesn't mean that it's helpful in test taking, or that you should simply accept it as part of your life. Anxiety can have a variety of effects. These effects can be mild, like making you feel slightly nervous, or severe, like blocking your ability to focus or remember even a simple detail.

If you experience test anxiety—whether severe or mild—it's important to know how to beat it. To discover this, first you need to understand what causes test anxiety.

Causes of Test Anxiety

While we often think of anxiety as an uncontrollable emotional state, it can actually be caused by simple, practical things. One of the most common causes of test anxiety is that a person does not feel adequately prepared for their test. This feeling can be the result of many different issues such as poor study habits or lack of organization, but the most common culprit is time management. Starting to study too late, failing to organize your study time to cover all of the material, or being distracted while you study will mean that you're not well prepared for the test. This may lead to cramming the night before, which will cause you to be physically and mentally exhausted for the test. Poor time management also contributes to feelings of stress, fear, and hopelessness as you realize you are not well prepared but don't know what to do about it.

Other times, test anxiety is not related to your preparation for the test but comes from unresolved fear. This may be a past failure on a test, or poor performance on tests in general. It may come from comparing yourself to others who seem to be performing better or from the stress of living up to expectations. Anxiety may be driven by fears of the future—how failure on this test would affect your educational and career goals. These fears are often completely irrational, but they can still negatively impact your test performance.

Elements of Test Anxiety

As mentioned earlier, test anxiety is considered to be an emotional state, but it has physical and mental components as well. Sometimes you may not even realize that you are suffering from test anxiety until you notice the physical symptoms. These can include trembling hands, rapid heartbeat, sweating, nausea, and tense muscles. Extreme anxiety may lead to fainting or vomiting. Obviously, any of these symptoms can have a negative impact on testing. It is important to recognize them as soon as they begin to occur so that you can address the problem before it damages your performance.

The mental components of test anxiety include trouble focusing and inability to remember learned information. During a test, your mind is on high alert, which can help you recall information and stay focused for an extended period of time. However, anxiety interferes with your mind's natural processes, causing you to blank out, even on the questions you know well. The strain of testing during anxiety makes it difficult to stay focused, especially on a test that may take several hours. Extreme anxiety can take a huge mental toll, making it difficult not only to recall test information but even to understand the test questions or pull your thoughts together.

Effects of Test Anxiety

Test anxiety is like a disease—if left untreated, it will get progressively worse. Anxiety leads to poor performance, and this reinforces the feelings of fear and failure, which in turn lead to poor performances on subsequent tests. It can grow from a mild nervousness to a crippling condition. If allowed to progress, test anxiety can have a big impact on your schooling, and consequently on your future.

Test anxiety can spread to other parts of your life. Anxiety on tests can become anxiety in any stressful situation, and blanking on a test can turn into panicking in a job situation. But fortunately, you don't have to let anxiety rule your testing and determine your grades. There are a number of relatively simple steps you can take to move past anxiety and function normally on a test and in the rest of life.

Physical Steps for Beating Test Anxiety

While test anxiety is a serious problem, the good news is that it can be overcome. It doesn't have to control your ability to think and remember information. While it may take time, you can begin taking steps today to beat anxiety.

Just as your first hint that you may be struggling with anxiety comes from the physical symptoms, the first step to treating it is also physical. Rest is crucial for having a clear, strong mind. If you are tired, it is much easier to give in to anxiety. But if you establish good sleep habits, your body and mind will be ready to perform optimally, without the strain of exhaustion. Additionally, sleeping well helps you to retain information better, so you're more likely to recall the answers when you see the test questions.

Getting good sleep means more than going to bed on time. It's important to allow your brain time to relax. Take study breaks from time to time so it doesn't get overworked, and don't study right before bed. Take time to rest your mind before trying to rest your body, or you may find it difficult to fall asleep.

Along with sleep, other aspects of physical health are important in preparing for a test. Good nutrition is vital for good brain function. Sugary foods and drinks may give a burst of energy but this burst is followed by a crash, both physically and emotionally. Instead, fuel your body with protein and vitamin-rich foods.

Also, drink plenty of water. Dehydration can lead to headaches and exhaustion, especially if your brain is already under stress from the rigors of the test. Particularly if your test is a long one, drink water during the breaks. And if possible, take an energy-boosting snack to eat between sections.

Along with sleep and diet, a third important part of physical health is exercise. Maintaining a steady workout schedule is helpful, but even taking 5-minute study breaks to walk can help get your blood pumping faster and clear your head. Exercise also releases endorphins, which contribute to a positive feeling and can help combat test anxiety.

When you nurture your physical health, you are also contributing to your mental health. If your body is healthy, your mind is much more likely to be healthy as well. So take time to rest, nourish your body with healthy food and water, and get moving as much as possible. Taking these physical steps will make you stronger and more able to take the mental steps necessary to overcome test anxiety.

Mental Steps for Beating Test Anxiety

Working on the mental side of test anxiety can be more challenging, but as with the physical side, there are clear steps you can take to overcome it. As mentioned earlier, test anxiety often stems from lack of preparation, so the obvious solution is to prepare for the test. Effective studying may be the most important weapon you have for beating test anxiety, but you can and should employ several other mental tools to combat fear.

First, boost your confidence by reminding yourself of past success—tests or projects that you aced. If you're putting as much effort into preparing for this test as you did for those, there's no reason you should expect to fail here. Work hard to prepare; then trust your preparation.

Second, surround yourself with encouraging people. It can be helpful to find a study group, but be sure that the people you're around will encourage a positive attitude. If you spend time with others who are anxious or cynical, this will only contribute to your own anxiety. Look for others who are motivated to study hard from a desire to succeed, not from a fear of failure.

Third, reward yourself. A test is physically and mentally tiring, even without anxiety, and it can be helpful to have something to look forward to. Plan an activity following the test, regardless of the outcome, such as going to a movie or getting ice cream.

When you are taking the test, if you find yourself beginning to feel anxious, remind yourself that you know the material. Visualize successfully completing the test. Then take a few deep, relaxing breaths and return to it. Work through the questions carefully but with confidence, knowing that you are capable of succeeding.

Developing a healthy mental approach to test taking will also aid in other areas of life. Test anxiety affects more than just the actual test—it can be damaging to your mental health and even contribute to depression. It's important to beat test anxiety before it becomes a problem for more than testing.

Study Strategy

Being prepared for the test is necessary to combat anxiety, but what does being prepared look like? You may study for hours on end and still not feel prepared. What you need is a strategy for test prep. The next few pages outline our recommended steps to help you plan out and conquer the challenge of preparation.

Step 1: Scope Out the Test

Learn everything you can about the format (multiple choice, essay, etc.) and what will be on the test. Gather any study materials, course outlines, or sample exams that may be available. Not only will this help you to prepare, but knowing what to expect can help to alleviate test anxiety.

Step 2: Map Out the Material

Look through the textbook or study guide and make note of how many chapters or sections it has. Then divide these over the time you have. For example, if a book has 15 chapters and you have five days to study, you need to cover three chapters each day. Even better, if you have the time, leave an extra day at the end for overall review after you have gone through the material in depth.

If time is limited, you may need to prioritize the material. Look through it and make note of which sections you think you already have a good grasp on, and which need review. While you are studying, skim quickly through the familiar sections and take more time on the challenging parts.

Write out your plan so you don't get lost as you go. Having a written plan also helps you feel more in control of the study, so anxiety is less likely to arise from feeling overwhelmed at the amount to cover.

Step 3: Gather Your Tools

Decide what study method works best for you. Do you prefer to highlight in the book as you study and then go back over the highlighted portions? Or do you type out notes of the important information? Or is it helpful to make flashcards that you can carry with you? Assemble the pens, index cards, highlighters, post-it notes, and any other materials you may need so you won't be distracted by getting up to find things while you study.

If you're having a hard time retaining the information or organizing your notes, experiment with different methods. For example, try color-coding by subject with colored pens, highlighters, or post-it notes. If you learn better by hearing, try recording yourself reading your notes so you can listen while in the car, working out, or simply sitting at your desk. Ask a friend to quiz you from your flashcards, or try teaching someone the material to solidify it in your mind.

Step 4: Create Your Environment

It's important to avoid distractions while you study. This includes both the obvious distractions like visitors and the subtle distractions like an uncomfortable chair (or a too-comfortable couch that makes you want to fall asleep). Set up the best study environment possible: good lighting and a comfortable work area. If background music helps you focus, you may want to turn it on, but otherwise keep the room quiet. If you are using a computer to take notes, be sure you don't have any other windows open, especially applications like social media, games, or anything else that could distract you. Silence your phone and turn off notifications. Be sure to keep water close by so you stay hydrated while you study (but avoid unhealthy drinks and snacks).

Also, take into account the best time of day to study. Are you freshest first thing in the morning? Try to set aside some time then to work through the material. Is your mind clearer in the afternoon or evening? Schedule your study session then. Another method is to study at the same time of day that you will take the test, so that your brain gets used to working on the material at that time and will be ready to focus at test time.

Step 5: Study!

Once you have done all the study preparation, it's time to settle into the actual studying. Sit down, take a few moments to settle your mind so you can focus, and begin to follow your study plan. Don't give in to distractions or let yourself procrastinate. This is your time to prepare so you'll be ready to fearlessly approach the test. Make the most of the time and stay focused.

Of course, you don't want to burn out. If you study too long you may find that you're not retaining the information very well. Take regular study breaks. For example, taking five minutes out of every hour to walk briskly, breathing deeply and swinging your arms, can help your mind stay fresh.

As you get to the end of each chapter or section, it's a good idea to do a quick review. Remind yourself of what you learned and work on any difficult parts. When you feel that you've mastered the material, move on to the next part. At the end of your study session, briefly skim through your notes again.

But while review is helpful, cramming last minute is NOT. If at all possible, work ahead so that you won't need to fit all your study into the last day. Cramming overloads your brain with more information than it can process and retain, and your tired mind may struggle to recall even previously learned information when it is overwhelmed with last-minute study. Also, the urgent nature of cramming and the stress placed on your brain contribute to anxiety. You'll be more likely to go to the test feeling unprepared and having trouble thinking clearly.

So don't cram, and don't stay up late before the test, even just to review your notes at a leisurely pace. Your brain needs rest more than it needs to go over the information again. In fact, plan to finish your studies by noon or early afternoon the day before the test. Give your brain the rest of the day to relax or focus on other things, and get a good night's sleep. Then you will be fresh for the test and better able to recall what you've studied.

Step 6: Take a Practice Test

Many courses offer sample tests, either online or in the study materials. This is an excellent resource to check whether you have mastered the material, as well as to prepare for the test format and environment.

Check the test format ahead of time: the number of questions, the type (multiple choice, free response, etc.), and the time limit. Then create a plan for working through them. For example, if you have 30 minutes to take a 60-question test, your limit is 30 seconds per question. Spend less time on the questions you know well so that you can take more time on the difficult ones.

If you have time to take several practice tests, take the first one open book, with no time limit. Work through the questions at your own pace and make sure you fully understand them. Gradually work up to taking a test under test conditions: sit at a desk with all study materials put away and set a timer. Pace yourself to make sure you finish the test with time to spare and go back to check your answers if you have time.

After each test, check your answers. On the questions you missed, be sure you understand why you missed them. Did you misread the question (tests can use tricky wording)? Did you forget the information? Or was it something you hadn't learned? Go back and study any shaky areas that the practice tests reveal.

Taking these tests not only helps with your grade, but also aids in combating test anxiety. If you're already used to the test conditions, you're less likely to worry about it, and working through tests until you're scoring well gives you a confidence boost. Go through the practice tests until you feel comfortable, and then you can go into the test knowing that you're ready for it.

Test Tips

On test day, you should be confident, knowing that you've prepared well and are ready to answer the questions. But aside from preparation, there are several test day strategies you can employ to maximize your performance.

First, as stated before, get a good night's sleep the night before the test (and for several nights before that, if possible). Go into the test with a fresh, alert mind rather than staying up late to study.

Try not to change too much about your normal routine on the day of the test. It's important to eat a nutritious breakfast, but if you normally don't eat breakfast at all, consider eating just a protein bar. If you're a coffee drinker, go ahead and have your normal coffee. Just make sure you time it so that the caffeine doesn't wear off right in the middle of your test. Avoid sugary beverages, and drink enough water to stay hydrated but not so much that you need a restroom break 10 minutes into the test. If your test isn't first thing in the morning, consider going for a walk or doing a light workout before the test to get your blood flowing.

Allow yourself enough time to get ready, and leave for the test with plenty of time to spare so you won't have the anxiety of scrambling to arrive in time. Another reason to be early is to select a good seat. It's helpful to sit away from doors and windows, which can be distracting. Find a good seat, get out your supplies, and settle your mind before the test begins.

When the test begins, start by going over the instructions carefully, even if you already know what to expect. Make sure you avoid any careless mistakes by following the directions.

Then begin working through the questions, pacing yourself as you've practiced. If you're not sure on an answer, don't spend too much time on it, and don't let it shake your confidence. Either skip it and come back later, or eliminate as many wrong answers as possible and guess among the remaining ones. Don't dwell on these questions as you continue—put them out of your mind and focus on what lies ahead.

Be sure to read all of the answer choices, even if you're sure the first one is the right answer. Sometimes you'll find a better one if you keep reading. But don't second-guess yourself if you do immediately know the answer. Your gut instinct is usually right. Don't let test anxiety rob you of the information you know.

If you have time at the end of the test (and if the test format allows), go back and review your answers. Be cautious about changing any, since your first instinct tends to be correct, but make sure you didn't misread any of the questions or accidentally mark the wrong answer choice. Look over any you skipped and make an educated guess.

At the end, leave the test feeling confident. You've done your best, so don't waste time worrying about your performance or wishing you could change anything. Instead, celebrate the successful completion of this test. And finally, use this test to learn how to deal with anxiety even better next time.

Review Video: Test Anxiety
Visit mometrix.com/academy and enter code: 100340

Important Qualification

Not all anxiety is created equal. If your test anxiety is causing major issues in your life beyond the classroom or testing center, or if you are experiencing troubling physical symptoms related to your anxiety, it may be a sign of a serious physiological or psychological condition. If this sounds like your situation, we strongly encourage you to seek professional help.

Online Resources

Due to our efforts to try to keep this book to a manageable length, we've created a link that will give you access to all of your online resources:

mometrix.com/resources719/nystcefamconsc

It's Your Moment, Let's Celebrate It!

Share your story @mometrixtestpreparation